W9-CMZ-436

WATER

ELEMENTS

EARTH

AIR

FIRE

WATER

WATER
ITS GLOBAL NATURE

MICHAEL ALLABY

Facts On File
New York • Oxford

ELEMENTS: WATER
Copyright © 1992 by Michael Allaby

Facts On File Limited   or   Facts On File, Inc.
Collins Street   460 Park Avenue South
Oxford OX4 1XJ   New York NY 10016
UK   USA

A British CIP catalogue record for this book is available from the British
Library.

A United States of America CIP catalogue record for this book is available
from the Library of Congress.

ISBN 0-8160-2526-6

Facts On File books are available at special discounts when purchased in bulk
quantities for businesses, associations, institutions or sales promotions. Please
contact the Special Sales Department of our Oxford office on 0865 728399
or our New York office on 212/683-2244 (dial 800/322-8755 except in NY,
AK, or HI).

Produced by Curtis Garratt Limited,
The Old Vicarage, Horton cum Studley, Oxford OX9 1BT

Picture research by Jennifer Garratt

Technical artwork by Taurus Graphics Limited
Pencil drawings by Paula Chasty

Printed in Hong Kong

10 9 8 7 6 5 4 3 2 1

This book is printed on acid-free paper.

(Previous pages, left) As well as contributing to the beauty of
wild country, a tumbling waterfall is an apt symbol of the vital
nature of water to all forms of life. This is Owhoroa Falls in New
Zealand. (Previous pages, right) And without water, an arid
landscape, such as this in Utah in the United States, is barren
indeed.

CONTENTS

INTRODUCTION

Water, air, earth and fire have been known throughout most of our history as the 'elements'. No one knows when these elements were first defined, but they were certainly being discussed around 600 BC and it was such discussions, of ideas that were developed and elaborated over centuries, which laid the foundations of the particular way of examining and thinking about natural phenomena we now call 'science'.

The word 'element' is used differently today, but its ancient meaning continues to haunt our language and culture. It suggests balance and justice, concepts which seem appropriate to our modern concern about the condition of the natural environment.

This is one of a series of four books, each of which describes one of the ancient elements, but in a modern way. You will read accounts of the substances which compose each of the elements, how they are formed, how humans have made use of them, ways in which we may be damaging them, and the steps that are being taken to render our exploitation of them more rational. The text deals with scientific and technological concepts, but places them in a cultural and historical context that to some degree restores the older images their names still conjure, even now, as we approach the end of the twentieth century.

Thales, who may have introduced the Greeks to geometry, which he learned in Egypt, came from Miletus, in Asia Minor. His dates are uncertain (according to Apollodorus he was born in 624 BC and according to Diogenes Laertius he was 78 when he died) but because he predicted an eclipse which is believed to have occurred on 28 May 585 BC, he must have been alive prior to that year. He was one of the Seven Wise Men of Greece, each of whom was renowned for one particularly wise saying. Thales's saying was that water is the primal substance from which all other substances are made. If this sounds extravagant to a modern ear, perhaps it is worth reflecting that water is composed of hydrogen and oxygen, which are found in all living and most non-living matter.

Anaximander (about 610-547 BC), a natural philosopher of the Milesian school and a younger contemporary of Thales,

disagreed. He held that the primal substance is eternal and indefinable, and is transformed into the substances we see around us. Each of the elements — earth, fire, air and water — is a god, seeking to expand his dominion, but this proves impossible because the proportion of each element is fixed and the balance cannot be disturbed. Fire produces ash, which is earth. When warmed, water becomes air, and when cooled air turns to water.

Some three centuries later, the philosopher Aristotle (384-322 BC) developed the idea further. He maintained that the elements are not eternal, but change from one to another and mingle under the influence of the approach and retreat of the Sun, and everything is in constant motion. Fire is absolutely light and moves upwards, air is relatively light, earth is absolutely heavy and moves downwards, and water is relatively heavy. All matter which exists below the Moon is composed of the four elements, and subject to change and decay, while matter above the Moon is made from a fifth, eternal element.

The ideas of Aristotle, expounded in his many writings, dominated European thought for 2000 years, and their influence was not wholly benign. Indeed, they became such a serious constraint on intellectual development that eventually innovative philosophers and scientists found themselves beginning their expositions by refuting one or another Aristotelian doctrine. Yet it was Aristotle who insisted that the route to understanding natural phenomena begins with detailed observation of them, which is the principle underlying all modern science.

Gradually, old ideas gave way to new. William of Occam (c.1290-1350), though an Aristotelian, contributed the maxim, known as 'Occam's razor', that explanations should be free from unnecessary hypotheses — the simplest explanation is likely to be the best one. Copernicus (1473-1543) and Galileo (1564-1642) demolished the Earth-centred view of the universe, and Johannes Kepler (1571-1630) discovered the laws of planetary motion. Francis Bacon (1561-1626) began the process of developing an inductive scientific system by which general

(Opposite) Aristotle (384-322 BC)

laws may be derived from observation and experiment. It was Robert Boyle (1627-91), regarded as one of the founders of modern chemistry, who, in 1661, first used the old word 'element' to describe a substance that cannot be separated into two or more simpler substances.

These books, then, aim to bridge the historical gap between ancient and modern views of the world. In *Water* , the story is told in four parts. The book begins by describing what water is, where it comes from, and its physical and chemical properties. It is these properties that make water essential for all living organisms and, in the second section, the book discusses the biological importance of water and water as a medium in which organisms live. The third section deals with the movement of water, through the air where it produces our weather, and in the oceans. The final section deals with the ways in which humans have used water, for transport — of substances as well as passengers and cargo — and as a source of power. The section ends by outlining the ways in which we pollute water, the significance of that pollution, and the reforms by which we may hope that pollution is gradually being brought under control.

Galileo (1565-1642) and (opposite) Francis, Lord Bacon (1561-1626).

PART 1

WHAT IS WATER?

WATER AND ITS PROPERTIES

A glance at any map of the world shows that most of the surface of our planet is covered by water. It is the characteristic that most obviously distinguishes the Earth from Mars and Venus, our close neighbours in the solar system.

It is not simply the presence of water that is unique, but its abundance. Almost three-quarters (70.8 per cent) of the total surface area of the planet is covered by the seas and oceans to an average depth of 2.3 miles (3.73 km), so together they contain 320.7 million cubic miles (1370 million cu km) of water. When the inland seas, lakes, glaciers and polar ice caps are included, the area covered by water amounts to 146.4 million square miles (379.3 million sq km), or 74.35 per cent of the Earth's total area.

The oceans and seas are contained in basins bordered by the continents. Were the solid surface of the planet level, without these contrasts in elevation, the Earth would be covered by one vast ocean, about 1.6 miles (2.7 km) deep.

The formation of the solar system is believed to have begun when a cloud of gas and particles condensed. Almost all of the mass became concentrated in the Sun, the remainder making up the planets, each of which began to grow as small pieces of matter collided and adhered to one another until, perhaps in as little as 10,000 years, they had grown into 'planetismals' — bodies up to 10 miles (16 km) in diameter — which crashed into one another, shattering into debris which then collapsed again under the force of gravity. The energy released in such violent impacts was suffi-cient to melt the matter from which the young Earth was made.

Most of the Earth's fresh water exists as ice and each summer some of this ice, from the edges of the polar ice sheets, breaks away and drifts towards warmer waters. This iceberg is in Antarctic water.

As the Earth grew, the heat generated by the conversion of the kinetic energy of impacting rocks was augmented by the radioactive decay of a number of unstable elements. These were formed, much earlier, when a star larger than the Sun exploded as a supernova, and they were present in the cloud out of which the solar system condensed. Together, the heat of impact and the much greater heat of radioactive decay were sufficient to melt the rocks of the new planet.

Free to move in relation to one another, the constituents of the molten rock sorted themselves by weight, the heaviest tending to move towards the centre. The densest, rich in the metals iron and nickel, accumulated to form the Earth's solid inner core and an outer core where, although extremely dense, the metals behave as a fluid. It is the flow of material in the outer core that produces the 'dynamo' which generates the Earth's magnetic field.

At the surface, where heat was radiated into space and so dissipated, the rocks cooled to form a solid crust resting on the hot, dense, plastic rocks beneath, but they did not solidify from an homogeneous mixture of ingredients. If you hold two different pieces of rock of the same weight one may be much larger than the other. The weight of the crustal rocks is much the same from one part of the world to another, but because of this difference in their densities their volume varies. The densest rocks, mainly basalt, form a relatively thin crust and the less dense, such as granite, form a much thicker crust. The surface of the thin crust is low-lying, that of the thicker crust rises much higher, and so the dense, thin crust provides the basins containing the oceans and the thicker crust forms the continents.

Most scientists believe the water that fills the ocean basins was released as vapour when the surface rocks cooled and as molten

The head of a comet is made mainly from pieces of rock bound together by ice — it is a 'dirty snowball'. Some scientists have suggested that bombardment by comets supplied much of the Earth's water. This is Comet Kohoutek, photographed in 1974.

hydrogen

oxygen

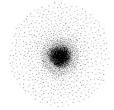

hydrogen

carbon

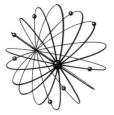

Atoms are often represented as small particles (electrons) orbiting a nucleus as above. In reality the electrons are not particles of solid material and may be better described as clouds surrounding the nucleus (top). The water molecule (below) consists of two hydrogen atoms attached to an oxygen atom.

rock erupted, and still erupts, through the weaknesses in the crust that allow volcanoes to form. Hydrogen and oxygen, the elements that comprise water, are very abundant in the universe and the cloud from which our world is made contained large amounts of them. Water accounts for about 5 per cent of the weight of rock and when molten rock flows to the surface and cools, some of the water evaporates from it.

Others have suggested that the Earth's water arrived, after the crust had partly solidified, as comets collided with the planet. Comets, most of which now reside in the furthest reaches of the solar system, are 'dirty snowballs' made from a rock surrounded by ice mixed with dust. Were they to have been much more numerous in our region of space then than they are today they could have contributed large amounts of water.

Although all the planets were formed by similar processes, Mars lost much of its water and what remains exists mainly as ice, while Venus lost virtually all of its water. It was only on Earth that the strength of the gravitational field, the temperature and the atmospheric pressure allowed water to be retained.

Molecules and atoms

A molecule of water consists of two atoms of hydrogen joined to one atom of oxygen. This gives the molecule, and therefore water itself, its familiar chemical formula of H_2O. The formula is familiar, but what does it really mean? What are hydrogen and oxygen and how do they combine?

An atom consists of a central nucleus surrounded by electrons. The nucleus has a

positive electrical charge, an electron has a negative electrical charge, and it is the attraction of opposite charges that holds the nucleus and its electrons together. Apart from their charges, electrons possess energy, and the more energy they have the further from the nucleus they are likely to be. If there are several electrons, each may possess a different amount of energy but, unless they are disturbed by some outside force, the particles that make up an atom will always arrange themselves so that their total energy is as close as possible to zero, rather in the way that spherical boulders would roll to the bottom of an incline provided the surface were smooth.

The electrons orbit the nucleus, but not in the way a planet orbits a star. It is more helpful to think of an electron orbit as a wave, with a length that depends on the velocity of the electron. If the length of the orbit is equal to a whole number of wave cycles, the crests will always occur in the same places, and this is a 'permitted' orbit. In a 'forbidden' orbit — one that cannot exist — the number of wave cycles contains a fraction. The permitted orbits, each corresponding to an energy level, because the wavelength of the orbital path depends on the velocity of the electron, form a series of shells around the nucleus.

A shell may be filled, so no other electron can enter, or it may have vacancies. Because the electrons fill the inner shells, with the lower energy levels, first it is the outermost shell that is most likely to have vacancies.

The atomic nucleus is itself composed of three types of particles, protons and neutrons, known collectively as 'nucleons' and 'prions'. Protons have a positive electrical charge, neutrons are electrically neutral, and prions hold the protons and neutrons together. The positive charge on a proton is exactly equal to the negative charge on an electron, so there can be as many electrons as there are protons. When there are, the atom as a whole is electrically neutral.

The mass of an atom depends on the number of nucleons in its nucleus. Prions have no measurable mass and that of an electron is so small it makes no appreciable difference. The chemical properties of an atom depend on the number of its protons.

Hydrogen has the simplest of all atoms, consisting of just one proton, no neutrons or prions, and one electron. Oxygen has a nucleus consisting of eight protons and

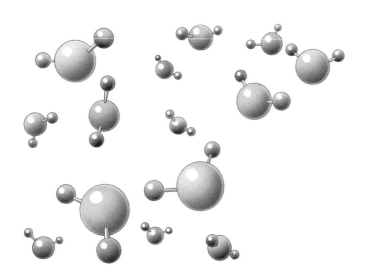

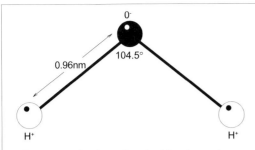

The water molecule: an isoceles triangle carrying a negative electrical charge at the (oxygen) apex and a positive charge on each hydrogen atom. (1 nm (nanometre) is one millionth of a millimetre, or 0.0000000394 inches)

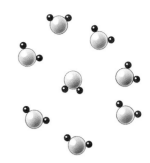

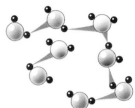

GAS. The molecules collide, but their kinetic energy is too great to permit them to bond, so they remain separate and fast moving.

eight neutrons. Despite the fact that the oxygen atom is 16 times more massive than the hydrogen atom, the diameters of the two are almost the same because the particles are very small indeed and the volume of an atom consists mainly of empty space.

The outermost electron shell of an oxygen atom has vacancies and the hydrogen atom can lose its electron rather easily. This is because the electron is held in place by only one proton and, because of the relatively large size of the hydrogen atom, its electron is a long way from the nucleus so the force retaining it is weaker than in any other atom. When hydrogen and oxygen atoms meet, the hydrogen electron jumps into the outermost shell of the oxygen atom. The acquisition of an electron gives the oxygen atom a negative charge, the loss of an electron gives the hydrogen atom a positive charge, and the two atoms are held together by the attraction of the opposite charges. An atom that acquires an electrical charge by the loss or gain of an electron is known as an 'ion', and so this joining of atoms is known as 'ionic bonding'.

It is not all that happens, however. The electron shells of the two atoms overlap, creating an area of negative charge between the two nuclei that attracts both of them. This is called 'covalent bonding' and it distorts the field, so the molecule formed by such a bond may not be symmetrical. In the case of water, the two hydrogen and one oxygen atoms form a V-shaped molecule with an angle of 104.5 degrees. This means, however, that although the molecule as a whole is electrically neutral, there is a small negative charge at the oxygen end balanced by a positive charge at the two hydrogen ends. This electrical polarity gives the water molecule some of its remarkable properties.

A water molecule never exists alone, of

course, and the molecules react with one another partly because of a third kind of bonding, known as 'hydrogen bonding'. The hydrogen atom can form ionic bonds between oxygen atoms belonging to two different molecules, linking the molecules together. This property, which is peculiar to hydrogen, also arises from the relative weakness with which the nucleus and electron are held together. Each of the molecules held by a hydrogen bond can form similar hydrogen bonds to two others, and so water molecules can form a structure that is very complicated but very open, because of the shape of the individual molecules.

The phases of water

Water freezes at 0 degrees Celsius (32 degrees Fahrenheit) and boils at 100 degrees Celsius (212 degrees Fahrenheit). Indeed, Anders Celsius (1701-44) used the melting and boiling temperatures of water to define his temperature scale. The temperatures are well known, but they are true only under certain conditions. The water must be pure, it must be saturated with dissolved oxygen, and the atmospheric pressure must be precisely 101,325 pascals (equal to 1.01325 bars, or one 'atmosphere'). This is the average pressure at sea level.

Depart from these conditions and water will not freeze or boil at exactly 0 and 100 °C. Because the actual atmospheric pressure very rarely corresponds to the average — as a glance at the weather map in a newspaper will confirm — and natural water contains impurities, so it is not pure H_2O, the water you boil in your kitchen or that freezes in your refrigerator hardly ever does so at the 'official' temperature.

The solid, liquid or gaseous state of a substance is known technically as its 'phase' and to understand how the atmospheric pressure affects it you must picture the way water molecules behave. You cannot see them, of course, because they are far too small to be visible even under the strongest microscope, but with a quite ordinary microscope you can see their effects. If you sprinkle a little dark-coloured, fine powder on the surface of a small beaker of water and watch the powder grains individually you will see they move about in a quite random fashion. Tap the side of the container to make waves in the water and it will have no appreciable effect on the powder. The

LIQUID. The molecules bond but the arrangement is constantly fluctuating, with the molecules separating and recombining. As the temperature falls, the molecules move closer together, reaching their closest positions at 39 °F (4 °C).

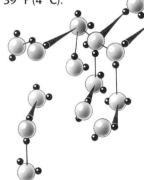

ICE. As they lock together to form a solid, the molecules are linked by hydrogen bonds. This produces a very open structure in which, although they are held firmly, the molecules are further apart than they are in water at 39 °F (4 °C).

random movements will continue un-changed. The first person to observe this, in 1827, was a Scottish botanist called Robert Brown (1773-1858) and so it is known as Brownian motion.

It occurs because the molecules in a liquid are constantly moving, colliding with one another and ricocheting in new directions until further collisions change their directions again. The result is entirely random, or Brownian, motion. The powder grains floating on the surface are battered by the molecules and so they, too, move erratically.

Some of the molecules break free from the surface of the liquid and enter the air. This is what happens when water evaporates. Leave water exposed to the air for long enough and all of it will evaporate, but it is a slow process. The molecules can move, but the attraction that binds one molecule to its neighbours keeps them close together. At the surface the attractive force from below, of the molecules in the liquid, is much stronger than that among the more widely spaced gas molecules of the air and so the liquid molecules find it difficult to escape. The molecules are not all moving at the same speed, however, and now and then one that is travelling especially fast may approach the surface almost at right angles and pass into the air. Even then it may be pulled back into the liquid. Only if it avoids this will it have evaporated, and it is still possible for it to collide with an air molecule that knocks it back into the liquid.

The molecules in a gas are much further apart than those in a liquid but, because of this, they can be forced closer together by pressure — a gas can be compressed. Think of an area of the Earth's surface and imagine the column of air above it, from the surface all the way to the top of the atmosphere. Air is a material substance and it has weight. The whole weight of the column presses down on the surface at its base. Because air can be compressed, the pressure exerted by the weight of the air column forces the air molecules closer together. The air is relatively dense at sea level but its density, and therefore the pressure exerted by the overlying column, decreases rapidly with increasing altitude. The average sea level air pressure is 101,325 pascals but at 5000 feet (1500 m) it is only about 840,000 pascals and at 30,000 feet (10,000 m) it is about 280,000 pascals.

The denser the air, the greater the chance that a molecule leaving the surface of a liquid will collide with a gas molecule that knocks it back again, but the lower the air pressure the more rapidly a liquid evaporates until a point may be reached where the atmospheric pressure is so low that a particular substance cannot exist at all in liquid form because it will evaporate instantly.

This is why liquid water cannot exist on the surface of the Moon or Mars, and it is also why carbon dioxide, whose molecules have more energy than those of water, cannot exist as a liquid on the surface of the Earth. The opposite effect also occurs. If moist air is compressed, say by a piston in a cylinder, liquid water will form as the vapour is forced to condense.

The amount of energy molecules have depends on the temperature. The warmer they are the faster they move. Continue heating a liquid and a point will be reached where, in local regions of the liquid, some molecules have enough energy to break free from one another and move further apart. In those regions the liquid becomes bubbles of gas and, being less dense than the surrounding liquid, the gas bubbles rise to the surface and burst, releasing the gas into the air. This is what happens when a liquid boils but, because the ease with which the molecules enter the air depends on the air pressure, the greater the air pressure the more energy, as heat, that must be imparted to the liquid to make it boil. In other words, the lower the air pressure, the lower the boiling temperature of water.

There is no part of Tibet that lies below about 12,000 feet (3650 m). Tea is the national drink and people like to drink it while the water is still boiling vigorously. At that altitude water boils at a comfortably warm temperature. There have been cases of Tibetans moving from their mountains to a much lower altitude and suffering severe scalding when they tried to drink their tea the way they were accustomed to drinking it.

A liquid will not boil, however, if the heat applied to it is enough only to raise its temperature to boiling point. The molecules require additional energy to allow them to break free from the attractive force that binds them together. This is called 'latent heat'. The amount needed varies from one substance to another and, in the case of water, it requires 2500 joules of energy to convert one gram of water into gas at its

boiling temperature (about 21 cal/oz). The same amount of heat is liberated when the gas condenses into a liquid. It is the release of the latent heat of condensation as raindrops form that warms the air inside storm clouds, causing the air to rise rapidly, cool as it rises so more water vapour condenses, and to generate the characteristic cumulus and cumulonimbus shapes.

As the temperature of a substance is reduced the energy available to the molecules is also reduced and they move more slowly. The attractive force between them draws them more closely together, the distance between each molecule and its neighbours eventually being limited by the repulsive force between the atomic nuclei. They cease to move about randomly and adopt fixed positions in which they continue to vibrate. Close together and unable to move freely, in this condition the molecules form a solid.

The molecules in a gas are completely disordered. Those in a liquid are ordered very locally because they are close together, with molecules within about one molecular diameter of their neighbours. Move further away and there is no evident order. In a solid, however, the molecules form regular patterns, called 'lattices'.

The boiling temperature of water depends on the air pressure. Tibetans, who live at a high altitude, are used to drinking their tea while it is still boiling. These people are at Xigaze.

Again, latent heat is involved. As the molecules move from the higher energy state of the liquid to the lower energy state of the solid, latent heat is released. In the case of water, 334.7 joules are released for every gram of water that freezes (2.8 cal/oz). This is why it feels warmer when water begins to freeze and it is also why it feels colder when the ice thaws, because the same amount of heat must be taken from the air to raise the energy level of the molecules enough for them to escape from the ice lattice. The amount of heat involved may sound small but, if the latent heat of melting were applied to liquid water at just above its freezing point, it would be sufficient to heat it to 176 °F (80 °C).

A direct change, in either direction, between the solid and gaseous states is called 'sublimation'. In the case of water it involves 2834.7 joules per gram (23.7 cal/oz), which is the sum of the latent heats of melting and vaporization.

In spring, as the ice melts on a pond and the warmth of the Sun causes evaporation, water exists in all three phases at the same time.

The universal solvent

If you mix a little salt, or sugar, or any of a very large range of other substances in water it will form a solution. This means that the substance you add to the water, the 'solute', becomes dispersed evenly throughout the water, the 'solvent', and it remains there. If you leave the solution to stand, the solute and solvent do not separate. It also means that if you sample the solution at any number of points you will find it always contains precisely the same proportions of solute and solvent. If you mix just a little salt or sugar with the water, then wherever you sample the water it will be just a little salty or sweet, and it will taste the same no matter where you take your sample.

Not all substances will dissolve in water. If you add powdered chalk, for example, you can stir the mixture until it looks milky but if you leave it to stand, before long the chalk will settle to the bottom and the water will contain no trace of it. Oil and water will not even form an apparently homogeneous mixture and if left to stand the two will separate, the oil floating on the top of the water. What appears as the quite different behaviour of chalk and water is really an illusion. When chalk is powdered

it forms minutely small particles. Disperse them throughout the water and although each particle of chalk remains quite intact they are too small, and moving too fast, to be individually distinguishable. Oil, however, being a liquid, forms droplets and these are much larger than chalk particles and easily visible. There are liquids that will form a solution in water. Two liquids that will mix to form a solution are said to be 'miscible' (the opposite is 'immiscible').

There is so much water on the Earth, and it is such a familiar substance, that we tend to take its remarkable properties for granted. Its ability to form solutions with so many different chemical compounds is one of those properties — and one on which all life depends. All the gases present in the air are slightly soluble in water, for example, and this provides the free oxygen needed by aquatic organisms. Most chemical reactions take place in solutions because it is in solution that molecules have the mobility they need to encounter one another.

When you take clothes to be dry-cleaned, solvents will be used, and many solvents are used in manufacturing industry, but such solvents are used only for special purposes, to dissolve compounds that are insoluble in water, many of them based on oils. Water is by far the commonest solvent in use, and water comes closer than its rivals to being a 'universal solvent' — an imaginary substance much sought by medieval alchemists that, were it to exist, would dissolve any container in which we might try to confine it.

The ability of water to dissolve most of the compounds that enter it is derived from several characteristics of the water molecule. The first is that water molecules are extremely small. As they move around, sliding past one another in the liquid, it is easy for them to slip between and around alien atoms. This gives them ready access to such atoms. That would avail them little were it not for their second important property — their polarity. Because of the three types of bonding that link its oxygen atom to its two hydrogen atoms, the water molecule is not symmetrical and its triangular shape leaves it with a positive electrical charge at the hydrogen ends and a negative charge at the oxygen end. These charges mean the molecule tends to form a bond whenever it moves close to an atom or molecule carrying an opposite charge and, because it has both a positive and a negative charge, that means any charge at all.

The third important property is the stability of the water. Under ordinary atmospheric pressure, if it is heated to 3632 °F (2000 °C) only 2 per cent of its molecules will dissociate into independent atoms of hydrogen and oxygen. Molecules of most compounds would not survive such treatment so well. As the temperature increases, their molecules acquire more energy and so do the atoms of which the molecules are composed until eventually the molecules break apart. This leaves each part as an ion — an atom or group of atoms carrying an electrical charge — and ions quickly bond to one or other end of water molecules.

At the same time, however, water itself becomes ionized to a small extent. In a bowl of water not all the molecules will be H_2O. Just a few of them will have separated into hydrogen atoms (H, and with a positive electrical charge and conventionally written as H^+) and hydroxyl ions (OH, with a negative charge, written as OH^-), while a few others will have formed H_3O, also with a positive charge because of the additional hydrogen atom. These ions form and reform but, as they do so, they will bond with any other ion of appropriate charge. In some cases, this property allows water not merely to dissolve a compound but to react with it chemically, altering it to a different compound with different qualities (a chemical reaction involving water is called 'hydrolysis'). If phosphorous chloride (PCl_3) is added to water, it is hydrolysed violently, to produce phosphonic acid (H_3PO_3) and hydrochloric acid (HCl).

The solubility of salt

Common salt is sodium chloride (NaCl) and it is so highly soluble in water as to be 'deliquescent' — meaning water vapour present in the air will dissolve it. Its strong affinity for water is due to a peculiarity of the sodium atom. This has only one electron in its outermost shell and consequently the bonds it forms with other atoms, including other sodium atoms, are very weak. Pure sodium is a white metal so soft you can cut it with a knife, and it is soft because of the weakness of its interatomic bonds. The outermost electron is easily lost, ionizing the atom (Na^+) and its bond with chlorine is

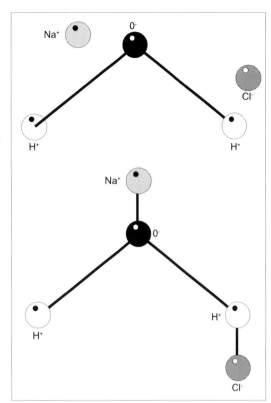

In a salt crystal, atoms of sodium (Na) are bonded to atoms of chlorine (Cl). When the salt dissolves in water, this bond breaks and the atoms separate.

Positively charged sodium atoms and negatively charged chlorine atoms then attach to water molecules, the sodium to the oxygen and the chlorine to the hydrogen.

easily broken, so the chlorine is also liberated as a free ion (Cl^-). Insert a water molecule between the sodium and the chlorine and much stronger bonds are made. The hydrogen bond contributes to the process. After the hydrogen (H^+) end of the water molecule has formed a bond with a chlorine ion (Cl^-), the hydrogen bond permits a second, but weaker, link with a second chlorine. This strips a chlorine from its sodium, leaving the sodium to bond with another water molecule. It explains why salt dissolves in water so rapidly.

To a chemist the word 'salt' means the compound that is produced when an acid reacts with a base (an alkali is one kind of base), and common salt (sodium chloride) is but one of many salts. The name 'common salt' is warranted, however, because sodium chloride accounts for almost 80 per cent of the total amount of all the salts dissolved in sea water.

Pure water is neither an acid nor a base. It is neutral and, indeed, it provides the standard against which acidity is measured on the standard 'pH' scale. Introduced in 1909 by S. P. Sørensen, the scale measures the 'potential of hydrogen' (hence the abbreviation) as hydrogen ions. Neutrality is set at pH 7.0, which is the value for pure water. A pH value lower than 7.0 indicates an acid, one higher than 7.0 a base.

(Opposite top) Ice is less dense than water at just above freezing temperature and, therefore, it floats. The surface of this Swiss lake is just starting to freeze. (Opposite bottom) Everything we drink consists mainly of water — including the world's most popular soft drink, here on sale in Kinshasa, Zaïre.

What is a solution?

A compound that has dissolved in water has not become a liquid. You can change salt from its usual solid condition into a liquid by heating it (but you should not attempt to do so because in the process the sodium becomes dangerously unstable and may explode), and you melt crystalline sugar, at quite a low temperature, when you make a caramel. All that has happened in a solution is that the constituents of the solute have become evenly dispersed in the solvent, water, which is a fluid. Should the water evaporate, the solute will be left behind in its original form. Evaporation occurs when fast-moving molecules escape from the surface of the liquid, but it is only molecules of the solvent that can escape in this way. Leave a saline solution to stand exposed to the air and, little by little, its volume will decrease as water evaporates, so that what remains will become saltier as the proportion of salt to water increases. This is why the water that evaporates from the surface and then condenses again to form clouds contains no salt — it is 'fresh' — and why the rivers, lakes and other bodies of inland water are always fresh (unless they are located close enough to a salt deposit to be affected by it).

As more and more of a solute is added to water, a point will be reached beyond which no more can be dissolved and undissolved solute starts to accumulate. With some substances solubility can be increased by raising or lowering the temperature. Cooling water increases the amount of dissolved oxygen it can hold, which is why discharging warm water into a river is regarded as a form of pollution — it reduces the oxygen available to fish.

The effects of temperature

An ordinary thermometer consists of a glass tube containing a liquid. If the liquid is silver in colour it is mercury — a metal that is liquid at any temperature above -38 °F (-38.87 °C). If it is red, the liquid is alcohol containing a red dye. When the temperature increases, the liquid expands to fill more of the tube. When the temperature falls, the liquid contracts and occupies less of the tube. The general rule, then, is that liquids expand as they become warmer and contract as they become cooler. The number of molecules does not change. Nothing enters or leaves the thermometer and, if you could weigh the liquid inside the tube, you would find its weight does not change. Nothing has been added or removed.

If you could sample the liquid, however, you would discover that one physical characteristic does change. Suppose you could remove and weigh just a small volume of the liquid while it is cold, then return it, increase the temperature, and remove and weigh a similar volume again. You would find that the cooler sample weighs more than the warm sample. The reason is quite straightforward. As the liquid cools, its molecules have less energy, move less vigorously and so are closer together. Because its molecules are closer together the liquid occupies a smaller volume. The opposite happens as the liquid warms, and it occupies a larger volume. Two samples, each of similar volume but taken at different temperatures, will have different weights because the two contain a different number of molecules — different amounts of the substance being sampled. You might summarize your findings by saying that *the density of a liquid (or gas) is inversely proportional to the temperature*. As the temperature increases, the density decreases and vice versa.

If you continue to cool the liquid, the density continues to increase until the substance changes phase and becomes a solid (in the case of alcohol at -272.2 °F, -169 °C). The molecules of the liquid move closer and closer together until they form a lattice, a network into which they are fixed and within which they have sufficient energy to vibrate but not to move independently of one another.

Most solids expand when heated because their atoms vibrate more vigorously, but under conditions in which the repulsive force between like charges that prevents them approaching one another too closely is greater than the attractive force of opposite charges that holds them together, so they vibrate quite a long way apart before their mutual attraction draws them together again. Because all the atoms or molecules behave in the same way, the entire piece of material expands when it is heated and contracts when it is cooled.

Imagine, now, a pool of any substance in which some of the liquid is relatively warm, some relatively cool, and some frozen into a solid. Leave the mixture to stand and it will form layers,with the densest and, therefore,

heaviest at the bottom and the least dense and, therefore, lightest at the top. The warm liquid will float above the cold liquid and the solid will sink to the bottom.

Up to a point, this is what will happen to water. Indeed, it does happen in the seas and during summer in some lakes. Quite distinct layers form, with warm water overlying cool water and little mixing between the two. When water freezes, though, its solid phase floats.

The water molecule, you will recall, consists of one hydrogen atom bonded to two oxygen atoms to form a triangle with the hydrogen at the apex, and water molecules are linked to one another by the hydrogen bond that allows a hydrogen atom to link two oxygens. As liquid water cools, the molecules move closer together and move less vigorously. The water becomes denser, just like any other liquid. At 39.2 °F (4 °C) the water reaches its maximum density. When molecules are repelled because similar electrical charges approach too close, they are free to move apart. Cool water below this temperature and the molecules start to become locked together in the form of ice. They are bound by the hydrogen bond, which links oxygen atoms, the oxygen atoms repel one another, but molecules have lost their freedom to move away from one another. The resulting structure is very irregular and also very open, with many empty spaces. This causes water to expand as it solidifies. As it expands it becomes less dense than liquid water. The change is no more than about 10 per cent but it is enough to ensure that the ice floats.

If the water is confined, within a section of pipe for example, the pressure it exerts as it expands is considerable. Under laboratory conditions, and at a temperature of -7.6 °F (-22 °C), the pressure amounts to about 55 tons per square feet (216 million pascals), although it exerts only about one-tenth of this pressure if it is unconfined. It is hardly surprising that the expansion easily bursts pipes.

Under high pressure and at much lower temperatures the character of ice changes. Ordinary ice, the kind that floats on water, is known as ice I, but there are eight other forms of ice in which the repulsion between molecules is overcome and they are packed together much more tightly. Such ices are denser than liquid water. They never occur in the presence of the liquid but, if they did,

they would sink to the bottom. Ice I can be converted to much denser ice III at around -4 °F (-20 °C) and a pressure rather more than 20 times average sea level air pressure. Such extreme conditions do not occur on Earth, but this and other forms of ice probably exist on some of the bodies in the outer regions of the solar system.

The ice from which glaciers and the polar ice caps are made does not form in the same way that ice forms when you make ice cubes in a refrigerator. In the refrigerator, liquid water is cooled until it freezes. An ice sheet begins as snow, made from tiny crystals of ice linked into loose, complex, and sometimes very beautiful shapes. The snow falls and later more snow falls to lie on top of it. As snow accumulates, year after year, the weight of the overlying snow packs the crystals together until they become a solid mass of ice.

So far as living organisms are concerned, the fact that ordinary ice floats on the surface of water is much more than an intriguing curiosity. We benefit from it greatly. In winter, water cools because the air in contact with the surface is colder than the water itself and heat passes from the warmer to the cooler medium. As the water cools it becomes more dense and sinks, being replaced by warmer water from below. The process might continue until all the water was chilled to the same temperature, but eventually the surface water is so cold that it freezes. The ice floats at the surface and may be chilled still more by the bitter winds that blow across it, but the water beneath the ice is protected. It cannot be cooled except by its contact with the surface ice, and as water freezes the latent heat released tends to warm the water immediately below it. In all but the shallowest bodies of water some liquid remains, and can support life. Were the lakes and seas to freeze solid, life in them would be destroyed. Indeed, had the seas frozen solid early in the history of the Earth it is very unlikely that life could have evolved at all.

Water's vital role

Its property of being a solvent for such a wide range of substances makes water very useful around the house, but it is much more important than that. Consider what happens when you water a plant. The water trickles down through the soil, around and between soil particles, dissolving chemical

(Opposite) The gases that form our atmosphere, including the water vapour, were originally erupted from volcanoes. This is Nyamulagira, Zaïre.

Sea water can be made drinkable if its salt is removed. This is a large seawater desalination plant near Acre, Israel.

compounds that are present in the soil, compounds you may have added yourself, as fertilizer. Then it bathes the fine hairs that grow from the plant roots. Now a chemical solution, the water enters the plant through its root hairs and, because the plant can use the substances dissolved from the soil for its nourishment, the watering helps it to grow and remain healthy. That is how all plants obtain most of their nutrients.

You and I are able to eat solid food, although we can subsist on a liquid diet if we must — and some invalids may have to

do so — but really dry food, containing almost no moisture, is rather unpalatable. It is unpalatable because, before we can digest our food, we must chew it into a pulp mixed with saliva and, if it is too dry, it may make excessive demands on the salivary glands in the mouth. It may be almost impossible to swallow food that is too dry. Saliva consists of a number of chemical compounds that kill bacteria and start the digestive process — dissolved in water, of course.

Despite our reliance on solid foods, we obtain a significant proportion of our

ever, and you will find that 87 per cent of it is water. In this case, the liquid is not a solution but an emulsion, in which the fats exist as globules larger than any molecule but much too small to be visible using an ordinary microscope, dispersed evenly throughout the water in which soluble substances are dissolved.

Beer also consists very largely of water. In this case the liquid is a solution — of a little alcohol, sugars, and a bitter flavour imparted by a very complex combination of resins, possibly tannins, and essential oils obtained by boiling the flowers of the hop plant. Beer drinkers are not necessarily seeking the nutritional qualities of their beverage, although many waistlines testify to the fact that these certainly exist. Wine is made from the fermented juice of the grape but, chemically, grape juice is a weak solution of sugars and other substances produced by the vine plant and stored in its fruit.

The only liquids we consume that are not made almost wholly from water are oils and, apart from the small quantities that some people take for medicinal reasons, we use oils only in cooking and dressings. Our drinks — all of them — are essentially water, usually with flavourings. The drinks may be intended to supply nutrients — ascorbic acid (vitamin C) is provided by fruit juices, for example — but it is water that we drink. The sensation of thirst, which impels us to drink, indicates a need for water. An adult human must consume at least 1.75 pints (one litre) of water a day, either by drinking or as an ingredient of food, and a person deprived of water will survive for no more than about six days, or in a hot environment perhaps for as little as two or three. A healthy person can survive for several weeks without solid food. It is hardly surprising that desert peoples picture paradise as a place of luxuriant, well-watered gardens.

nutrients in liquid form. The dairy industry encourages us to drink milk, in quantities that may or may not be wholly beneficial to our health, by advertising the high nutritional value of its commodity. Many years ago, children of impoverished families, living in industrial cities, suffered from rickets, a disease caused by a deficiency of vitamin D, obtained from the ultraviolet radiation in sunlight, and of calcium. Milk is an excellent source of calcium and so for some years free milk was supplied to British schoolchildren. Analyse cows' milk, how-

The water must contain very little salt (for reasons explained on page 69), and people adrift at sea in lifeboats without fresh water, or the means to remove salt from sea water, may die from thirst. The aridity of desert islands is due to their lack of fresh water, yet they are surrounded on all sides by sea water. Sea water can be converted to fresh water, most simply by evaporating the water and trapping and condensing the vapour, but on a large scale the process is very expensive.

THE WATER YOU NEVER SEE

During a severe drought, water evaporates from the ground surface and the soil dries. Plants wilt, and eventually die, because the soil within reach of their roots contains insufficient water for their needs. If the soil is mainly clay, cracks may appear in it. Drought does not crack a sandy soil because the large sand grains simply fall together. Clay particles are much smaller and pack together. Separate them and they turn into dust.

The cracked surface of a clay soil presents a dramatic picture of drought, immediately recognizable and evocative of hardship and hunger. The picture is true, of course, but perhaps not quite so true as it seems. If you were to take a sample of soil from that parched land and bake it in an oven, with some device to trap any gases emitted from it, you would collect a surprisingly large amount of water. Water accounts for rather more than 17 per cent of the weight of clay, no matter how dry the soil from which it is taken.

This water is of no value to plants because it is bound firmly to the surface of clay particles. Most soils hold water in this way, but the amount is related to the size of the particles. The larger the particles, the less water they will hold. Sand, whose grains are large, really can become very dry indeed.

Soil particles are made from a range of chemical compounds, but all of them contain oxygen. A hydrogen atom in a water molecule can bond with an oxygen atom in the molecule of a mineral, and that is how water attaches itself very securely to the surface of soil particles, often forming a layer around the particle, like a skin, one molecule thick.

The reason that a soil composed of large particles holds less of this bound water than a soil composed of small particles is a matter of geometry. The smaller the particle the greater surface area it has in proportion to its volume. A given volume of, say, a clay soil will contain far more small particles than a similar volume of, say, a sandy soil,

When clay soil dries, it shrinks and cracks appear, but a considerable amount of water remains, as a chemical constituent of the minerals themselves.

and so it will provide a much larger total surface area to which water can bind itself.

The difference in particle size is considerable. In the system of measurement used in Britain (a slightly different system is used in the United States), sand, which can be graded from 'very coarse' to 'very fine', consists of grains whose diameter is between 62.5 and 2000 microns (a micron is one-millionth of a metre, so sand grains are from 0.002 to 0.08 in in diameter). Clay particles, in contrast, are less than 4 microns (0.0002 in) in diameter — one-five hundredth to one-fifteenth of the size.

Bound water is not the only soil water whose use is denied to plants. The words 'clay' and 'sand' refer only to the size of the particles, not to their composition, and the classification also includes 'gravel', 'pebbles' and 'boulders'. Most of the minerals whose particles form clay are hydrous aluminium silicates, although magnesium or iron may substitute for some of the aluminium. This means they consist of alternate layers of alumina (aluminium oxide, Al_2O_3) and silica (silicon dioxide, SiO_2), but with some of the oxygen atoms being replaced by hydroxyl (OH) groups. In other words, water forms part of the chemical compound and its molecules help to give the mineral its particular structure.

We cannot use such 'locked-up' water directly, but there are many very common minerals whose molecules include water. Some of them are very valuable to us. Gypsum, for example, is used in building and in the manufacture of Portland cement, but in one of its naturally occurring forms it is called alabaster, and used for statuary. Gypsum is calcium sulphate dihydrate ($CaSO_4.2H_2O$) — a molecule of calcium sulphate securely attached to two molecules of water. Heat it to drive off one of the water molecules and it becomes a hemihydrate, $CaSO_4.H_2O$, better known as plaster of Paris. The paper on which this book is printed contains kaolin (china clay), as a filler between the vegetable fibres, as a whitener, and to provide a non-absorbent surface suitable for printing fine lines and colour. Kaolin is obtained from the mineral kaolinite, which is another hydrous aluminium silicate, $Al_2Si_2O_5(OH_4)$.

Sometimes it is useful to add water, and hydrate a compound. This is how lime is made, used mainly to neutralize acid soils and acid lakes. Lime begins as limestone, a very common rock that consists mainly of calcium carbonate ($CaCO_3$). The rock is crushed and then heated in a kiln. This drives off carbon dioxide (CO_2), leaving calcium oxide (CaO), or quicklime. The quicklime is then doused with water. This produces a rapid, violent reaction, with the emission of heat, at the end of which the oxide has become a hydroxide, $Ca(OH)_2$, which is the slaked lime that is sold to farmers and that you can buy from any garden supplier.

Washing soda, sometimes called soda ash, is also a hydrate, of sodium carbonate ($Na_2SO_4.10H_2O$). In the days before modern detergents it was widely used for washing clothes and you can still buy it at any hardware store. Industrially, in the late eighteenth century it became one of the raw materials for the manufacture of soap and, because of its commercial importance, the production of soda ash was the foundation

Ordinary agricultural and horticultural lime is sold as a dry powder. It is a hydrated mineral, however, and water forms part of its constituent molecules.

on which the modern chemical industry was built.

Movement of water

When rain falls on the land, or snow melts, much of the water runs off immediately, flowing down the slope to enter the river which drains that particular area. Severe rain storms increase the amount of water carried by rivers, and in extreme cases can overflow their banks to cause flooding. The spring thaw brings more predictable volumes of meltwater.

Rivers are supplied by water that drains from the surrounding land, so you can think of a river — even a very small one — as lying at the bottom of a 'drainage basin'. Small drainage basins are often linked into larger ones, as small rivers feed into larger rivers.

If the rivers mark the lower boundaries of a drainage basin, the upper boundary is marked by high ground, from which some water will flow to one side and some to the other. The area drained by a particular flow of water is called a 'catchment' (or in the United States a 'watershed') and its uppermost boundary is a 'divide'.

As it flows across the surface the water collects any loose material it can carry. The size and number of the particles it can transport depends on the energy the water has — the rate at which it flows. The amount can be substantial and surface run-off is a powerful agent of erosion on vulnerable soils. Soil particles are carried away to the river and then carried by the river, sometimes to be deposited much further downstream, where the river is wider and flows more slowly, or perhaps in the estuary. That is where salt water from the sea meets fresh water in the river. Negative chlorine ions (Cl^-) bond with positively charged soil particles, linking them together into clumps. The process is called 'flocculation' and it increases the size and weight of the silt particles, causing them to settle. This is why mudflats, made from accumulated river-borne silt, are such a common feature of estuaries. Soil that is not deposited is carried out to sea. In the Bay of Bengal, soil carried by the Ganges and Brahmaputra rivers has been accumulating for centuries. The sea offshore is less than 600 feet (183 m) deep for more than 100 miles (160 km), and the Mahanadi, Godavari and Krishna rivers have built huge deltas in the west of the

Bay. Where the accumulation of silt ends, the water depth more than doubles.

Erosion is most severe on steep slopes where there is no vegetation and soil is exposed. It can be minimized by maintaining a permanent vegetation cover, so plant roots trap and hold soil particles, and by reducing the angle of slope — by terracing, for example — on cultivated soils.

Not all of the run-off flows across the surface of the land. If you watch the rain falling on a field, even one where the soil is bare, you may see a few rivulets flowing along furrows but it will be obvious that most of the water, and perhaps all of it, is soaking into the ground. It still flows more or less directly down the slope, however, but it does so below the surface, moving through the soil rather than over it. If there is a ditch along the lower side of the field you may see the water collecting in it.

Measure the amount of water falling on the field, however, and compare it with the amount entering the ditch; you will find the figures do not tally. Some of the water will be evaporating from the surface, of course, but, even when you have made an allowance for that, you will discover that not all the rain is finding its way to the ditch.

The 'missing' water percolates downwards through the soil. The ease with which it does so depends on the character of the soil, but all soils are more or less porous and permeable — the two are not the same and it is possible for a soil to be both porous and impermeable.

Composition of soil

Soil is composed of mineral grains whose size and shape vary widely. When they are packed together, as they are in a soil, there are small spaces left among them and these spaces, or pores, are more or less linked. Water can fill the pores and it can also flow from one to another. The total amount of pore space determines the amount of water the soil can hold — its porosity. The extent to which the pores are linked, so they can become channels, determines the ease with which water can percolate through the soil — its permeability.

Two samples of soil of equal volume but quite different types — say a sandy soil and a clay — may contain similar amounts of total pore space. You can understand this apparent paradox if you picture two boxes of equal volume. You are to fill both boxes with ball bearings, small ones, say with a diameter x, in one box and large ones, say with a diameter $2x$ in the other, in such a way as to leave the same amount of air space, say 10 per cent, in each box. Measure the volume of a box, deduct 10 per cent, and what remains is the volume you must fill with ball bearings. Calculate the volume of a large and a small ball bearing, divide the volume you must fill by the volume of each type of ball bearing and the result will be the number of ball bearings of each size that will fill the allotted space. The 'grains' will be of greatly different size, but they will occupy the same volume and there will be the same volume of air space among them. That is how it can be that a volume of a sandy soil and the same volume of a clay soil can contain equal volumes of pore space.

Pour a little water on to each sample and measure the time it takes for the water to reach the bottom of the box and you will find that, although the samples are equally porous, they are not equally permeable. The smaller the ball bearings, or soil grains, the smaller are the pore spaces, the smaller the channels linking them, and the greater the resistance they offer to the flow of water.

You will see the implications of this if, next time you visit the coast, you pour water on to dry beach sand. It will vanish immediately and, in a very short time, the sand will be quite dry again. Pour water on to a clay soil and it will take much longer to disappear.

The character of most soils changes with increasing depth. The uppermost layer, where plants grow and life is abundant, contains large amounts of organic material, which modifies the texture of the soil, usually making it more porous but less permeable, so it tends to retain water. Lower down the soil is more mineral, but organic matter will have been washed into it from above. At the lowest level, the soil is affected mainly by the underlying rock from which its minerals are derived.

As water percolates downwards, eventually it must reach a layer of impermeable material. This may be closely packed clay, or it may be the underlying rock itself. When it arrives at this level it moves no further downwards and will flow downhill. It will move much more slowly than water at the surface, because it must percolate through material the grains of which are packed together closely by the weight above them,

and the gradient may be shallower than the surface gradient. The water that flows over the surface of the impermeable layer is called the 'groundwater' and it does not flow in streams, like rivers, but more or less in broad sheets defined by the boundaries of the drainage system and the contours of the ground it crosses. The material through which the groundwater flows is called an 'aquifer'.

The surface over which the groundwater flows is shaped by the rocks — either those which compose the surface or those that lie beneath it. Where there are depressions in the rocks, water will accumulate to form subterranean pools — not of free water, of course, but of soil material that is saturated. Just as the depth of a lake varies from place to place according to the level of the lake bed, so the depth of groundwater varies from place to place and, but less like a lake, it has an upper surface. This is the 'water table', a somewhat indistinct boundary below which the soil is saturated and above which, although not saturated, the soil is very wet. The level of the water table falls in very dry weather, when the rate at which water drains from the soil exceeds the rate at which the rainfall contributes to the groundwater. In very wet weather the water table rises and in some places and at some times it may reach ground level, waterlogging the upper layers of soil. The sedges, rushes, and very tussocky grasses you often find growing on low-lying land are plants that can tolerate water around their roots. They are good indicators of a high water table and land that floods from time to time.

If you bore a hole through the soil, deep enough for it to penetrate below the water table, the bottom of the hole will fill with water. This is then a well and, if it is deeper than the lowest level to which the water table falls during dry spells, the well will seldom be dry. To obtain the water you will need to install either a pump or a bucket you can lower on a winch. For most of history, in most of the world, this is how people obtained their water if they did not live beside a river.

Not every aquifer has a water table. When

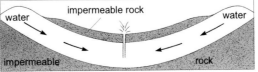

Ground water may be held between two layers of impermeable material. If there is a depression, like a basin, in both layers, the water between them will drain to the lowest region and fill it. When a hole is drilled from the surface through the upper impermeable layer, water will 'find its own level' by flowing more rapidly down the slope and up the drilled hole. This is an artesian well, where water flows to the surface without being lifted.

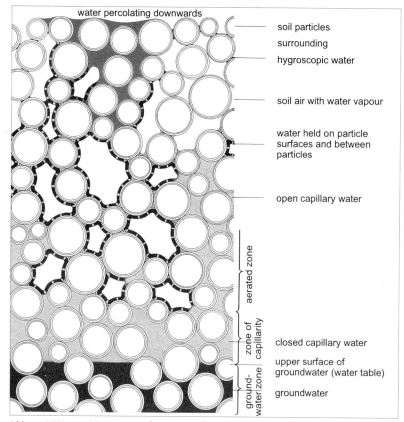

water percolating downwards

soil particles
surrounding

hygroscopic water

soil air with water vapour

water held on particle
surfaces and between
particles

open capillary water

aerated zone

zone of capillarity

closed capillary water

upper surface of
groundwater (water table)

ground-water zone

groundwater

(Above) Water falling on the ground surface moves downwards between the soil particles until it reaches a layer of impermeable material, where it accumulates as groundwater. The indistinct upper surface of the groundwater is called the 'water table'. As the upper layers of soil dry, water is drawn from below by capillary attraction. Above the water table there is a layer in which all the capillary spaces are filled and, above that, a layer where they are only partly filled. Higher still, water is held on the surface of soil particles, but soil spaces are filled with air and, above this layer, water exists as vapour.

(Opposite) Most wells, like this one in Burkina-Faso, differ from artesian wells (see also previous page) in that the water must be pumped to the surface.

the upper limit is defined by a water table, it is said to be 'unconfined', but there are also 'confined' aquifers, that flow between two impermeable layers. The water in a confined aquifer may be held under considerable pressure. In some cases the pressure is such that, were the confining layer to be removed so the water could find its own level, the water table would be above ground level. If you sink a well that punctures the uppermost impermeable layer of such an aquifer, the water will rush to the surface without pumping. This is an 'artesian' or 'overflowing' well.

The groundwater also forms a reservoir that can be tapped by plants. In dry weather, water evaporates from the soil surface leaving vacancies among the pore spaces. The very smallest of these spaces can be filled by water drawn upwards from the water table. The process is called 'capillary action', or 'capillarity', and it is caused by surface tension. (This is explained below.)

At the boundary between a liquid and air, the attractive force holding water molecules together is much stronger below than above. This has the effect of increasing the strength with which the surface molecules are bonded to the molecules on either side of them. The result is that the surface molecules form a layer, almost like an elastic

skin, held together by molecular forces. This phenomenon is called surface tension, and in water the layer is strong enough to float a needle that is laid on it gently enough for it not to break the surface.

Like stretched elastic, the tension draws in the surface layer, trying always to adopt the most economical shape. Release the elastic and it will contract. Separate a small amount of any liquid and at once its own surface tension will compel it to adopt the shape that has the smallest surface area — a sphere. The liquid will form a drop.

The surface molecules can also bond with the minerals at the sides of the pore spaces and they do so with an attraction stronger than that between water molecules. Water bonds to glass in the same way and you can see it as a 'meniscus', where the water curves up the glass. In the soil, water climbs the sides of pores provided the force exerted by the weight of the water involved is less than that of the molecular attraction. It can occur, therefore, only in the smallest of soil pores.

There is a capillary zone above the water table and in dry weather this can extend upwards a surprising distance, but it depends critically on the size of the pore spaces, which depends in turn on the size of the soil grains. In sand, with pores of about 0.00008 inches (0.02 mm) diameter, water may rise about 4 inches (10 cm). In clay, where pore diameters may be about 0.000002 inches (0.0005 mm), water may rise 10 feet (3 m). Plants can reach water, therefore, provided their roots are within the capillary zone, and they are more likely to achieve this in a clay soil than in sand.

Eventually, of course, the flowing groundwater enters rivers and so returns to the sea, but it can take many years.

Connate water
Very occasionally an aquifer may form that is more than confined. It is sealed permanently, to remain undisturbed, isolated from its surroundings, for millions upon millions of years. Such water is called 'connate', from the Latin *connatus*, meaning 'born with, and implying that the aquifer and the rocks in which it is sealed formed together and at the same time.

The soil that is washed from the land by the rain enters rivers. The larger and heavier particles do not travel far. A fast-flowing mountain stream is energetic and

Connate water is sealed from the outside world for a very long time. (1) Its formation begins with the deposition of sediment above a layer of impermeable rock in which there is a depression. The weight of accumulating sediment squeezes out water, which moves downwards. (2) The upper layers of the sediment then begin to consolidate. The pressure they exert forces some of the trapped water back through the overlying layer, leaving behind the dissolved salts, so the remaining water becomes increasingly saline. (3) The overlying sediment is converted into a cap of impermeable rock and the very saline water is held between it and the base of the depression in the underlying rock.

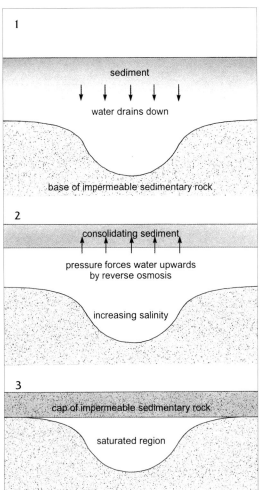

their courses, so they discharge into different sea areas. The sea level may rise or fall, altering the dynamics of water circulation.

The weight of a thick bed of sediment compresses the lower layers. Formerly soft, fine mud, they are packed down into a very soft rock. Mudstones and shales are sedimentary rocks, and so are the beach rocks, made from partly consolidated sand, on which you may stub your toe as you walk across a beach because the rock — on its way to becoming a proper sandstone — looks much like the sand in which it lies. You can crush such rocks between your fingers and scratch them with a fingernail but, nevertheless, they are rocks and their initial compaction marks the start of a process called 'diagenesis' by which the sediment is transformed into a sedimentary rock which, in time, may become quite hard. Limestone is a sedimentary rock and some limestones are used widely as a high-quality building stone.

The process may involve chemical changes, as the constituents of the sediment react with one another and with substances present in the water around them. If crustal movements carry the material close to an area of volcanic activity, or to rocks that are cooling after having been released from below the crust, the resultant baking may effect further changes. As the temperatures and pressures involved increase, diagenesis grades into 'metamorphism' — although there is no clear boundary between the two types of processes — and a sedimentary rock is altered into a metamorphic rock by partly melting and then cooling, and during this process new groups of minerals crystallize. This may produce a very hard, impermeable rock such as slate, which began as mud and makes an excellent roofing material.

The sediment is very porous while it is settling on the sea bed. Sea water completely saturates it, all the way down to the impermeable and non-porous rock at its base. When the sediment is compressed, however, it loses its permeability, because the packing together of the microscopically small particles from which it is made reduces the size and number of pore spaces and of the channels linking them.

In most cases, the conversion of sediment to rock squeezes the water out of the pore spaces. Consider what may happen, however, if the sediment has filled a depression in the underlying, impermeable rock until a

can transport all but the larger pebbles, which accumulate on its bed. Further downstream, as the river grows deeper and wider, it flows more slowly. The water has less energy to transport solid particles and the heaviest settle on the bottom. By the time the river reaches the sea, only the finest particles remain. Many of these are deposited in the estuary, but some of the silt reaches the sea. There the mixing of salt and fresh water causes even that silt to flocculate and settle, as mud on the sea bed, mainly in fairly shallow water.

The mud is deposited day after day, year after year, and the layer of sediment it forms grows ever thicker. Sedimentation is partly a chemical process, affected by the chemical composition of the water, and so scientists studying ancient sediments can learn much about the kind of environments in which the sediments were deposited. Sedimentation may continue for just a few years or for many millions, but eventually it ceases. The pattern of sea currents may change, because of changing climates perhaps, or of upheavals in the Earth's crust. Rivers may change

level surface is produced above it. When the sediment is compressed most of the water will be squeezed out, but the water held by the sediment in the depression may remain because there is nowhere it can go — the sides of the depression are impermeable and, by the time the pressure is sufficient to remove the water, the overlying layer may also be impermeable. So the water is re-tained, trapped. The water and the rock have formed together. The water is connate.

Sedimentary rocks rarely remain in the places where they were formed. Movements of the Earth's crust push them this way and that. They can be buckled, twisted, raised on end, or turned upside down, and shifted considerable distances. Finally, they may be thrust high above sea level to form moun-tain chains. If they contain connate water, the water travels with them.

Meteoric water

The process described above involves the entrapment of sea water, but scientists now believe fresh water can be trapped in the same way. Sediments also form on lake beds and connate water held in a lake-bed sediment — called 'meteoric' water — would be fresh. 'Meteoric' is an adjective, derived originally from the Greek *meteoros* meaning 'lofty', that is applied to things, like rain, which fall from the sky.

It is not easy to tell the origin of connate water because, regardless of its source, its chemical composition is altered radically by the conditions to which it has been ex-posed. Invariably it is extremely saline — commonly containing about seven times the concentration of salt that is found in sea water. In some cases the salt may have been dissolved out of surrounding rocks, but it would be a curious coincidence if all connate water were to have obtained so much salt in this way, and there is another possibility.

The process of osmosis is described on page 69. Essentially, it occurs when two solutions of different strengths are separated by a membrane that permits the passage of molecules of the solvent, but not of the solute. Solvent passes from the solution of lower strength to that of higher strength, concentrating the former and diluting the latter, until the two are of similar strength. Osmosis can occur in reverse, however, provided the stronger solution is held under much greater pressure than the weaker. This

forces solvent molecules to pass in the opposite direction — from the higher to the lower concentration — so that the stronger solution becomes more concentrated and the weaker solution less so.

As a sediment is compacted and its permeability steadily decreases, perhaps it passes through a stage in which it acts as the kind of semi-permeable membrane that is needed for osmosis to occur. This stage would be reached — if it is, for no one can be certain — when the pore spaces had been reduced to an extent that permitted the passage of water molecules, but of nothing larger. The lower layer of sediment, in which water was trapped, would be held under great pressure that would increase as sediment continued to be deposited far above to add to the weight. Were the pressure to reach a sufficiently high value, at the same time as the porosity of the sedi-mentary layer immediately above it gave it the properties of a semi-permeable mem-brane, then water might be forced upward, through that layer, but leaving behind the molecules of any substance dissolved in the water. If this is what occurred, it would explain how connate water comes to have a salinity which is not only higher than that of modern sea water, but of sea water at any time in the history of the planet.

Water for health

Many years ago, a farmer in northern Germany noticed that his pigs often went to drink from a particular spring, and that some time after they had drunk from it their skins bore a pale, almost silvery sheen that soon disappeared. One day, overcome by his curiosity, he decided to sample the water. It was very salty. The pigs were enjoying the taste of the salt — and of the many other minerals in the water — and as they drank they splashed around and became wet. As the water dried, the salts were left behind as a film on their skins. The farmer, or more correctly his pigs, had discovered the natural mineral spring on which the prosperity of the city of Bad Oeynhausen came to be based. In gratitude, the citizens placed a statue of him, with his pigs, in the centre of the town, standing appropriately in a pool fed by a fountain.

Such mineralized waters have been known to possess therapeutic properties, at least since Roman times. Today, the waters are bottled and marketed, but in the past people

Bad Oeynhausen, Germany, owes its prosperity as a spa town to a local farmer and his pigs who discovered the first mineral spring. The grateful citizens erected this statue to commemorate the discovery.

(Opposite) The mineralized waters at Bath, England, have been prized since Roman times.

could sample them only by visiting the towns that grew up around the springs where they occurred — towns that usually included the word 'Spa' in their names in England, or 'Bad' in Germany. In Germany the waters are still known as *Heilwasser*, 'healing waters'. Belief in their properties is not unfounded. They really do benefit sufferers from certain ailments.

As groundwater flows through the soil, chemical compounds contained in the rocks, and from grains in which the soil is composed, dissolve into it. The chemical content of the water varies widely from place to place, depending on the local chemistry of the rocks but, in some places, the water becomes a complex solution of many minerals.

The flow follows the gradient of the underlying, impermeable rock and often emerges at the bottom of valleys. In many places, though, the impermeable layer does not have an even surface. It is buckled or folded, and it may also have joints and cracks through which water can pass. Groundwater can reach the surface at such places and, wherever it does so, it 'springs' from the ground. This is a spring, despite the fact that in most cases the water merely seeps rather than springs.

Where the rock is deeply fissured, groundwater may descend by one fissure, flow through crevices in the rock itself, and

emerge again from another fissure. Such water is usually warm, and the Germans, who take such matters seriously, define a 'thermal' spring as one whose temperature is not less than 68 °F (20 °C). In practice it can be much higher. The thermal spring in Bath, England, for example, issues from the ground at 114-120 °F (45-49 °C).

The water is warmed by its contact with the surrounding rocks. The temperature of crustal rocks increases with increasing depth. The rate of this 'geothermal gradient' varies quite widely from place to place, but on average it is 58-116 °F/mile of depth (20-40 °C/km). It is caused almost entirely by the decay of radioactive elements dispersed throughout the rocks themselves, and it increases with depth, because heat can escape from rock only by conduction upwards, towards the surface, because the crust lies above the much hotter material of the Earth's mantle. When water flows through the rock itself, and at some depth, it passes through an environment which is markedly warmer than that above. Ordinary groundwater, on the other hand, is insulated from the ground surface, which is warmed by the Sun, and is in contact only with the surface of the impermeable rock. The temperature of the rock remains constant throughout the year, and because this is also the temperature of the groundwater, in summer the water is usually several degrees

cooler than water at or close to the surface. This is why most spring or well water is refreshingly cool on a hot day.

Geysers

In certain places, however, very hot water may emerge from the ground, sometimes under pressure. Such eruptions of water are known as 'geysers', a word derived from the Icelandic word *geysir* which means 'gusher'. Geysers occur in many parts of the world, although the most famous ones are in Iceland, New Zealand and Yellowstone National Park, in Wyoming, United States, and they are all associated with areas of recent volcanic activity.

The Strokkur geyser, in Iceland, erupts every three minutes and feeds a pool warm enough for bathing.

The temperature of the volcanic rocks below ground level increases with depth much more rapidly than the usual geothermal gradient. Groundwater flows at depth into a system of fissures in the rock, the fissures being connected to a central shaft that opens at ground level. The water is heated more strongly at the bottom of the shaft than at the top. As the water boils, bubbles rise through the shaft, expelling some water and reducing the pressure under which the water is held. The reduction in pressure reduces the temperature at which the water will boil, so boiling intensifies until the whole column of water is expelled as a spout. Then more water enters the fissures, is heated, and the process repeats itself. The geysers in the Yellowstone National Park erupt to heights of about 150 feet (45 m), but the greatest of them all, at Waimangu, New Zealand, spouted to more than 1600 feet (about 500 m). Its activity began in 1900, following a volcanic eruption in 1886, but by 1904 it had lowered the water table to such an extent that it ceased to spout.

Geyser water contains many chemical compounds dissolved from the surrounding rocks, and sometimes it carries solid material as well. The Waimangu geyser ejected mud and stones as well as water. As the hot water evaporates from the ground around the geyser mouth, the dissolved minerals are left behind to form accumulations of rock, called 'siliceous sinter' (siliceous because of the large proportion of silica it contains).

The configuration of the fissures in which the water is heated may not produce the conditions necessary for eruptions. Then, instead of a geyser, hot springs occur, or small pools of hot — sometimes boiling — water, or boiling mud. Because of their high mineral content, such waters are also valued for their therapeutic properties.

There are other places, not necessarily associated with recent volcanic activity, where the geothermal gradient is anomalously high, and reservoirs of water may be held trapped, far below the ground. By drilling through the overlying rock this water can be released, so it rises to the surface under its own pressure. It can then be used to heat other water, as a source of energy. This is the most usual form of 'geothermal energy', and because the source of heat is radioactive decay, this is a form of nuclear energy.

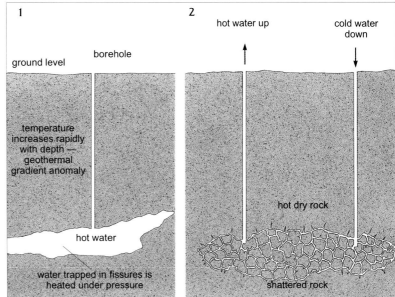

Energy can also be extracted from such anomalously hot rocks that are dry. Two holes are drilled from the surface into the hot rocks, and explosive charges are detonated at the bases of the shafts to shatter the rocks between them. Water is then pumped down one hole. It moves through the shattered rock, being heated as it passes, and emerges from the second hole.

Geothermal reservoirs, of water or of hot rock, are limited in extent, and the extraction of heat cools them until they are at the same temperature as the surrounding rock. They are not an inexhaustible source of energy and, of course, geothermal energy is available only in certain places which may not be in populated areas where the energy can be used. Nor is this source of energy particularly 'clean'. The water extracted from the rock contains substances that make it highly corrosive and poisonous, so it must be kept isolated from the surface environment.

The search for petroleum
Occasionally you see people, probably wearing overalls and hard hats, taking mysterious measurements on the ground. Or you might see a low-flying aircraft trailing a curious, bullet-shaped object some distance behind it. You might not know the purpose of such activity, but you would feel more confident were you to see a derrick, and drilling in progress. These are all methods used in 'geophysical exploration' — the scientific search for useful subterranean or submarine resources. These days the search is likely to be for petroleum.

(1) Where the rate at which the temperature of rocks increases rapidly with depth, water trapped in the hot rock will be heated. It cannot expand because it is confined, so the pressure is high. A borehole sunk into the reservoir will allow the hot water to escape to the surface.
(2) Where the anomalously hot rock contains no water, two boreholes are drilled. Explosives detonated at the bottom shatter the rock, making it permeable. Cold water pumped down one hole flows through the fissures, is heated, and emerges from the other hole.

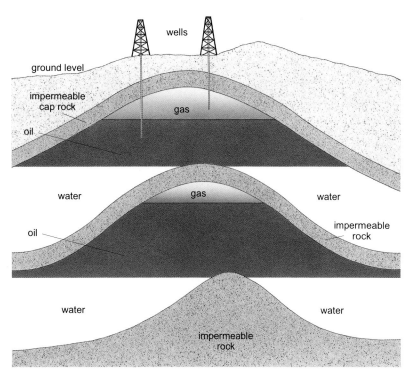

Oil and gas reservoirs begin to form from the accumulation of sediment mixed with the remains of marine organisms. Other sediments then form an overlying impermeable layer. Isolated from the outside environment, the decomposition of the organic material may then resume, followed by the formation of another impermeable layer. This process is repeated several times. Movements of the Earth's crust deform the layers, often forming a domed shape into which sediment drains, and heat the material, altering its composition. The mixture of salt water, mineral grains, gases, liquids and solids is now petroleum under pressure.

(Opposite) Oil and gas, confined in reservoirs below the sea bed, can now be exploited. This is the Shell/Esso Brent 'B' oil production platform in the North Sea. The vessel in the foreground has just delivered supplies.

Different types of rock have different densities. This can produce minor, local variations in the Earth's gravitational field that can be detected using sensitive instruments. Some rocks contain more magnetite than others. Magnetite, or 'lodestone', is an iron oxide and its presence can distort the magnetic field locally, again to an extent that can be detected. Rocks vary in the ease with which they conduct electricity, and in the way shock waves travel through them. These differences, too, can be detected.

The scientists looking for petroleum hope to find an area where permeable rock, such as limestone or sandstone, is surrounded and overlain by an impermeable rock such as slate, and preferably where the structure forms a pronounced dome. This is the kind of place where petroleum may be found, and where it may be worth drilling. The purpose of drilling is to obtain samples of the rock at varying depths. The samples are examined closely and, in particular, they are studied for the fossils they contain. Petroleum is the partly decomposed remains of once-living organisms, but the presence of rocks which contain certain kinds of fossils may justify drilling deeper. The scientists are not looking for water, which is worthless, but if they find petroleum there will be water associated with it and, if they are unlucky, water is all that their eventual well may yield.

As marine organisms die, their remains sink slowly towards the sea bed. Many will be eaten by other organisms, but some will reach the bottom where tides and currents may sweep them to places where they accumulate and become mixed with the sediment that is forming at the same time. Sometimes the sediment contains a large proportion of sand grains, or of shells made from calcium carbonate. The layer of mud continues to accumulate until conditions change, and a different type of sediment, with much finer particles, forms above it. This upper layer may then be compressed into an impermeable sedimentary rock, leaving the mixture of organic matter and sand or calcium carbonate trapped beneath it. The trapped mud also contains a high proportion of sea water, held just as connate water is held (see page 28).

Movements of the Earth's crust may then twist and distort the rocks, and at some stage may expose them to high temperatures. This transforms the rocks from sedimentary to metamorphic types, and it also 'cooks' the organic material still held in the trap. This 'cooking' transforms the organic remains into a mixture of gas and liquids — some of them so viscous as to be almost solid — composed mainly of hydrocarbons, compounds of carbon and hydrogen, together, of course, with the water that is trapped with them. The liquids have been converted to petroleum, and the gas is mainly methane (CH_4) or 'natural gas'

The fluids can move through the porous sandstone or limestone made from the sand grains and shell remains with which they are mixed. Over a long period they will tend to flow downhill, to accumulate in depressions, where they form reservoirs of oil, gas and water, the impermeable rocks above them forming a 'cap'. Should the deformation of the structure cause it to bulge upward, so the cap rock forms a dome, the volume of the reservoir will be increased, and more material is likely to accumulate in it — which is why scientists are especially excited when they locate a dome.

Exploitation of the reservoir involves drilling a hole into it, through the cap rock and all the rock above it. Released from the pressure under which it has been held, the hole becomes a well and the contents of the reservoir rush to the surface — and much of what arrives at the wellhead is extremely saline water.

FRESH WATER AND SALT WATER

Hardness and acidity

If you move from one part of the country — any country — to another you may well find that the water which flows from the taps changes. It may taste different from one place to another, may or may not leave a 'fur' (see below for explanation) inside kettles and hot-water pipes, and you will notice a marked difference when you wash with it. Some water readily makes a lather with soap, so you need little soap to wash, but other water is much more reluctant to lather, you need more soap and, after you have washed, you will find a residue of scum on the sides of the basin. The contrast is between 'hard' and 'soft' water, and it arises from differences in the rocks over and through which the water flows before it is abstracted.

The story begins with carbon dioxide (CO_2), a gas that is weakly soluble in water. As water vapour condenses to form clouds, a little atmospheric carbon dioxide dissolves into it, to form H_2CO_3. This is carbonic acid, and all rain and snow is naturally acidic. When it flows across and through the ground, the water encounters more carbon dioxide, a by-product of the decomposition of organic material — the remains of plants and animals in which bacterial action oxidizes the carbon to carbon dioxide. So the concentration of carbonic acid increases somewhat.

What is now a weak acid flows through the soil, in contact with the mineral particles from which the soil is made, and it is able to react with some of them. If it encounters grains containing calcium or magnesium it can form calcium or magnesium carbonate ($CaCO_3$ or $MgCO_3$), calcium or magnesium bicarbonate ($Ca(HCO_3)_2$) or $Mg(HCO_3)_2$. The carbonates are insoluble, but the bicarbonates dissolve in the water and become part of it. The water will also dissolve the chloride and sulphate of calcium and magnesium, as well as iron oxides. The reactions 'use up' the acid, so the pH increases and the water becomes slightly alkaline.

This hard water occurs only in regions where it comes into contact with chalk, limestone or other sedimentary rocks rich in calcium and magnesium. The hardness

caused by calcium bicarbonate is called 'temporary' because, when the water is boiled, the bicarbonate is changed to carbonate. This is insoluble, and is precipitated as the scale or fur that accumulates in kettles and pipes. The other ingredients cause 'permanent' hardness, and can be removed only by filtering the water through substances that bond to them. Magnesium and calcium chloride and sulphate also react with the fatty acids in soaps to form the tough, insoluble scum that is deposited in fabrics during washing, and on the sides of washtubs and basins — a problem which does not occur with modern detergents.

The extent to which water is hard is measured as the ability of the water to form a scale when it is boiled. In the German grading system, the concentration of ingredients causing temporary hardness is measured, then an adjustment is made so the bicarbonates can be regarded as oxides — calcium oxide (CaO) and magnesium oxide (MgO) respectively — to avoid counting the carbon dioxide which is an ingredient of all water. One degree of hardness is then equal to 10 milligrams per litre (which is the same as 10 parts per million) of CaO or 7.19 milligrams per litre of MgO.

Water that flows over hard rocks, such as granite, encounters little or no calcium or magnesium compounds with which it can react. It remains weakly acidic, forms no scale when it is boiled because there is no carbonate to be precipitated, and does not form a scum with soap. It is 'soft' water. There is some evidence to suggest that the incidence of heart and circulatory diseases is lower in regions where the water is hard than in those where it is soft, but no explanation has been found for this observation.

River and lake systems are more or less discrete. That is to say, the water in an area drains into particular channels that converge in one major river. Large rivers may merge further downstream, so waters from different drainage basins may mix, but even then the drainage basins are likely to be adjacent to one another, with similar geology and vegetation. Because water is affected so strongly by the substances it encounters, the chemical composition of river and lake water varies widely from place

(Opposite) Rivers and lakes often form an intricate network of waterways, draining the surrounding land and returning water to the sea.

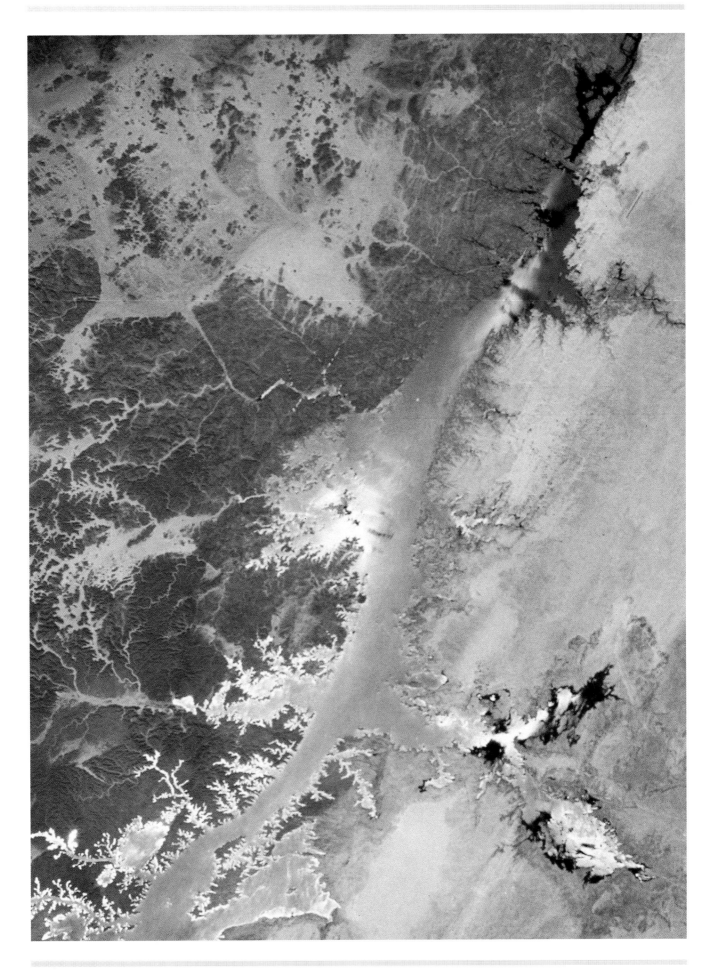

As the sea level falls, small areas may become partly cut off from the main body to form almost land-locked seas. Their waters have only limited contact with those of the ocean and, therefore, their chemical composition may be markedly different.

to place. It is possible only to suggest an average acidity, between pH6 and pH8, and an average content of dissolved material. As parts per thousand by weight, with the percentage of the total dissolved material in brackets, typical river water contains:

bicarbonate	58.5	(48.6)
calcium	15.0	(12.5)
silicate	13.1	(11.0)
sulphate	11.2	(9.3)
chloride	7.8	(6.5)
sodium	6.3	(5.3)
magnesium	4.1	(3.4)
potassium	2.3	(2.0)
nitrate	1.0	(0.8)
iron	0.7	(0.6).

Salinity and acidity of the sea

Rivers discharge into the sea, so all the material dissolved in their waters reaches the sea, where it would accumulate were it

not for the mechanisms that transfer chemical compounds from the sea back to the land (see page 47ff). Unlike rivers and lakes, however, the seas and oceans are linked to one another and, to some extent, water is exchanged among them. The rate of exchange is slow but, over the millions of years the oceans have existed, their waters have mixed sufficiently for their chemical compositions to be similar, although they are not identical. In particular, the concentration of the ingredients (although not the proportions of one ingredient to another) of seas which have only a restricted contact with the oceans, such as the Black Sea and Mediterranean, may differ substantially from that of the oceans.

The most obvious characteristic of sea water is its salinity — its 'saltiness'. This can be measured in two ways, as chlorinity (salt is sodium chloride), or salinity. The chlorinity measurement counts iodine and bromine as well as chlorine, and is the quantity, in grams, contained in 1 kilogram of water. If you multiply this measure by 1.80655, the resulting number represents the salinity, which is a measure of the total amount of dissolved solids contained in the water. As with the measurement of the hardness of fresh water, the salinity measurement regards carbonate as oxide (to avoid counting carbon dioxide). It also regards iodine and bromine as though they were chlorine, and it assumes all organic matter has been fully oxidized. Conventionally, salinity is counted in parts per thousand ('per mille'). In the oceans, salinity ranges between 33 and 38 parts per thousand, and it averages 35 parts per thousand.

A variety of substances contribute to the salty taste of sea water. If you have ever kept an aquarium for marine species, you will know that if you add 35 measures of common salt to every thousand measures of fresh water the resulting solution will taste like sea water, but fish will be unable to survive in it. The method by which chlorinity and salinity are measured provides a clue to the complexity of sea water. Eleven ingredients account for 99.99 per cent of the dissolved material. In parts per thousand by weight, with the percentage of the total of dissolved material in brackets, these are:

chloride	18.980	(55.05)
sodium	10.556	(30.61)
sulphate	2.649	(7.68)
magnesium	1.272	(3.69)
calcium	0.400	(1.16)
potassium	0.380	(1.10)
bicarbonate	0.140	(0.41)
bromide	0.065	(0.19)
borate	0.026	(0.07)
strontium	0.008	(0.03)
fluoride	0.001	(insignificant).

The total quantity of dissolved material varies somewhat, altering the salinity of the water, but the proportions of the ingredients are almost constant.

Clearly, some ingredients have disappeared. The seas receive their water from rivers — all of their water, for there is no other source of any importance. The rivers carry iron, silicate, and over the years they should have contributed much more bicarbonate than the 0.41 per cent found in the sea. The silt they carry must contain aluminium, which is the third most common element in the Earth's crust and accounts for 8 per cent of the crust by weight.

Sea water is alkaline, with a pH between 8.0 and 8.4, and under alkaline conditions, calcium and bicarbonate react to form calcium carbonate which is insoluble and so ceases to count as an ingredient of the water. Silica is removed by aquatic organisms which have many uses for it. Aluminium and iron, carried as oxides, are removed by reactions with other ingredients that cause them to coagulate and sink. The water finally contains only those dissolved substances for which there is no effective removal mechanism, together with the surplus that remains of those that are partly removed.

The sea as a sink

For many people, an idyllic rural scene is almost certain to include certain 'standard' components. There will be rolling fields, some with ripe corn, others meadows with tall grass and a riot of wild flowers. There will be cows and perhaps sheep and, somewhere in the background, there may be a farmyard with a few chickens. Certainly there will be hedges and trees and some of the trees will line the banks of a small river. There are other components the picture will have excluded — necessarily because of the requirement for it to be 'idyllic' — but they are there just the same. There is a major road, busy with traffic, for example, and a major industrial complex, and a sewage

As a river flows through farmland, as here in the English Lake District, plant nutrients drain into it. These support aquatic life but can cause pollution if the amounts are excessive.

works. They are out of sight, but they exist. Visible or not, all these components, and more, contribute substances to the river. The river drains the land and, like a familiar household drain, it carries materials away, eventually to the sea, and the sea is the sink into which all the world's drains flow.

Apart from carbonic acid and the dissolved substances gathered from the rocks, other material is added by the ordinary activities of living organisms. In case of humans, this includes industrial activities.

The river rose in the hills where a spring issued from a rock fissure, with groundwater drained from the hill tops through the thin, acid soil. After it has flowed a short distance, the river may be discoloured, 'peaty', because of the presence of humic acids. The composition of these is unknown, but certainly it is extremely complex. The acids are produced by the decay of plant material to humus and under certain circumstances, involving their exposure to alkaline water,

they can be released in soluble form. It is said to be the contribution from the humic acids released from the peats of western Scotland that produces the unique quality of the water necessary for the distillation of Scotch whisky.

Still further downstream, the river receives water draining from farmed land and containing plant nutrients. Plants take up nutrients in the form of a solution of simple compounds and, because they are accessible to plants only when they are in a soluble form, inevitably a proportion of the total amount is lost as soil water drains into the nearest river. The process is called 'leaching' and, over a long period, it can seriously deplete the store of nutrients held in most soils unless these are replenished. The most important plant nutrients are nitrogen, in the form of nitrate (NO_3) or ammonium (NH_4), phosphorus, in the form of orthophosphates (mainly H_2PO_4 and HPO_4), and smaller amounts of potassium, magnesium, calcium and sodium, all of which are taken up as positively charged ions.

Plant nutrients are unlikely to remain in the river water for long. They are utilized by the aquatic and riverside plants that, in turn, feed the animals which live on, in and beside the river. The supply of nutrients can become a form of pollution, in extreme cases causing 'eutrophication' (see page 187), but only where they are discharged in relatively large amounts into still or slow-moving water. In most waters, most of the time, a constant supply of them is essential to living organisms. The discharge of human sewage adds to the quantity of plant nutrient, especially of nitrate, ammonium and phosphate.

There is nothing surprising in the idea that rivers carry substances dissolved, or carried in suspension, from the surrounding land. That is the main source of such substances, but it is not the only one. A significant amount of material is carried in the air.

Carried on the wind

You may recall that in 1965 traces of insecticides, including DDT, were found in the bodies of six Adélie penguins and one crabeater seal, at Cape Crozier, on Ross Island, Antarctica. A later study found DDT in Weddell seals and in skuas. The amounts were far too small to harm them, but what interested scientists was the fact that these animals lived 620 miles (1000 km) from the nearest land — Cape Horn — and twice that distance from most other inhabited land. It is possible that the animals had been exposed to insecticides carried there inadvertently by humans (there are no insect pests in Antarctica, and the use of insecticides on the continent is forbidden by the Antarctic Treaty), but it is more likely that

Mountain streams, like this one in the Swiss Alps, flow across and beside rocks from which they collect only very small amounts of plant nutrients, but their turbulent flow allows them to become rich in dissolved oxygen.

they were carried in the air. DDT molecules are able to adhere to soil particles by a type of bonding. The phenomenon is called 'adsorption', and it forms a layer over the surface of the particle. Thus firmly attached, the molecules are carried with the particle wherever it may go — and, although usually they do not remain airborne for long, occasionally soil particles can travel long distances.

Under certain atmospheric conditions, dust from the surface of the Sahara Desert can be lifted high into the air, carried across Europe, and then washed out in 'red' rain as far north as Britain. It is said that battles fought in North Africa during the Second World War raised dust that produced spectacular sunsets as far away as the Caribbean. It is not only desert soil that can be carried away by the wind. The 'dustbowl' conditions which devastated farms in parts of the United States in the 1930s occurred on what had been ordinary agricultural soil — and dust from one storm, in 1933, was traced for some 1300 miles (2100 km). Even in climates that ordinarily have ample rain, a short spell of dry weather can produce conditions in which dust storms can occur on light soils, where the particles are not protected by a cover of vegetation. There have been moderately severe dust storms in parts of eastern England.

Some of the airborne particles fall over land but, because the greater part of the Earth's surface is covered by water, most enter the sea. The quantities are impressive. It is estimated that each year about 43 million tons falls over the United States alone — and about one-third of all the dust in the air is there as a result of human activity. Not all dust consists of soil particles, of course. Pollen grains are also transported in this way, and the seas make their own contribution. As spray is blown from the tops of waves, it breaks into small droplets, some of which evaporate before they have time to return to the sea. Their evaporation leaves crystals of salts suspended in the air. The crystals, mainly of sodium chloride, calcium chloride, potassium bromide and magnesium chloride, are extremely small but, over the world as a whole, the total amount is estimated to be about 2 billion tons a year. Most return to the sea, of course, but some is carried over land, and enters fresh water.

The air itself also adds to the content of water. The carbon dioxide that is present in all water affects the other ingredients in several ways (see page 38). Nitrogen in the air, oxidized by lightning into a soluble compound, is washed to the surface in storms. Oxygen is also slightly soluble in water. It dissolves into raindrops, and more is added wherever the water splashes — over waterfalls and in the 'white water' of river rapids, for example — and some dissolves into any surface where water and air are side by side.

Amino acids — the building blocks of life
Every cell in the body of every living organism, from the humblest bacterium to the giant redwood and the blue whale — and including you and me — contains protein. There are many types of proteins, but all of them have large and very complex molecules constructed from arrangements of units, called 'amino acids'. An amino acid molecule consists of a number of amino groups (NH_2) and carboxyl groups (COOH). Some amino acids are made by green plants, using simple inorganic compounds as raw materials. Animals obtain many of those they need by consuming plants, and they are able to synthesize others in their own bodies.

All amino acids contain nitrogen (N), and certain of them that are essential for protein synthesis also contain sulphur, so there is some sulphur in all proteins. Sulphur accounts for about one-fifth of the weight of human hair and the feathers of birds, for example. It is also found in many enzymes, and in thiamin (vitamin B_1). Phosphorus is also an essential ingredient of some proteins, including the nucleic acids, one of which is DNA, the molecules of which carry the genetic code. Phosphorus is also involved in the chemical reactions, between adenosine diphosphate (ADP) and adenosine triphosphate (ATP), whereby energy is transported inside organisms and released where it is needed.

Carbon, hydrogen and oxygen are the elements that are used in the largest amounts in all living tissues. These are supplied from the carbon dioxide in the air and from water. Nitrogen is also obtained from the air, but by a somewhat indirect route. Apart from these four, there are 14 other elements that occur in all living organisms, and 21 that are used by some organisms, but not all.

(Opposite) Surface waters also accumulate substances delivered by air and sometimes, as you can see from this tornado damage in Sri Lanka, the wind can deliver quite large objects.

The sulphur cycle

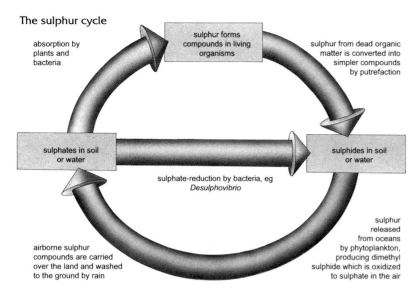

absorption by plants and bacteria

sulphur forms compounds in living organisms

sulphur from dead organic matter is converted into simpler compounds by putrefaction

sulphates in soil or water

sulphides in soil or water

sulphate-reduction by bacteria, eg *Desulphovibrio*

airborne sulphur compounds are carried over the land and washed to the ground by rain

sulphur released from oceans by phytoplankton, producing dimethyl sulphide which is oxidized to sulphate in the air

Plants are able to manufacture sugars, proteins, fats and other chemical substances from simple compounds. Animals cannot construct all these substances for themselves, so they must obtain them by eating plants. Carnivores obtain the materials they need by eating herbivores. When the plants and animals die, their tissues are consumed by another hierarchy of organisms, and the combined effect is to break down the complex molecules into simpler ones that can be taken up again by plants. The elements essential to life are cycled and recycled endlessly.

This makes the process seem straightforward, but there is a problem. Plant roots can absorb nutrient elements only from solutions. This means the nutrients must be in a

The phosphorus cycle

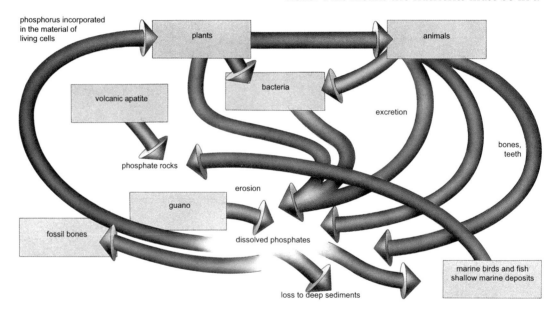

phosphorus incorporated in the material of living cells

plants

animals

bacteria

volcanic apatite

excretion

phosphate rocks

bones, teeth

erosion

guano

fossil bones

dissolved phosphates

marine birds and fish shallow marine deposits

loss to deep sediments

The nitrogen cycle

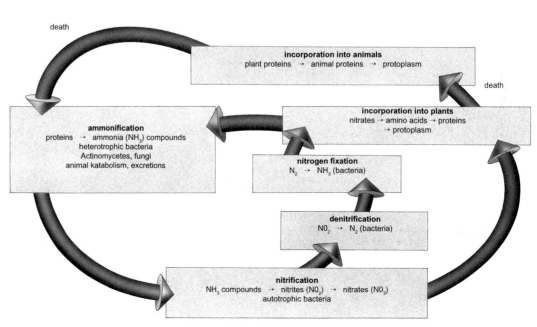

The food we eat, from which our bodies are made, is composed of elements that are cycled constantly between the soil, water, air and living organisms. Sulphur (top) and nitrogen (right) are constituents of proteins. Phosphorus (middle) plays an essential role in the transport of energy in living organisms and is an important ingredient of bone.

death

incorporation into animals
plant proteins → animal proteins → protoplasm

death

incorporation into plants
nitrates → amino acids → proteins → protoplasm

ammonification
proteins → ammonia (NH_3) compounds
heterotrophic bacteria
Actinomycetes, fungi
animal katabolism, excretions

nitrogen fixation
N_2 → NH_3 (bacteria)

denitrification
NO_2 → N_2 (bacteria)

nitrification
NH_3 compounds → nitrites (NO_2) → nitrates (NO_3)
autotrophic bacteria

soluble form, and anything in the soil that is soluble is prone to leaching. A proportion will be carried away in the water, eventually to the sea and, over millions of years, the soil might be expected to lose all of its nutrients. The fact that it has not done so, and that plants continue to thrive, indicate the existence of mechanisms whereby nutrients can be cycled on a global scale, through 'biogeochemical cycles' that transport elements vast distances by land, sea and air.

The smell of the sea

If you plan a visit to the coast, probably you will enjoy looking forward to your first smell of sea air. The sea does have a smell sometimes — and it is not the very different smell of ozone that people once imagined. It is a subtle smell, not present everywhere or all the time and, in part, most probably it is diluted dimethyl sulphide. What your nose detects is that stage in the sulphur cycle in which sulphur is being transported from the sea back to the land. Most of the component of the smell that is not part of the sulphur cycle is part of the iodine cycle.

Sulphur is absorbed by plant roots from the soil solution as sulphate (SO_4) ions. Inside plant tissues the sulphur is incorporated into amino acids and built into proteins. Some of these proteins return to the soil immediately the plant dies, others are first consumed by animals, which postpones their return, but does not cancel it. When at last the sulphur returns to the soil, bacteria oxidize it back into sulphate which, being soluble, dissolves in the water present in the soil. Each time this happens a proportion is lost by leaching, which makes it available to aquatic organisms. Eventually, as part of the general accumulation of organic wastes, some of the sulphur becomes incorporated in muds on lake beds and river estuaries. Much of it remains there, reacting with metals to form the insoluble sulphides that are common constituents of sedimentary rocks, but some is recycled.

Muds are airless places, inhabited by organisms which find oxygen poisonous. They feed on the wastes, and one by-product of their activity is hydrogen sulphide (H_2S) gas. The hydrogen sulphide bubbles out of the mud, sometimes all the way to the surface, and a certain amount of sulphur is returned to the land by this route, with the hydrogen sulphide oxidized to

sulphuric acid (H_2SO_4) or sulphate. You may have detected the unmistakable, 'rotten eggs', smell of hydrogen sulphide in the vicinity of stagnant ponds or mud.

The importance of seaweeds

There is no doubt that it is as sulphuric acid dissolved in rain water that sulphur returns from water to the land, but the principal route does not involve hydrogen sulphide. The sulphur is carried to the sea, where it is taken up by marine plants. Down near the low-tide mark, growing on rocks or sometimes on other seaweeds, you may find a small, red, rather feathery seaweed. It is called *Polysiphonia*, and it is interesting because 15 per cent of its dry weight consists of a chemical compound called dimethyl sulphonium propionate, or DMSP. The seaweed releases DMSP into the water where it breaks down to yield dimethyl sulphide, or DMS. Some DMS breaks down in the water, into compounds that can be taken up by plants, but some enters the air, where it reacts further, eventually yielding sulphate, but this time as microscopically small crystals on to which water vapour can condense.

It may be that *Polysiphonia* produces DMSP because its presence helps protect cells against desiccation in environments, such as rock pools, where the salinity fluctuates widely. No one knows whether this explains its production by a wide range of other marine plants, most of which are single-celled and form part of the 'phytoplankton' (from the Greek *phuton* 'plant', and *plagktos*, 'wandering') that floats in the surface layers of the sea. The release of DMSP and its conversion to DMS and then to sulphate are the principal means by which sulphur moves from the oceans back to the land. Over the open oceans, far from land, the sulphate crystals supply a large proportion of the particles that are necessary for the condensation of water vapour, and the formation of cloud over the remoter areas is due in no small part to this planktonic activity. It also explains the presence of a significant proportion of the dilute sulphuric acid that causes 'acid rain'.

Under suitable conditions, the phytoplankton proliferates rapidly to form 'blooms'. Over the last 20 years or so the frequency of such blooms has increased, most noticeably in the North Sea, but more recently blooms have been observed in the

North Atlantic, especially in the region south of Iceland. These algae release DMS, and those in the Atlantic, known as coccolithophorids, are particularly productive. Apart from their undoubted contribution to 'acid rain', these blooms may well have increased the amount of cloud over the Atlantic, and perhaps over other oceans where the blooms have not yet been identified. This may be a response to global warming — some scientists have suggested feeding nutrients to the phytoplankton to encourage them to remove carbon dioxide from the air and to increase cloud cover, which shades and so cools the Earth's surface.

Phosphate discharges

Some people worry about the apparently careless way we discharge phosphates into waters. We are urged to buy detergents that do not contain them. In fact, the fears are greatly exaggerated. Phosphate pollution is serious only locally, and detergents are not the principal source, so using 'phosphate-free' products contributes little or nothing to environmental protection. Phosphates are present in sewage, and because a large proportion — but not all — of sewage is discharged into water, some phosphates reach surface waters by this route, but not all of them. If the sewage is exposed to the air, about half its phosphate content is lost because bacteria convert it to a (poisonous) gas, phosphine, one of the phosphorus hydrides (PH_3). The phosphine escapes into the air and disperses, but it is slightly soluble in water and eventually it is washed down by the rain.

Compared with most of the elements needed by living organisms, phosphorus is rather scarce. Its average concentration in soils and rocks is about 0.12 per cent. Apart from its important role in the chemistry of all living cells, as the compound calcium phosphate, phosphorus is the major ingredient, with calcium carbonate, of the 'hard parts' of animal bodies — bones, teeth, fish scales and the shells of many invertebrates. These accumulate in sediments, and eventually form part of a range of sedimentary rocks. Some limestones are rich in phosphate and the action of rain water, removing calcium and magnesium bicarbonates, leaves the phosphatic compounds as pellets. Phosphorus is also recycled by another biological route involving sea birds. They

feed on fish but nest, and to some extent roost, on land, so their droppings — which in some places may accumulate to form 'guano' — returns phosphorus from the sea to the land, but mixed with a wide range of other compounds. If the guano is exposed to the rain, after a time many of those compounds are leached from it, leaving a more concentrated deposit of calcium phosphate.

Apart from carbon, hydrogen and oxygen, nitrogen is the element organisms need in the largest quantity, because, in amino groups, it forms part of all proteins. Nitrogen gas accounts for rather more than 78 per cent of air by volume, but, at ordinary atmospheric temperatures and pressures, pure, gaseous nitrogen is chemically inert. There are, however, two mechanisms by which it may be oxidized to nitrate (NO_3), and nitrate is soluble in water.

Nitrogen will react with oxygen at a high temperature or when exposed to a powerful electric spark. Nowadays, we release large amounts of nitrogen oxides from high-temperature industrial furnaces and internal combustion engines, and the industrial manufacture of nitrogen fertilizers involves the oxidation of nitrogen at high temperature and pressure.

Oxidation also occurs naturally, however, during very intense forest and bush fires and during thunderstorms, when lightning supplies electric power. The application of either form of energy oxidizes nitrogen to nitric oxide (NO) which rapidly oxidizes further to nitrogen dioxide (NO_2), or directly to nitrogen dioxide. Both oxides are soluble in water and dissolve in rain drops — almost immediately during a thunderstorm — to become nitric acid (HNO_3) which is washed to the surface as another source of acidity in natural rain. Once in water, the nitrate ion (NO) becomes accessible to plants. Clearly, it is the fate of gaseous nitrogen to be converted to soluble nitrate, and during the billions of years in which atmospheric nitrogen has been exposed to lightning flashes and fires, all of it should have been washed into the sea. Nitrogen is released by volcanic eruptions, but much of that is emitted as oxides and the rate of removal far exceeds the rate of emission from this source.

Nitrogen fixation

If you grow peas, beans, lupins or any of the other plants known as legumes, you will

(Opposite) Beneath the surface, mudflats provide an airless environment inhabited by bacteria which move elements between water and air. The pits in these mudflats, in North Carolina, were made by people digging for clams.

know that they enhance the fertility of the soil. Indeed, they are often grown for this purpose. They are able to do so because their roots harbour colonies of bacteria, living in nodules, that are able to use gaseous nitrogen directly. In doing so, they convert it into soluble compounds that become available for other organisms when the bacteria die. The process is called 'nitrogen fixation' and if you dig up a leguminous plant, taking care not to damage the roots, then gently shake off loose soil, you will be able to see the pale nodules quite clearly. There are several bacterial species, but the most common is *Rhizobium leguminosarum*.

The bacteria that inhabit the root nodules of leguminous plants are incapable of living in any other way. It is a truly symbiotic relationship in which the plant benefits from nitrogen, fixed by the bacteria, which passes into its root hairs, and the bacteria are supplied with carbohydrates, formed by the plant during photosynthesis. These are not the only organisms capable of nitrogen fixation, however. Other bacteria and some fungi, that are able to live independently, can do so, but only when they form a symbiotic association with the roots of a plant. Alder, sea buckthorn and bog myrtle are among the plants that can form such a relationship. Other bacteria, especially *Clostridium* and *Azotobacter*, are entirely free-living and can fix nitrogen, and so can some cyanobacteria ('blue-green algae') such as *Anabaena* and *Nostoc*.

The chemistry of nitrogen fixation is not understood fully, but what is known is that the bacteria use the nitrogen, together with carbohydrates, to produce amino acids. When the bacteria die, the amino acids from their cells undergo the series of processes to which all decomposing proteins are subjected. The first step is 'ammonification', in which the amino acids — including those from dead plants and animals and organic wastes of all kinds — are converted into ammonia (NH_3). A wide variety of organisms perform this process, by consuming the proteins and excreting ammonia. Human urine contains some ammonia, derived originally from the proteins in food. Ammonification is followed by 'nitrification', in which specialized bacteria, including *Nitrosomonas*, *Nitrobacter*, *Nitrospora*, and others, first oxidize ammonia to nitrite (NO_2), then oxidize the nitrite to nitrate

(NO_3). These reactions liberate energy that is available inside the cells where they occur. Nitrate is taken up by the roots of plants, and so is made available to animals once more.

The cycle is completed by the return of gaseous nitrogen to the air. This is 'denitrification', performed by bacteria such as *Thiobacillus denitrificans*. These bacteria live in environments, such as those found well below the surface of soft mud, where there is little oxygen. To compensate for this they are able to reduce nitrate (NO_3) to nitrite (NO_2), ammonia (NH_3), or free nitrogen, releasing the oxygen to be used to break down sugars from which the bacteria then synthesize more complex substances.

Once gaseous nitrogen has reacted to form a compound, all of the subsequent processes occur in water. Indeed, they can occur only because the compounds are soluble. The cycle involves removing nitrogen from the air, passing it through the cells of living organisms, and then returning it to the air again. The balance between the removal of nitrogen from the air and its return is of great ecological importance. Where a plant succession is developing towards a climax, for example, the total mass of all the plants in the area (the 'biomass') will be increasing, and this is possible only if nitrogen is available. (It will be available provided it is being removed from the air faster than it is being returned.) When the two parts of the cycle are in equilibrium there can be no further increase in biomass. Nitrogen can leach in from an adjacent area, but this can provide only local assistance, because the leaching that enriches one group of plants must deprive another.

Biochemical factories

Estuarine muds may not look particularly attractive, and many a tourist developer would love to convert them into dry land on which hotels and other holiday amenities could be built, but they are critically important in the cycling of elements. It is no exaggeration to describe them as 'biochemical factories', where some of the nutrients being carried from the land to the sea are trapped and returned to the land.

Smooth, and shining wet at low tide, mudflats may look like deserts, but the enormous numbers of wading birds that feed on them prove that, although they support a fairly small number of invertebrate animal species below the surface, the individuals of those species are present in truly vast numbers. They are feeding on nutrients made available by the 'factory', and the 'factory workers' are the bacteria, deep down where there is no air. We would be well advised to protect such wetlands, and their birds. The birds are not merely ornamental. Their droppings and corpses fall on dry land, and that is one important way nutrients are returned.

We should also keep a watchful eye on the agricultural chemicals with which we treat farm land. Were farmers to start killing in significant numbers the bacteria that process nitrogen in the soil, the cost would be high, for the nutrient supplied free of charge by natural processes would then have to be manufactured industrially as fertilizer. Apart from the immediate and obvious cost, who knows what wider consequences might ensue from such interference with so complex, subtle, and vital a system?

A proportion of the soluble nitrogen, as well as some of the nitrogen oxidized in the atmosphere, finds its way to the sea. There it nourishes marine plants, but in the open sea these plants are very small. Most consist of only one cell. They can live only in surface waters, down to the greatest depth to which sufficient light penetrates for them to be able to photosynthesize. Nutrient compounds, including those of nitrogen, are heavier than sea water and sink slowly to the sea bed. This removes them from the upper layers, which are consequently depleted of nutrients. This is why in the open sea the planktonic plants, and the animals feeding on them, are small. In relatively shallow coastal waters, however, wave and tidal movements and, in some places, upwelling currents (see page 90) bring nutrients closer to the surface, with the result that inshore waters are far more productive than the open ocean.

Iodine

It is not only the major nutrients that move through biogeochemical cycles, although it is their cycles which are better known. Consider, for example, the element iodine. Animals need iodine, but in very small amounts. The body of an adult human contains between 0.0007 and 0.00175 ounces (20-50 milligrams) of iodine. It is a small, but vital ingredient of the hormone thyroxin ($C_{15}H_{11}I_4NO_4$) which regulates

the rate at which we convert the food we eat into energy and, therefore, the efficiency with which we maintain our body temperatures. It also regulates various growth processes, and a deficiency of it causes goitre and other ailments. In amphibians iodine regulates metamorphosis from the larval to the adult form. Deprive tadpoles of iodine, and therefore of thyroxin, and they fail to develop into frogs or toads. Supply iodine to the axolotl, on the other hand, which usually spends its entire life as a larva, living in water and breathing with gills, and it will change into a perfectly ordinary salamander, equipped with lungs, and will move happily between water and dry land.

Iodine is dissolved out of rocks and taken up by plants, but not all rocks contain it, and so iodine deficiencies occur in some areas. It is carried to the sea where, because sea waters mix, it becomes distributed evenly. Sea water contains about one part of iodine to every 8000 parts of chlorine. This is quite adequate for the needs of aquatic organisms. Some iodine, combined with sodium as sodium iodate ($NaIO_3$), occurs in deposits of Chile saltpetre (sodium nitrate, $NaNO_3$) that are precipitated when sea water evaporates. So we can, and do, mine for iodine. We can, and do, also obtain it by processing seaweeds, which are rich in it, and it is also a by-product of oil refining — still present in the petroleum made from the remains of once-living organisms.

This is all very well for modern humans but, for most of our history, people living far inland had, at best, limited access to such resources, and non-humans had no access at all. In fact, they needed none because the seaweeds return iodine themselves. They emit molecules of methyl iodide (CH_3I), with the distinctive 'seaweed' smell that contributes so much to the joy of seaside holidays. The joy may be misplaced, because methyl iodide is very poisonous if it should become concentrated. Much of the methyl iodide reacts with chlorine from the sea to form methyl chloride (CH_3Cl), the iodine forming a soluble oxide that returns to the sea, but some is carried back over the land. Interestingly, methyl iodide also works as a catalyst in the reaction by which DMS is oxidized to yield sulphate crystals, so the seaweeds may also play a part in the formation of clouds and 'acid rain'. While we are protecting estuarine muds, we would do well to afford similar protection to the offshore seaweeds, and especially to the kelp beds, on which land-dwelling species depend for their iodine.

Sodium

We also need sodium, which is involved in the transmission of impulses in nerve cells and in maintaining the correct acidity of body fluids, and chlorine, whose presence in the stomach is essential to digestion. Together, sodium and chlorine ions help regulate the passage of molecules across cell membranes.

Humans have a great liking for salty tastes, and so do many other mammals. Indeed, people have often relied on their livestock to find sources of salt. The story of the pigs whose craving led to the prosperity of Bad Oeynhausen has been repeated countless times in the course of history, though not always to such spectacular commercial advantage.

Mineral springs apart, most of our salt is obtained either by mining deposits of halite, or 'rock salt', or by evaporating sea water. No matter how it is obtained, those who trade in salt are extremely careful to prevent it from coming into contact with water. It is so highly soluble, that even humid air will dissolve it. Indeed, naturally occurring salt deposits provide one of the favoured geological structures for the long-term storage of nuclear wastes. They are favoured partly because the mere fact that they contain crystalline salt proves their complete isolation from water — and the contamination of water is the principal hazard against which storage technologies must guard — and partly because salt is rather plastic and, if it is ruptured, it will tend to seal itself again.

Because it is so readily soluble, salt is regularly washed into the sea. You might expect, therefore, that after millions of years of this process salt deposits on land would be extremely uncommon, and that the salinity of the sea would have been increasing steadily throughout the history of the planet. In fact, this has not occurred. The salinity of the sea varies a little from place to place, but only between quite narrow limits, and there is good reason to suppose it has remained constant, if not for the whole of history then at least since living organisms became established. Almost all living cells are highly sensitive to quite small changes in salinity. Dump a load of salt into

a river and the fish will die — along with all the other species living in it. Allow sea water to flow inland, contaminating fresh groundwater, and crops grown on land supplied by that groundwater will fail. This is one of the fears arising from the threat of sea-level rises due to climatic warming. Place marine fish in fresh water and they will die. Fossils of the earliest marine organisms include some that are similar to species that are alive today, and it is reasonable to suppose they were no more tolerant of salinity changes than their modern descendants.

Salt is washed into the sea and the sea loses water only by evaporation, which removes fresh water and leaves behind the dissolved salts. Yet the salinity remains constant.

Seas are not of the same depth everywhere, and there are many places where an arm of the sea — and perhaps a large one — is almost trapped in a fairly shallow basin. Should the sea level fall just a little, a situation may arise in which water floods into the basin at high tide but, as the tide falls, the basin is isolated and water cannot flow out of it. After each high tide the basin will lose water by evaporation, and it will be filled again at the next high tide. Sea water feeds the basin, fresh water is lost by evaporation and so, over the years, the water in the basin will become increasingly saline. A further small fall in sea level will isolate the basin even from high tides, the water will evaporate and the salt will remain as a deposit of halite.

A fall in sea level indicates that the total volume of the oceans is decreasing. The removal of salt at such a time prevents an increase in the salinity. Should the sea level rise, so the sea salt is more diluted, the halite deposits will be flooded, the salt will dissolve, and its immediate transport back into the sea restores the salt and prevents ocean salinity from falling.

Salt may also be trapped more permanently, as a 'salt dome' — often indicating the presence of petroleum — when the formation of impermeable sedimentary rocks traps porous material, saturated with water whose salt is then concentrated into a layer, commonly many miles thick, as water migrates from it by osmosis. In a process called 'diapirism', the heavier sediments may then sink around the lighter salt, forcing it upwards into a dome shape.

(Opposite top) Phytoplankton in the Atlantic, as seen by the Nimbus-7 satellite. Increasing sunshine in spring causes the phytoplankton to bloom dramatically. The colours are false. The most dense blooms are red and density decreases through yellow, green and blue, to violet. (Opposite bottom) Kelp (*Laminaria digitata)* grows in large 'forests' close to the shore and is exposed at low tide. Kelp is an alga, despite its size.

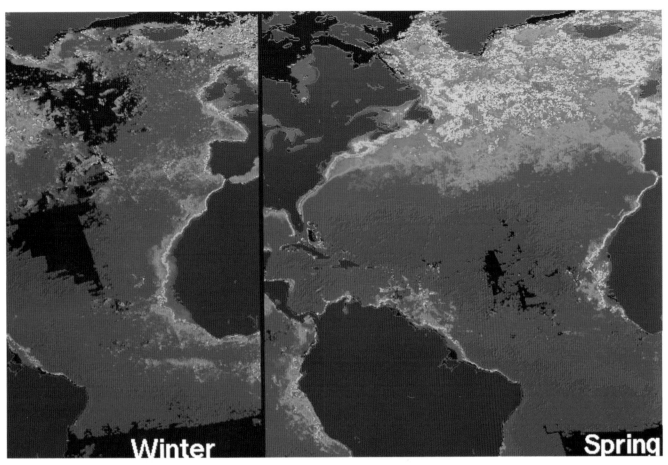

Winter

Spring

WATER IN LIVING ORGANISMS

Scientists who seek evidence of life elsewhere in the universe do so by monitoring radio waves. They hope that one day they may detect radio signal patterns indicating that they were transmitted deliberately by intelligent beings. The method is efficient although, so far, it has produced no result, but whether it is efficient or not, the scientists have no alternative. They cannot identify, far less study, such planets as may orbit distant stars, and it is only on planets that life, as we understand the word, may be expected to occur.

Were we able to study planets other than those in our own solar system — all of which are lifeless, apart from Earth — we would concentrate on those which satisfied certain criteria. It is difficult to imagine how life might develop on a planet that is very hot, for example, because high temperatures tend to break the bonds that make it possible for large, complex molecules to form and survive. Nor should the planet be very cold, for then the chemical reactions on which life depends would proceed much too slowly. Finally, the planet should possess water, as a liquid, which means it must also possess an atmosphere.

The existence of an atmosphere does not imply the existence of liquid water, but the existence of liquid water does imply the existence of an atmosphere. Without an atmosphere to exert pressure, water molecules are too freely mobile to be held in the liquid phase and, depending on the temperature, water can exist only as a solid or as a gas (see page 13). An atmosphere may also be necessary to provide a shield that absorbs excessive X-ray and gamma radiation from the star. Such high-energy radiation ionizes atoms, making them intensely reactive, and splitting molecules to release 'free radicals' and free electrons. All of these interfere with, and eventually destroy, the complex molecules from which living organisms are constructed.

Water provides a neutral medium in which chemical reactions can occur through chance encounters among freely moving molecules. The only other requirements are an 'energy gradient' — a difference in energy levels that can be exploited, and an adequate source of 'raw materials'. Some

scientists suggest that suitable conditions might have existed on the surfaces of clay particles, and in the interstices between them, and that the first chemical steps towards what we might recognize as life took place there, through the growth of increasingly complex crystals. The more general view is that the first necessary reactions took place in water. No one knows which view is correct, but we do know that life was present very early in the history of our planet and that it inhabited water.

The beginning of life on Earth
Conditions on Earth today are quite unlike those that existed billions of years ago, but you can still see the kind of environment in which life may have begun, and in which it is still abundant. Find a tidal creek or inlet where the climate is warm and the water is shallow. Probably the tidal range will be fairly small, so that each high tide brings in a little water to replace that which was lost by evaporation, but without disturbing the site too violently. The sea will bring in a load of chemicals on each tide and, between high tides, the water will be warmed sufficiently to encourage reactions. Allow, also, that thunderstorms produce nitrate and that from time to time the water is struck by lightning, to supply some electrical energy. In these conditions quite complex molecules form reasonably readily.

Life will not be evolving anew in tidal creeks today — or anywhere else so far as we know — because it exists already in such abundance, and the chemical raw materials are taken up and utilized before there is time for them to start the evolutionary process all over again. It is not difficult to gain an impression of the extent of this abundance. Take a sample of the water, collected at random in a jar, and watch it carefully with a strong magnifying lens or, better still, under a microscope. The tiny particles, moving about rapidly, are living organisms. Or use the lower leg and foot of a nylon stocking to make an improvised, but effective, plankton net, with a ring of wire to hold the end open and a handle to hold it. Trail your net through the water, and then rinse its contents into the jar of water you

(Opposite top) Rich in minerals, seaweed is harvested in many parts of the world, for use as fertilizer or for supply to the chemical industry. Here, seaweed is being gathered in Spain. (Opposite bottom) After processing, seaweed is marketed as a range of products.

A sheltered tidal creek in Devon, England. Creeks often accumulate nutrients, and many scientists believe it was in such places that life first appeared on Earth.

collected from the creek. Study it now and you will see much more.

There is no proof that this is where and how life on Earth began, and some scientists are coming to the view that the early part of the process took a short cut. Complex, carbon-based molecules, resembling tars, are known to exist in comets and in some meteorites. The early bombardment of the Earth may very well have injected large amounts of these chemicals. Most would have been destroyed by the heat generated by the friction of their passage through the atmosphere and by the impact, but if the density of the atmosphere was markedly greater then than it is now — which it may have been — the bodies would have been slowed down, perhaps sufficiently to permit a proportion of their large molecules to survive. If this is what happened, it would have supplied ready-made a stock of substances necessary to the emergence of living organisms that otherwise would have taken a long time to form and accumulate.

The idea of such a short cut helps to explain how it was that life appeared on Earth so soon after the planet formed, and

we can be very certain that it did, and that it was associated with water.

Some of the oldest rocks in the world have been found in western Greenland. They have been dated as 3800 million years old. The Earth itself is believed to have formed about 4600 million years ago and so the Greenland rocks were formed when our planet was a mere 800 million years old. The rocks are sedimentary. This means they were made by a process that began with the erosion of hard rocks, partly by water, the transport of rock particles, mainly by water but partly by air, and the accumulation of the particles as silt, forming a sediment — which can occur only on the bed of a body of water. The existence and reliable dating of the rock proves that liquid water was present on Earth in substantial amounts 3800 million years ago, that weather systems existed because wind and rain are necessary agents for rock erosion, and that the water had already been present long enough for erosion and particle transport to have led to sedimentation. If these implications of the Greenland rock seemed startling, there is more to come.

Isotopes

The Greenland rocks are enriched in carbon-12. That is to say, they contain a higher proportion of carbon-12 in relation to carbon-13 than is found in ordinary, atmospheric carbon dioxide.

The atoms of elements can exist in subtly different forms, called 'isotopes', that are alike in the number of (positively charged) protons contained in their nuclei, but that differ from one another in their number of (electrically neutral) neutrons. This means the isotopes differ in the mass of their atoms, which may influence their physical behaviour, but not in their chemical behaviour because this is determined by the number of protons. Some isotopes are stable and others are radioactive and, therefore, unstable, decaying to stable forms. Carbon has two stable isotopes, carbon-12 and carbon-13, and a number of unstable, radioactive ones (of which the best known is carbon-14).

The proportions of the two stable isotopes is constant in the carbon released into the atmosphere from volcanoes, but in the first stage of photosynthesis carbon-12 is used in preference to carbon-13. The discovery of carbon-12 enrichment in the Greenland rocks, therefore, suggests very strongly indeed that photosynthesis was established at the time the rocks formed. Not only was liquid water present on Earth 3800 million years ago, but living organisms were also present and had been present long enough for photosynthesis to have evolved.

The first life

This does not mean the Earth was populated by large plants. The organisms responsible were minute — and probably they still exist. When the sea looks green, its colour is imparted mainly by single-celled organisms that contain chlorophyll and manufacture sugars by photosynthesis. The smallest of them are the prochlorophytes, each of which is about 0.7 microns in diameter — 36,000 of them set side by side would make a row one inch (25.4 mm) long. Their existence was discovered only a few years ago, but it must be their small size that allowed them to hide, for no one could describe them as rare. In sea water samples, 60 million of them were measured in one pint (100,000 in 1 ml).

Such small cells subsisted principally by absorbing molecules of the compounds they required for the construction of the larger molecules from which their contents were made. Compared with inorganic molecules that comprise just a few atoms, and sometimes no more than two or three, the molecules found in even the simplest cells are impressively large. A molecule of chlorophyll *a*, for example, which is the commoner of the two types of chlorophyll that occur today in green plants, comprises 55 atoms of carbon, 72 of hydrogen, one of magnesium, four of nitrogen, and five of oxygen. The nucleic acids, such as DNA (deoxyribonucleic acid) and RNA (ribonucleic acid) have molecules much larger than this.

A time came when cells began to link with other cells, perhaps by ingesting them. Cells that contained chlorophyll were incorporated into larger cells and eventually lost their ability to live independently. In the cells of green plants, other than cyanobacteria ('blue-green algae') in which chlorophyll is distributed around the cell edges, they became chloroplasts, the internal cell structures where photosynthesis is performed. Other 'organelles' — the bodies inside plant and animal cells that perform particular functions, like the organs of an animal — may also have originated as independent, free-living organisms.

There are two types of cells, called 'prokaryotes' and 'eukaryotes'. Prokaryotes form the older group and, although most occur as single cells, they combine in some organisms — co-operation began very early in the evolutionary story. They are cells that have no distinct nucleus. They contain

Surface waters teem with life. Many of its organisms are microscopically small, but very beautiful. This sample of plankton includes diatoms, radiolarians and dinoflagellates.

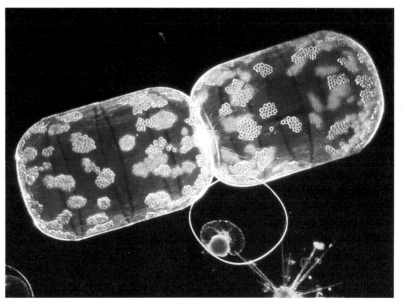

DNA, but in the form of a loop, rather than as chromosomes inside a membrane. Bacteria and cyanobacteria (blue-green algae) are prokaryotes. A eukaryote has a distinct nucleus containing its DNA, and also organelles to perform particular functions. Protozoons, such as the amoebae, as well as all the fungi, plants, and animals are composed entirely of eukaryotic cells. Scientists believe that many, and perhaps all, of the organelles are descended from free-living prokaryotes. Some contain their own DNA or RNA, for example, which is separate from that of the cell nucleus, and others bear a striking resemblance to free-living prokaryotes that still exist.

The emergence of multicellular organisms

The route which led to the emergence of multicellular organisms began when large, complex cells united. No record remains of this development, although it must have occurred, but animals still exist that have ways of life which may resemble those that were common when multicellular plants and animals were just starting to emerge. These animals are confederations of cells, each of which is more or less capable of living independently. Slime moulds, for example, live for much of the time as groups of amoeba-like cells, each of them moving about and feeding by itself. Then, for purposes of reproduction or when it is time to move to a new source of food, these independent cells join together to make a 'pseudoplasmodium' — a structure that behaves like a single, multicellular animal, looking rather like a tiny slug. Slime moulds are sometimes classified as fungi (hence the name 'mould'), but probably they are not related to fungi and, indeed, may have no animal or plant relatives at all. They are an evolutionary 'dead end' that developed so far, but no further — perhaps because they were astoundingly successful at the level they had reached.

Sponges are also at an evolutionary dead end, with no relatives, and they, too, are congregations of semi-autonomous cells. They are much bigger than slime moulds, of course, and more elaborately organized, although they have no specialized bodily organs or tissues. Essentially, a sponge is a network of tubes with openings to the exterior of the animal that give sponges their scientific name of Porifera (from 'pores'). Currents of water are wafted through the tubes by the movement of flagella — whip-like or tail-like cell appendages whose ancestors may also have once lived independently — and the cells collect particles from the passing stream. A sponge has a skeleton of sorts, made from small slivers ('spicules') of silica, or of a chalky material, or of 'spongin' which is made from collagen, a fibrous protein found in the bodies of most animals.

Chop a living sponge into small pieces, force the pieces through a fine sieve, and the water containing the sponge will become cloudy. Leave it to stand and, little by little, the cells will move together and take up positions that will restore the whole animal to very like its former shape.Sponges vary widely in shape and size, but the limit is not determined genetically, as in other animals and plants, but simply by the food and space available.

The Portuguese man-of-war (*Physalia physalis*) takes this kind of co-operation a stage further. The animal looks like a jellyfish, most people regard it as a jellyfish, and it can sting like a jellyfish, although, in fact, it is not a single animal at all but a community of individuals each of which has sacrificed a degree of autonomy by becoming specialized for a particular function that serves the colony as a whole. One type has a single tentacle it can extend or contract, and stinging cells. Up to 150 of these individuals collaborate to form a very effective fishing net. This type passes the food it catches to another type, which has a mouth and can eat and digest it. Yet another type specializes in reproduction, and one, from which all the others develop by budding, forms a gas-filled float surmounted by a structure that serves as a sail by which it is propelled at an angle of 45 degrees to the wind.

Some relatives of the Portuguese man-of-war, though not *Physalia* itself, can regulate the amount of gas in the float, enabling them to move vertically in the water, and some have 'swimming bells' — a ring of individuals that can squirt out water through a tube so the colony can 'jet propel' itself. This allows it to haul in its tentacles, move to a new location, then lower its 'net' and resume fishing.

Such delicate animals can exist only in water, and it was in water that all the present-day groups of animals first evolved. Today, many live only on land, but their

(Opposite) The Portuguese man-of-war (*Physalia physalis*) is not one animal but a colony in which each individual has a special part to play. The 'sail' helps the man-of-war to control its direction of movement.

ancestors were aquatic. Almost all insects dwell on land, but insects are arthropods — animals with external skeletons and jointed limbs — and arthropods lived in the sea for some 200 million years before they emerged into the air. To this day, the group includes the crustaceans — such as lobsters, crabs and shrimps — as well as the insects, mites, spiders and scorpions, and, although insects are terrestrial as adults, many of them — including mosquitoes, some flies, mayflies, dragonflies and damselflies, for example — must lay eggs in water and spend their larval stages there. Eurypterids, or 'sea scorpions', which appeared about 500 million years ago and became extinct some 270 million years later, were aquatic carnivores that had walking legs — one pair of which became modified for swimming in some species — and resembled modern scorpions and spiders in some respects. Many sea scorpions were 2 to 4 inches (5 to 10 cm) long, but some were very large and one (*Pterygotus deepkillensis*) grew to a length of almost 10 feet (3 m). Mammals evolved on land, though some subsequently took to living in water, but the ancestors of mammals were reptiles, which evolved from amphibians, which evolved from fishes. Fishes, amphibians, reptiles, mammals and also birds are all 'chordates', animals with a rod of nerve fibres, the 'notochord', running longitudinally through the body, and this feature may link all of them, perhaps evolutionarily, with the sea squirts (urochordates) in which the tadpole-like larvae also have a notochord.

Moving from water to land

Many groups of plants and animals remained aquatic but, for those that moved away from water, the escape was difficult and incomplete. The cyanobacteria may have been the first, although bacteria must have been blown ashore from the surface of the sea and some of them would have survived. The cyanobacteria joined with bacteria and other single-celled organisms to form large, complex, hump-shaped colonies in shallow water. The colonies probably projected above the water surface, at least at low tide. Their fossil remains are called 'stromatolites' and are found in rocks about 3000 million years old. Similar colonies are alive today, in a few places along coasts in Central America and Australia.

The first large plants — in some species up to 20 inches (50 cm) tall — established themselves on land rather less than 400 million years ago. When you consider the age of the Earth, and the 3800 million years during which it has supported life, this first substantial colonization of dry land took place very recently. Even then it was rather tentative, for the plants concerned could grow only in swampy ground. The great proliferation of plants that occurred around 325 million years ago, during the Upper Carboniferous (Pennsylvanian), was possible because at that time much of what are now Europe and the eastern part of North America were joined together in a vast region of tropical swamp. It is the remains of those plants that provide us with many of our rich coal measures.

Animals may have visited the shore briefly, but they could not live there permanently until plants were established to supply food. Once the plants arrived, however, the potential food source was immense, and it did not take animals very long to discover ways of exploiting it. Fossil dragonflies have been found in Upper Carboniferous coal. They were probably the largest insects the world has ever seen, with wingspans of up to 27.6 inches (70 cm). They cannot have been alone, for all dragonflies are carnivores, feeding on insects they capture in flight. There must have been other species of flying insects, as prey for these formidable hunters.

The insects were followed by fish, probably species that looked and behaved much like mudskippers, which use their fins and tails to move short distances across dry land, and sometimes bask in the sunshine with only their tails in the water. They can breathe air, but many fish can do this, especially those which live in shallow pools where the water is often depleted of dissolved oxygen. The swim bladder, a gas-filled sac found in many fish species and used to give the fish neutral buoyancy, is believed to have evolved from an organ used to assist in respiration.

Adapting to life on land called for solutions to much more serious difficulties. The most obvious was locomotion. Fins had to evolve into properly articulated limbs, supported by bones and operated by muscles, which required major modifications to the skeleton. In amphibians, such as the salamander, the transition from the pelvic fins of a fish has produced limbs that project

(Opposite) Life began in water but, in the course of their evolution, plants and some groups of animals have colonized dry land. The scorpions were among the first invertebrates to do so, about 400 million years ago, and giant dragonflies, which lived about 300 million years ago, were the first airborne predators, although dragonfly larvae are aquatic and adults must return to water to lay their eggs. The first land-dwelling vertebrates may have been fishes rather like mudskippers. Their descendants — the amphibians — represented today mainly by the salamanders and frogs — developed limbs, but remained semi-aquatic. Although the crocodile spends much of its time in or beside water, it breathes with lungs and is a true land-dweller. One line of reptilian evolution led to the birds, such as the chicken, and another led to the mammals, the group that includes the chimpanzee and its close relative, the human.

human

dragonfly

chicken

scorpion

chimpanzee

mudskipper

salamander

bony fish

crocodile

almost horizontally from the body and become vertical at the knee and elbow joints. Such limbs make it impossible to move easily and quickly. It was not until the appearance of the dinosaurs that there were land animals with limbs projecting downwards and positioned beneath the body. This highly successful arrangement also occurred in the mammals, which evolved separately from dinosaurs, and in the birds. *Archaeopteryx lithographica*, an animal about the size of a modern chicken which lived about 140 million years ago, had feathers and a furcula (wishbone) like a bird, with the teeth and long, bony tail of a small dinosaur, but its long legs were beneath its body. *Archaeopteryx* was probably a weak flier, but it could walk and run well.

Dehydration was a major hazard for animals living out of the water, because their skins were permeable. This was an advantage in wet surroundings, because it allowed them to exchange gases through their skins. Frogs release more carbon dioxide through their skins than they do from their lungs. The drawback, though, was that water vapour could also pass through the skin, leading to a serious loss of body fluid. Amphibians must not allow their skins to become too dry. The difficulty was overcome in reptiles by the development of a much more impermeable skin. Reptiles can live in deserts.

The final difficulty, and the most serious of all, was that eggs had to be laid in water, and the larvae that hatched from them were entirely aquatic. In most amphibians they still are, of course, and this is another reason for them to remain within easy reach of water. Again, the solution appeared first in the reptiles, whose eggs contain an 'amnion' — a fluid-filled sac in which the young can pass through the aquatic stages of their development, so they look like small duplicates of their parents by the time they hatch. Surround the amniotic egg in a tough protective shell, and the link with the aquatic past is broken — by providing an aquatic environment inside the shell.

Life's dependence on water
The evolution of land plants provides many parallels. In their own ways, plants also had to reduce their dependence on water, especially for reproduction and seed dispersal and, like animals, they did so by enclosing and conserving it. Life began in water

and, to a large extent, our success in moving away from water is measured by our ability to take the water we need with us.

Living cells, regardless of where they occur, have never lost their dependence on water. This is not because life evolved in the sea, and land-dwellers have been only partially successful in severing this link with their evolutionary past, but because of the characteristics of water itself. It is those characteristics that favoured the chemistry which led to the emergence of self-replicating molecules, and the subsequent development of more complex structures. It is not our link with the oceans that we retain, but our use of water as the medium for our body chemistry, and no other naturally occurring substance can provide a substitute. It is inconceivable that any evolutionary line could ever lead to organisms that had no need for water — although many plants and animals are very economical in its use, and some cells can survive desiccation and revive when moistened.

It is easy to see that a jellyfish, or Portuguese man-of-war, almost transparent and drifting in the sea, consists mainly of water and, if you have seen jellyfish on the beach, marooned by the tide, you will know that once removed from the sea they soon dry out and die. It is less obvious that fishes are also mainly water, and less obvious still that so are land animals, including the mammals, yet water accounts for most of the content of all cells and, in animals, of most of the blood and other body fluids. A cow may secrete as much as 13.2 gallons (60l) of saliva a day, for example, and about two-thirds of the weight of a human body is water. An adult male human has about 8.8 pints (5 l) of blood, an adult female about 7 pints (4 l), and children proportionately less.

While cells are free-living, they are able to absorb the substances they need and remove waste products simply by passing molecules in and out through their walls. In an animal such as a sponge, which consists of a colony of semi-autonomous cells, the overall arrangement allows each cell to be in contact with circulating sea water. Where the cells are specialized, and joined together to form the body of a larger animal, however, they have no such direct contact with the outside environment, and some mechanism is required to convey to them the molecules they need, and to remove wastes that might otherwise accumulate until they reached concentrations that were harmful to the cells themselves. Body fluids, which are mainly water, provide the medium in which products can be transported.

The circulatory system

The blood is a kind of all-purpose medium. It transports nutrients to cells and wastes from them, destroys alien cells and, of course, it delivers to tissues the compounds that will react to provide energy where it is needed.

In arthropods — the large group that includes the crustaceans, insects, mites, scorpions and spiders — the blood circulation is 'open'. The heart pumps blood into the body cavity rather than into a system of tubes. The blood circulates because the rigid external skeleton forms a container firm enough to withstand the pressure. If you imagine a pump taking the place of the cook's spoon, the blood moves about the cavity in much the same way as soup will move around a saucepan when it is stirred. Were the outer skin supple, it would simply bulge, and the fluid would pulse in and out rather than moving around.

Soft-bodied animals, such as worms, have a circulatory system in which blood is carried away from the heart in arteries and back to the heart in veins, much as it is in vertebrate animals like ourselves, although the other body fluids, mixed together, fill each segment. Apart from transporting nutrients and wastes and destroying alien cells, the fluids in the interconnecting, segmental body cavities of a worm serve to give the body its rigidity and assist in its movement. A worm moves, not so much by wriggling as by alternately contracting and relaxing its muscles in such a way as to force fluid into segments, making them swell, and then to flow out of them so the segments contract, while at the same time another set of muscles alternately elongate, and contract, the body.

The echinoderms — the large group, of about 6000 species, that includes the starfishes, sea urchins, sea cucumbers and sand dollars — use a much more sophisticated version of this technique. Alone among animals, they operate hydraulically, by means of a 'water-vascular system'. This consists of a circular 'ring canal' from which 'radial canals', with lateral branches, lead into each part of the body. The lateral

canals lead to 'tube feet', which are small protrusions from the underside of the shell, often flattened at their ends to form suckers. The entire system connects to the outside environment, allowing water to enter and leave. The water, almost identical to sea water in its chemical composition, is moved through the canals by the beating of cilia — hair-like structures on the surfaces of cells — and its progress is regulated by valves. The water-vascular system allows echinoderms to move about, although they are not able to move very quickly.

Cells obtain the energy they need by a complex series of chemical reactions. In most plants and animals, several of these reactions involve the oxidation of compounds, so oxygen is needed, and yield carbon dioxide as a by-product which must be removed. The overall process is cell, or tissue, respiration and the act of breathing is the means animals employ to obtain oxygen from the air and rid their bodies of carbon

We still rely on water to transport oxygen and nutrients and to remove waste products. The blood circulation system is centred on the heart and lungs and extends to every part of the body.

1 carotid artery
2 subclavian artery
3 aorta
4 pulmonary artery
5 brachial artery
6 coeliac trunk
7 superior mesenteric artery
8 radial artery
9 ulnar artery
10 femoral artery
11 external jugular vein
12 internal jugular vein
13 subclavian vein
14 pulmonary vein
15 cephalic vein
16 iliac vein
17 femoral vein
18 great saphenous vein

dioxide. The oxygen and carbon dioxide are conveyed to and from bodily tissues by the red blood cells (known technically as 'erythrocytes').

The erythrocytes are red because they contain the 'respiratory pigment' haemoglobin, which is red. This consists of two pairs of 'polypeptides' — long molecules each of which is made up of many amino acids joined end to end in a chain. These chains comprise the globin, and each of them is folded in such a way as to provide a site to which a molecule of haem is attached, a large molecule that includes one atom of iron. The iron can be oxidized, converting the haemoglobin into oxyhaemoglobin, but the bond is weak. If a nearby molecule is depleted of oxygen, it will attract the oxygen atom away from the haem.

One fluid ounce of blood contains about 128 million erythrocytes (4.5 million/ml), and blood can contain oxygen equal to about one-fifth of its own volume. This is about 60 times more oxygen than will dissolve in an equivalent volume of water.

Haem will also bond, and more strongly, with carbon dioxide to make carboxyhaemoglobin, and more strongly still with carbon monoxide — so the haem is unable to carry oxygen to tissues, which is why carbon monoxide is poisonous. Haemoglobin occurs in the blood of vertebrates, but it is not the only respiratory pigment. Some arthropods and molluscs use haemocyanin, for example, which contains copper instead of iron, and is blue rather than red.

Erythrocytes contain no water, but they are carried in the blood plasma, which is water in which proteins, sugars, hormones, vitamins, excretion products and many other substances are dissolved, and tiny globules of fat are carried in suspension. In particular, the plasma contains sodium chloride (common salt), potassium chloride, and sodium and potassium bicarbonates. Blood plasma is similar in composition to the lymph, or 'tissue fluid', which bathes all the cells inside the body, and drains from them through a system of vessels, the lymphatic system, to enter the bloodstream close to the heart.

Body fluids taste salty. Some people entertain the romantic notion that this is because the evolution of life began in a marine environment where the salinity inside and outside cells was much the same (they were 'isotonic'), and their land-dwelling descendants have retained this feature. The composition of our body fluids is thus a relic of an ancient ocean. Unfortunately, the idea is profoundly wrong and the truth is much more prosaic. Sodium, potassium and chlorine are essential ingredients of all cells because of the electric charges their ions carry in solution. They are involved in the movement of molecules into and out of cells, for example, and sodium is necessary for the building of proteins and for cell division. Body fluids taste salty because they contain sodium chloride, but it is pure coincidence that sea water is also salty.

Sodium also plays a vital role in the 'sodium pump' mechanism by which urine is concentrated in the kidneys by extracting water from it. You might picture the body of an animal as a water container, but it is a leaky container, and some animals are more efficient than others at holding water. A cat needs to drink, but in relation to its size it drinks much less than a human. We are very leaky animals, mainly because we perspire more efficiently than most animals, using the latent heat of evaporation of water to prevent ourselves from over-heating in hot weather.

Some desert animals do not drink at all. They obtain all the water they need from the plants they eat and then retain it. The sodium pump, which is an adaptation to life away from water, helps them in this. A kangaroo rat, for example, which needs to conserve water, excretes urine 10 times more concentrated than that of a beaver, which is semi-aquatic. Truly aquatic animals, such as fishes and amphibians, have no such mechanism and are unable to concentrate their urine. In humans, the sodium pump adjusts the concentration of urine that is excreted according to the concentration of the urine when it enters the kidney. The less dilute the urine, the more the kidneys concentrate it to conserve the little water it contains. A person who drinks ample amounts of fluid will excrete copious quantities of dilute urine. Someone whose body is dehydrated will excrete much smaller amounts of much more concentrated urine.

A human cannot survive for very long without water to drink (see page 23) because, although our kidneys can help reduce water loss, they cannot prevent it. Each time we exhale, the breath leaving our lungs carries water from the moist tissues lining our respiratory passages — you can see it condense if you breathe on to a mirror, even in the driest weather — and while we may keep ourselves cool to reduce perspiration, there is nothing we can do to prevent ourselves breathing. As water continues to leave the body, the concentration of the body fluid solution increases until water starts to drain from cells by osmosis (see page 69).

So large is our demand for water — for many industrial uses and domestically for cooking and washing as well as for drinking — that, even in high latitudes, and in climates such as that of Britain, where a relatively high average annual rainfall is distributed fairly evenly throughout the year, water shortages are quite common. After a few weeks without rain, in summer when the rate of evaporation is high, reservoirs are depleted, river levels low, and some form of rationing must be introduced.

In 1976, a drought meant that the household water supply had to be turned off in parts of Devon, England, and people obtained their water from standpipes in the street.

A dew pond, dug by farmers to collect water for their livestock.

In extreme cases, domestic supplies must be disconnected so that householders are compelled to collect water from street standpipes.

We fear drought, but not because it brings a risk of dying from thirst. Indeed, the need for drinking water does not enter into the definition of a drought. Crops fail and there is starvation long before supplies of drinking water are exhausted.

A drought will occur if the amount of water reaching the ground as rain over a given period is less than the amount that, were it present, would evaporate from the surface during the same period. Obviously, a drought is more likely in hot weather but, if the rainfall is low enough, it can occur anywhere in the world. In the Gobi Desert, the average July temperature is only 71 °F (21.7 °C) and in January it is 20 °F (-6.7 °C). The region is a dry desert because only about 2 inches (51 mm) of rain falls in a year. When the rate of evaporation exceeds the amount of water falling as rain, water is drawn upwards through the soil, only to evaporate from the uppermost layers. This depletes the groundwater, and the

water table falls until it lies below the reach of plant roots and, although water continues to move by capillary attraction (see page 28), as the soil dries, the resistance to such movement increases rapidly. At this point the vegetation begins to suffer and, unless water is supplied, the plants will die. The safety margins are narrow and ripening crops benefit from irrigation during dry weather that falls far short of drought.

Vascular plants

Most of our common plants — trees, grasses, crop plants and our garden plants, apart from the simpler types such as mosses and liverworts — are 'vascular'. That is to say, they contain tubes, or 'vessels', through which water passes. The stem has parallel, vertical vessels which branch repeatedly at both ends — the lower end in the root region and the upper end at the leaves. Plant cells literally gorge themselves with water. This distends them and makes them fairly turgid — rigid, like tiny inflated balloons. Like the earthworm, a plant uses water to give its tissues rigidity. If the flow of water is insufficient, cells are unable to remain turgid. They relax, the structures they comprise become limp and, except in the case of trees and shrubs, whose mechanical support is provided by wood, made from accumulated dead cells, the entire plant wilts. The plant will recover rapidly if water is supplied to its root area, although not in the case of 'temporary' or 'midday' wilting (see page 70).

The plant also requires water for photosynthesis, the chain of reactions in which glucose is synthesized from simple ingredients using the energy of sunlight and chlorophyll as a catalyst. The process is very complicated, but can be summarized as the breaking down of one molecule of carbon dioxide (CO_2) and two molecules of water ($2H_2O$) to produce one molecule of CH_2O, one molecule of water (H_2O), and one molecule of oxygen (O_2) — which is released into the air. Join six CH_2O molecules together, and the result is glucose ($C_6H_{12}O_6$).

We usually associate dry conditions with summer and warm sunshine, so it can come as a surprise to learn that the arctic regions of North America, Europe, Asia and Antarctica, are also dry deserts. Precipitation, mainly as snow, of course, is sparse and, although snow and ice cover much of the surface, this is of no use to plants, which require liquid water. Bordering these regions of extreme climate, the temperate zones support abundant plant life, but of plants that have adapted to the regular winter drought, when water is frozen.

Different groups of plants have adopted two distinct strategies. In one, the leaves are covered with a waxy substance that reduces the amount of water passing out of them so that, in effect, the plant can seal itself to retain an adequate water content. Holly is a familiar plant of this type — a broad-leaved evergreen. Conifers combine this with drastically reducing the size of their leaves until they are needles. Because the stratagem is equally effective whether the drought be accompanied by warm weather or cold, conifers flourish in Mediterranean climates as well as in the pine forests of the north.

Hamish Miller, a water diviner or 'dowser', seeking water in Cornwall, Britain.

The alternative is to dispose of leaves altogether during the dry season. As winter approaches, a deciduous plant withdraws nutrients from its leaves. They wither and, as the chlorophyll breaks down, other pigments dominate to change their colours. Finally, the plant secretes a hormone that breaks the leaf attachment and it falls. Most, but not all, deciduous plants are broad-leaved.

Evolution on land has taken plants and animals into most parts of the world, but it has not reduced their dependence on water. It could not, for life without water is inconceivable.

Osmosis and osmo-regulation
The cry of 'Land Ho!' from the crow's nest must have brought a smile to the lips of many a sailor in the days when sailing ships spent months at sea crossing uncharted oceans. A landfall brought the promise of many things, but the most important gift the land could offer mariners was also the simplest — water. Water is heavy, bulky, easily lost from leaking barrels, and ships must carry with them enough of it to last until stocks can be replenished. Should

storm or misadventure far out at sea make it necessary to abandon the ship, water had to be loaded into the lifeboats, for without it their occupants would not survive, despite the fact that they rode on the surface of countless billions of gallons of water. Today, the lifeboats would not carry water, because they are equipped with devices the passengers can use to render sea water drinkable.

The image of people dying from thirst in the middle of the ocean has been used with considerable dramatic effect in many movies. It has a companion, and rival image — the desert island. Here the movies usually cheat, for the islands they depict are idyllic and in no sense deserts. A genuine desert island would be one with no springs to supply fresh water and, therefore, no vegetation and no animal life.

Everyone knows that humans, like all land animals, cannot quench their thirst with salt water. Those who persist in the attempt eventually die — from dehydration. If that looks like a paradox, there is another. The physical characteristic that makes salt water poisonous to us is also one that makes life possible at all.

Evolution probably began when molecules

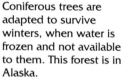

Coniferous trees are adapted to survive winters, when water is frozen and not available to them. This forest is in Alaska.

developed that were able to replicate themselves. The next step occurred when these molecules acquired a protection from chemical compounds that might disrupt their structure. The protection took the form of the cell, in which the molecules could be isolated from the outside environment. The isolation was provided by a membrane that formed a complete envelope. The isolation could not be total, however, for the cell required substances with which to maintain itself, and so the cell membrane evolved in such a way as to permit certain molecules to pass through it, but to exclude others. The membrane was semipermeable, and every cell is bounded by such a membrane.

The process that allows it to function is partly diffusion and partly a process related to diffusion. If you drop a sugar cube into a cup of hot water, the sugar will dissolve. If you wait a little while and then taste the water you will find it is sweet. The sugar molecules have dispersed themselves evenly throughout the water, rather than dissolving and then remaining as a region of very sweet water surrounded by water containing no sugar. Indeed, the mixing is complete and the sweetness of the water is exactly the same throughout the solution.

The explanation is simple. As the sugar molecules separate and mix with the water molecules they move at random, being buffeted this way and that as they collide with water molecules and with one another. Because there are many fewer sugar molecules than there are water molecules, the chance that a sugar molecule will become surrounded by water molecules is greater than the chance that it will become surrounded by sugar molecules. In time it becomes overwhelmingly more likely that the sugar molecules will be dispersed evenly throughout the water. It is theoretically possible that they might accumulate in one place, but no one has ever known it to happen, and it is so improbable as to be not worth considering. In practice, molecules in this situation always diffuse from the region of higher concentration to that of lower concentration.

You might picture the cell membrane as having pores so tiny that only very small molecules can pass through it. The cell requires oxygen and there is less oxygen dissolved in the fluid inside the cell than there is in the fluid outside bathing the cell.

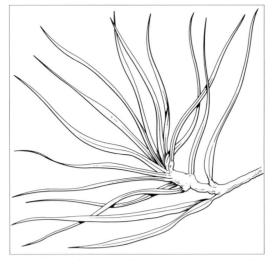

Oxygen molecules, which can pass through the cell membrane, enter the cell, diffusing from the region of higher concentration to that of lower concentration. The cell contains carbon dioxide, a by-product of its own chemical processes, and this diffuses out of the cell by the same means.

Water molecules can also pass through the cell membrane, but the much larger molecules of substances dissolved in the water cannot. If the solutions to either side of the membrane are of the same strength, no molecules cross the membrane but, if their strengths are unequal, there will be a tendency for them to equalize. This cannot be achieved by ordinary diffusion because the solute molecules cannot pass, but it can be achieved by the passage of water molecules in the opposite direction — from the region of lower concentration to that of higher concentration. The process is called 'osmosis', and it continues until the solutions are of equal strength.

If you drink enough salt water (and manage not to vomit), it is possible for your body fluids to become more saline than the fluid inside the cells of your body. Should this happen, water will move by osmosis out of the cells and the cells will dehydrate. It is clearly vital to the health of cells that the concentration of substances dissolved in body fluids is held constant. The process in called 'osmo-regulation', and in mammals it is performed by the kidneys.

This is also the fate awaiting a freshwater fish that enters salt water. It will die from dehydration. Should a sea fish enter fresh water the opposite will occur. The fluid inside its cells will be more saline than that outside. Water will enter the cells and continue to do so until the cells rupture.

Pine needles are leaves that have evolved to minimize the loss of water from the plant. They are very narrow and have a waxy surface that allows them to seal themselves.

In a solution, the random motion of particles ensures that molecules of the dissolved substance (solute) become evenly distributed throughout the solvent. If two solutions of the same substance at different strengths are separated by a membrane that permits the passage of molecules of solvent, but not of solute (top), molecules of solvent will pass through the membrane from the weaker to the stronger solution (bottom) until the two solutions are of equal strength. This is osmosis, exploited by all living cells to regulate their contents.

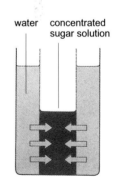

water   concentrated sugar solution

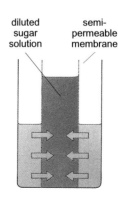

diluted sugar solution   semi-permeable membrane

Most aquatic animals maintain their body fluids at concentrations very close to that of the water in which they live although some, such as eels and salmon, are able to move between fresh water and the sea.

The walls of plant cells are reinforced by cellulose, making them much tougher than the membranes surrounding animal cells. The solution inside a plant cell is usually more concentrated than that of the fluid outside it, and so water enters. This fills the cell and makes it swell, but it does not burst as an animal cell would because the cellulose wall is too strong. It is their cellulose walls that give leaves the rigidity they need to expose themselves to sunlight, and that allow non-woody plants to stand erect.

When you cut flowers to decorate your home you place them in water in order to 'make them last'. Eventually, of course, they will wilt, lose their colour and their petals, and their stems will become limp. The cells will have died, but the availability of water delays the process.

Xylem and phloem
Plants are filled with water. They require it

to make their cells rigid enough to provide mechanical support, to convey nutrients in solution, and as a raw material in its own right, essential for photosynthesis. All in all, plants require a great deal of water, and they obtain it from the soil in which they stand. It is possible to grow plants without soil, but not without water. The technique is called 'hydroponics', and involves bathing the root system in a solution containing precisely calculated amounts of nutrient. It is not suitable for all plants, but for some it can be very effective. Many aquatic plants grow naturally in this way. Some of the large seaweeds you find at the seaside have what look like roots, but they are 'holdfasts', used only to anchor the plant and not to absorb nutrients, which is the task of specialized cells throughout the plant, working in much the same way as those of a simple, colonial animal.

In the more advanced 'vascular' plants, water, with its nutrients carried in solution, is transported by vessels, which together comprise the 'xylem'. The products of photosynthesis are carried from the leaves to the other tissues where they are needed by

(Opposite) The natural supply of rain is often insufficient for farm crops and irrigation is needed. This field is in the United States. (Below) Far from land, seafarers must carry with them the fresh drinking water on which their lives depend.

another system of vessels, called the 'phloem'. The xylem and phloem vessels lie parallel to one another, forming 'vascular bundles'.

In the trunk of a tree, the phloem is in the bark, outside the xylem, which explains why a tree will die if it is 'ring-barked'. The phloem carries the sugars made by photosynthesis. A continuous cut around the trunk, right through the bark and, therefore, through the phloem, interrupts the downward transport of sugars. The root starves and, as its cells die, the tree loses its ability to transport water and nutrients upwards from the soil. This kills the entire tree.

The xylem vessels are made from long, cylindrical cells, joined end to end. The cell walls at the ends of each cylinder more or less break down, and the cells themselves die so the structure forms a continuous, hollow tube of dead tissue. While this is happening, wood is deposited on the sides of the cells, strengthening them, but leaving many small pits where there is no wood and through which water can pass into and out of the tube. The xylem also contains 'tracheids', which are similar to vessels except that in cross-section they are usually polygonal, rather than circular, and the end walls of their cells are tapered and have many pits, rather than being lost altogether.

The system of xylem vessels and tracheids is superficially similar to the system of blood or lymphatic vessels in an animal, but there is one very important difference. The xylem is not a circulatory system. It is open at both ends, and water moves in one direction only, from the soil, through the plant, and then out of the plant. In every vascular plant, from the daisy growing on the lawn — and the grass around it — to the tallest tree, water is being moved from the ground to every part of the plant and then to the outside air. The xylem is made from dead tissue, and the movement of water through it is entirely mechanical. Dissolve a poison in water in a concentration sufficient to kill the plant, and it will be transported like any other solution. Cut off a part of the plant — such as a flower and its stem — and it will retain its ability to conduct water for several days.

Botanists puzzled for a long time over the apparent mystery of the xylem. How does the plant manage to raise water all the way to the top of a tree? The tallest tree in the world is believed to be the coast redwood

(*Sequoia sempervirens*), one of which grew to nearly 370 feet (113 m). If you place one end of a tube in water and use a pump to evacuate the air from the top, water will rise up the tube, but not very far. The water is not 'sucked' up the tube, but pushed up by the pressure of air on the water outside the tube once the pressure is reduced inside. Use mercury instead of water, and at sea level it will rise a mere 30 inches (762 mm) because the apparatus is actually a barometer, measuring atmospheric pressure. Capillary attraction will raise water to a greater height than atmospheric pressure (see page 28), but not to the top of even a small tree.

The solution to the puzzle is somewhat tentative for much has still to be learned about the way water is moved inside plants. Probably the living cells of the plant aid the process, but in ways that are not understood. Tentatively, then, the solution has two parts. The first, as sometimes happens in science, is that the original question was misleading. Trees and other plants do not start as full-sized, but empty vessels into which water must be drawn. They are full of water from the moment their seeds germinate. It is not difficult to understand how a young, and very tiny, plant can be filled with water. As the plant grows it remains filled. The second part of the solution concerns the leaves.

The leaves are the principal site of photosynthesis, and to perform photosynthesis the leaf cells must be able to take in carbon dioxide from the air and release oxygen. Gases enter and leave through extremely small pores, called 'stomata', on the surfaces of all leaves, usually more on the lower than the upper surface. The stomata are very numerous. On the underside of a leaf from an apple tree, for example, there are up to about 26,000 per square inch (400 per sq mm). This is about the average, but over a wide range. The spider plant (*Tradescantia*), for example, has only about 3500 per square inch (14 per sq mm), while the Spanish oak (a cross between the Turkey oak, *Quercus cerris* and cork oak *Q. suber*) has about 305,000 per square inch (1200 per sq mm). Because the plant, including its leaves, is filled with water, water also evaporates through the stomata, which can be opened and closed to allow gases to be exchanged, but the loss of water minimized. Some loss of water from the plant is unavoidable, but it cools the leaves

(Opposite) Coral reefs are possibly the richest of all ecosystems. This is part of the Great Barrier Reef.

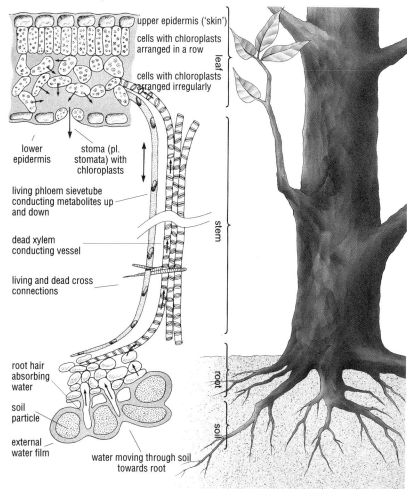

upper epidermis ('skin')

cells with chloroplasts arranged in a row

leaf

cells with chloroplasts arranged irregularly

lower epidermis

stoma (pl. stomata) with chloroplasts

living phloem sievetube conducting metabolites up and down

stem

dead xylem conducting vessel

living and dead cross connections

root hair absorbing water

soil particle

external water film

root

soil

water moving through soil towards root

Movement of water through a plant. Water containing dissolved nutrients and adhering to soil particles is absorbed through the root hairs and more soil water is drawn towards the roots to replace it. Inside the plant, the water moves upwards through the xylem vessels to the leaves. There, sugars are made by photosynthesis, dissolve in the nutrient solution and are carried by the phloem to all parts of the plant. The continual flow of water is sustained by the evaporation of water through the stomata.

through the latent heat of vaporization, just as perspiring cools our skin.

Succulent plants, such as the cacti, which are adapted to hot, dry climates, conserve water by opening their stomata as little as possible. This causes them to heat, but they can tolerate high temperatures. It also reduces the exchange of gases, however. Despite being exposed to intense sunlight, in air containing no less carbon dioxide than air anywhere else, a low rate of photosynthesis is the price they pay for conserving water. They grow very slowly, but under conditions in which other plants could not survive. If the plant must choose between carbon dioxide and water, water is the more important.

If the amount of carbon dioxide in the air increases, plants can obtain as much of it as they need by reducing the time their stomata are open. This, in turn, reduces the amount of water they lose by evaporation. One consequence of the industrial emissions of carbon dioxide is to reduce the quantity of water needed by plants for healthy growth.

Transpiration

The stomata are very small and within them water molecules will adhere strongly to the sides. As water evaporates, the force of adhesion draws more water molecules towards the surface to replace those which have departed. Because the stomata are linked to vessels and, eventually, to the vascular bundles in the xylem, all of which are filled with water, the force of adhesion constantly draws water upwards. The mechanism would fail were the column of water, extending from the leaves to the ground, to be broken at any point, but the force of adhesion is complemented by the force of cohesion, by which liquid water molecules are attracted to one another.

This movement of water from the soil, through the plant, and by evaporation into the air, is called 'transpiration'. Its rate varies from one plant species to another, according to the temperature and humidity of the air, and it occurs mainly in daytime, when stomata must be opened to permit photosynthesis, but the amount of water involved can be very large. It is, after all, proportional to the size of each stoma — which ranges widely, from about 0.00016 inches (4 μm) to 0.01 inch (250 μm) — multiplied by the number of stomata on each leaf, multiplied by the number of leaves. It has been estimated that a birch tree, with some 250,000 leaves, transpires about 79 gallons (360 l) of water a day.

When you measure the weight of water a plant transpires, and compare this with the dry weight of matter the plant produces, the transpiration ratio is typically between about 300:1 and 700:1. The calculation is used in determining which areas are suitable for particular crops. If you wish to grow oranges, for example, quite apart from warm weather and sunshine, you will need a place where the amount of water available is equal to a rainfall of not less than about $1/2$ inch (12.5 mm) a day because that is the quantity of water the crop requires. From sowing to harvesting, a crop of maize needs water equivalent to about 10 inches (250 mm) of rain. Where the rainfall is insufficient, but the climate is suitable in other respects, the crop can be grown with the help of irrigation.

The rate at which plants transpire water far exceeds the rate at which it will evaporate from bare ground or even from the surface of a lake. This must be so because the total area of all the transpiring leaf surfaces is much larger than the area of ground on which the plant stands. One consequence of this is that the air immediately above vegetation is more humid than air above bare ground.

This phenomenon is seen most dramatically in tropical rain forests, where the rainfall is heavy, the temperature consistently high, and the vegetation very luxuriant. So dense is the foliage that, although it is so intense, the rain drips from leaf to leaf as it travels from the canopy to the forest floor, and from there it is quickly transported back to the leaves, and transpired back into the air. Many scientists fear that widespread clearance of the forests will disrupt this cycle. Instead of being transpired, rainwater will drain into rivers — eroding soils in the process — so reducing the humidity of the atmosphere. The climate will become drier, and this may affect climates far beyond the boundaries of the humid tropics.

Transpiration by plants also affects the movement of water in the soil. Where the vegetation cover is abundant, rain penetrates the ground and begins to drain horizontally and vertically (see page 27) but, before it can travel far, a large amount of it is intercepted by plant roots and removed. The amount of rainwater entering the groundwater and draining to rivers is therefore only a proportion, and perhaps a small proportion, of the total amount that falls. Transpiration by freshwater aquatic plants, on the other hand, can remove so much water as to dry out shallow lakes. Indeed, this is a natural ageing process by which shallow lakes eventually become dry land.

If the vegetation cover is removed, the proportion of rainwater draining into the groundwater and rivers increases. On low-lying land, perhaps some distance from the area of bare ground, this may lead to rises in the water table that are high enough to cause waterlogging of soils, and increase the risk of flooding.

There are ways transpiration can be exploited to advantage. Plants with roots that can tolerate being submerged in water from time to time, and that have a high transpiration rate, are often used to drain wet land. Alder (*Alnus*) and willow (*Salix*) species — which grow naturally along river banks — are often used in this way.

Trees move water from their roots to their leaves, where it evaporates, and forests strongly influence their local climates. This tropical rain forest is in Venezuela.

OCEAN LIFE

A three-dimensional world

People enjoying themselves at a swimming pool spend almost all their time at the surface of the water. We need to breathe, of course, but this is only one reason for the short time humans can spend at the pool bottom. When the lungs are filled with air a human body is less dense than water. Being very buoyant, we tend to bob to the surface like corks and this makes swimming under water rather hard work.

Most of the ray-finned fishes, forming the subclass (Actinopterygii) that includes the great majority of fish species, are able to control their buoyancy by means of a swim bladder, a thin-walled sac containing as much gas as the fish needs to make its body density equal to that of water. The fish achieves neutral buoyancy: in effect, it is weightless and moves in three dimensions more freely even than a bird in the air. Because water pressure increases with depth, the fish adjusts the volume of gas in its swim bladder according to the depth at which it is swimming. Some species are able to gulp air at the surface and burp to release it again.

The swim bladder evolved from an organ used to assist in respiration, from which the lungs of land-dwelling vertebrates may also have evolved. The first fishes with swim bladders lived about 400 million years ago, in the Devonian Period, in seas that by then supported a great variety of organisms, including another group of fishes, some of which were the ancestors of the sharks. They first appeared at about the same time as the ray-finned fishes but they never acquired swim bladders. Sharks can also achieve neutral buoyancy, with the help of the liver. It can account for up to one-quarter of the total body weight of a shark and it contains an oil, squalene, that is lighter than water. The more squalene the liver contains, the more buoyant the shark will be. A tiger shark, 13 feet (4 m) long, weighs about 990 pounds (450 kg) on land, but less than 8.8 pounds (4 kg) in water.

Animals that live on the sea bed have bodies denser than the water above them, but the great majority are very nearly weightless and weightlessness brings other advantages. An aquatic animal cannot be injured by falling, and it does not need a rigid skeleton and powerful muscles to support it. The skeleton and muscles increase mobility by allowing an animal to swim, but they can be reduced to a minimum.

Squids are molluscs, related to land-dwelling snails and slugs. The earliest molluscs all had shells. Most slugs have lost the shell, and in squids it is reduced to a horny 'pen'. Squids have more rigid bodies than slugs because they have evolved plates of cartilage that make a kind of skeleton and also protect the brain. They swim by drawing water into a body cavity, then contracting muscles that expel it forcibly through a funnel to the rear. They are, literally, 'jet propelled', and a pair of fins at the rear of the body helps stabilize them. They can swim very fast. Some have been known to leap on to the decks of ships more than 12 feet (3.5 m) above the water surface. Yet they can also cruise slowly and, because the funnel can be directed this way or that, they are highly manoeuvrable and can swim either forwards or backwards.

Squids feed by pursuing their prey, but an animal which feeds among the masses of minute organisms that comprise the plankton (from the Greek plagktos, meaning 'wandering'), floating near the sea surface, does not need to be a strong swimmer. Jellyfish have no control over their travels. They float near the surface, wandering where wind, current and tide carry them. Technically, a jellyfish is known as a 'medusa' (from the name of the Greek Gorgon who had snakes where most of us have hair). In many species, the free-floating medusa is one stage in a life cycle most of which is spent as a small, sedentary polyp, but the jellyfish (Scyphozoa) spend most of their lives as medusae and only a brief larval stage as polyps. Most are small but not all. The float, or 'bell' of Cyanea capillata can reach a diameter of 6.5 feet (2 m). Beneath the bell hang the long tentacles, often armed with stinging cells (nematocysts), with which the animal gathers its food. Some have stings which can be serious to humans. The most dangerous of all marine animals is probably Chironex fleckeri, a jellyfish found near the Australian coast. Its sting can be fatal,

(Opposite) An animal that lives in water is almost weightless. The jellyfish drifts or swims weakly, but fishes, such as the sharks, are powerful swimmers, highly manoeuvrable and capable of impressive turns of speed. Whales are the most fully aquatic of all the mammals that have returned from the land to the sea, and include some of the largest animals that have ever lived. Fish and whales are vertebrates, but a skeleton is not essential for swimming. The squid is an invertebrate that swims very fast by a type of jet propulsion.

within up to 20 minutes and sometimes in seconds.

In this three-dimensional world animals expend little energy combating gravity. This advantage, and the abundance of food, drew some animals back to the sea long after their ancestors had taken up life on land. It is perhaps 60 million years since a group of porpoise-like, carnivorous mammals adopted an aquatic way of life. Their descendants are the whales, which have adapted fully to the marine environment, although they must still breathe air. Being weightless, there was no limit to the size they could attain, and the blue whale, more than 100 feet (30 m) long and weighing about 140 tons on land, is about the size of 30 average elephants.

Life in polar regions
In the sea just below the permanent Antarc-

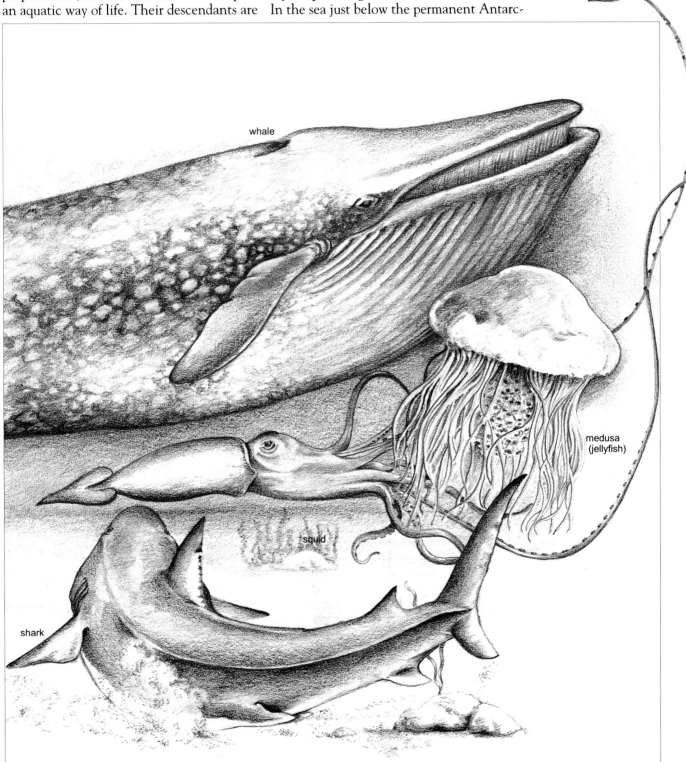

sea otter

Galápagos penguin

Many land animals have found ways to exploit the rich food resources of the sea. (Right) Penguins swim well but can no longer fly. (Left) The sea otter is very well adapted to its marine environment and rarely comes to shore even to sleep.

tic ice sheet the water is very cold indeed. It is more saline than most sea water, because fresh water has frozen out of it, and so its freezing temperature is well below 32 °F (0 °C). This presents a problem for an animal with body fluids that are less saline, and so freeze at a higher temperature, and that has no means of regulating its body temperature. It should freeze but, in fact, those Antarctic waters are among the most productive in the world. They support relatively few species, but those which have adapted to the temperature are very abundant. Vast quantities of nutrients, brought close to the surface by upwelling currents (see page 90), sustain large growths of phytoplankton — but only in certain places and near to the coast — and the phytoplankton provides food for animals.

The cod icefish, or Antarctic cod, (*Notothenia coriiceps*) is one of nearly 60 species comprising the family Nototheniidae, and together they are the most numerous of all Antarctic fishes. It is about 2 feet (60 cm) long and feeds on invertebrates. Despite its name, it is not related to the cod of temperate waters. The cod icefish is able to survive the cold because its blood contains a glycoprotein — a compound of a protein and a carbohydrate. This lowers the freezing temperature of the blood. In effect, it is an antifreeze and many Antarctic fishes make use of it.

The solubility of oxygen is greater in cold water than in warm, and Antarctic waters are rich in oxygen. They carry so much oxygen that fish of some species have very little haemoglobin in their blood, and one species, the icefish (*Chaenocephalus aceratus*), has blood that contains no haemoglobin at all — its blood is white and almost transparent. The fish is sluggish, so its oxygen requirement is modest, and the oxygen dissolved in its blood plasma is sufficient for its needs.

The most abundant animal of all, however, is the krill (*Euphausia superba*), an almost transparent crustacean, about 2 inches (5 cm) long, which looks like a shrimp. Shoals of krill are often hundreds of yards across, more than 15 feet (4.5 m) thick, and in the densest upper layers may contain as many as 75,000 individuals per square yard (63,000 per sq m). The krill feed on the phytoplankton and most other animals feed on the krill. A blue whale may take a ton of krill at a single meal, and enjoy four meals a day.

Food is plentiful, but only in the sea, for the land has little to offer, and all the birds and mammals of Antarctic regions are aquatic. At the other end of the world, in the Arctic, another group of animals has evolved in parallel. The two groups are largely isolated by the great distance between them, and by the waters of low latitudes, which provide much less food and which some of them would find intolerably warm. Whales move between polar and subtropical or even tropical waters (see page 80), but as distinct populations that have little contact with one another, and, although they may approach close to the Equator, only rarely do they cross it. The whales of the two hemispheres seldom meet.

Penguins, of which there are 18 species, occur only in the southern hemisphere, but not exclusively on the continent of Antarctica. They are found along the shores of all the southern continents and islands, some of them far to the north. The Humboldt (*Spheniscus humboldti*) and Galápagos (*S. mendiculus*) penguins live quite close to the Equator — but they do not cross it.

The Antarctic penguins are hunted by leopard seals (*Hydrurga leptonyx*), but the largest carnivore of the Arctic is not a seal, it is the polar bear (*Thalarctos maritimus*), the biggest of all bears, and it feeds mainly on seals. Seals, too, occur in both hemi-

spheres. Some, like leopard seals in the south and common seals (*Phoca vitulina*) in the north, never move far from the coast. Others, like the Arctic harp seal (*Pagophilus groenlandicus*) and the Antarctic Weddell seal (*Leptonychotes weddelli*), live in the open sea and rarely leave the water, except now and then to lie on ice floes. Elephant seals occur in both hemispheres but, although they are much the same size and similar in appearance and are classified as belonging to the same genus (*Mirounga*), they are placed in different species and occupy different habitats. The northern species (*M. angustirostris*) occurs along the Californian coast, the southern (*M. leonina*) mainly around the Falkland Islands (Malvinas). The Arctic equivalent of the elephant seals is the walrus (*Odobenus rosmarus*), which uses its tusks — in fact, overgrown canine teeth — to stir up food from the sea bed, prize molluscs from rocks, and to heave itself out of the water. Walruses are so well insulated by their thick blubber, that they

Sea fish have adapted to the waters in which they live. The Atlantic herring lives in large shoals that travel long distances, but always in temperate waters (see page 83). The ice fish avoids freezing in the Antarctic waters it inhabits by having an antifreeze compound, but no haemoglobin, in its blood. The barracuda lives in warmer waters, where it is a powerful predator.

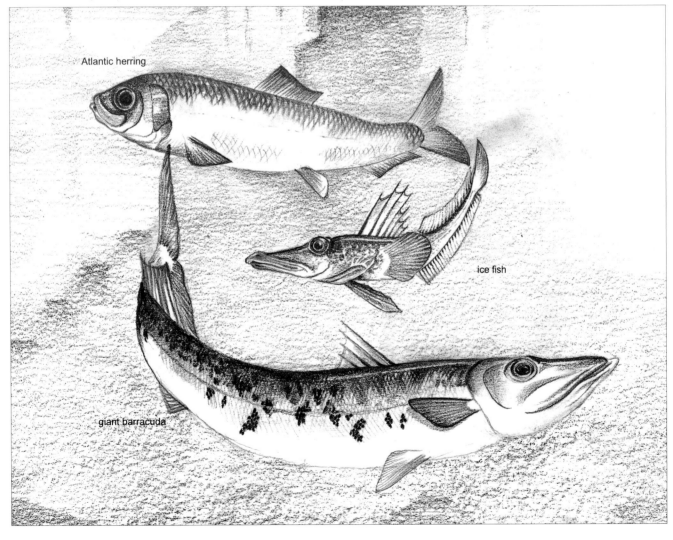

Atlantic herring

ice fish

giant barracuda

can doze contentedly with their skins frozen hard.

Walruses feed on invertebrates, as do the sea otters of the Pacific. Again, one species (*Enhydra lutris*) lives in the northern hemisphere and another, the smaller marine otter (*Lutra felina*), in the southern. In some ways, the sea and marine otters are more completely aquatic even than seals. They rarely come ashore, even to give birth to their young, and they sleep in the water, tangling themselves in seaweed so they will not drift. The sea otter is also remarkable in that it uses tools. During its dive for food, it collects a stone from the sea bed, then lies on its back on the surface with the stone on its chest and beats its prey against the stone to break the shell. A few years ago, the Californian sea otter was threatened with extinction, but protection from hunting and careful conservation saved it, and now its population is quite large and increasing.

Distribution of species

The factors that govern the distribution of species in water are no different from those which obtain on dry land. In general, where resources — such as food and nesting sites — are available, species will arrive or evolve to exploit them. Once those species are there, and their needs are satisfied, there is no reason for them to leave. Where the living conditions are similar in different, widely separated places, it is quite usual to find similar but unrelated species occupying them. Such species are rarely able to move from one habitat to another because, quite apart from the inhospitable regions they may have to cross between the two areas, there is no room for the would-be immigrants in the other habitat. Many species have moved through the Suez Canal from the Red Sea into the eastern Mediterranean, from a region with a wide diversity of species to one with far fewer species. Presumably this allowed them to escape from overcrowding and to exploit available resources, but few Mediterranean species have managed to move in the opposite direction and establish themselves in the fully exploited Red Sea.

The diversity of species is usually higher in warm climates than in cold, but there are exceptions. There are more species of seals in polar regions than in lower latitudes, for example, and in temperate regions the diversity of all kinds of species is lower than

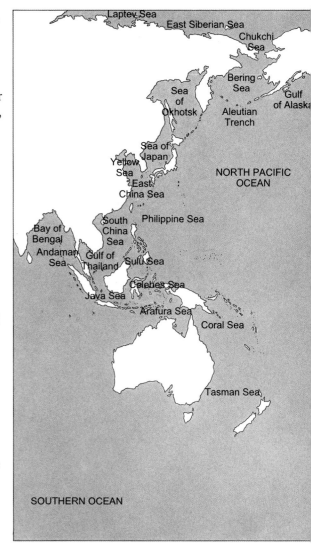

might be expected. Probably this is because conditions in the temperate regions are much less stable than those in either polar or tropical regions. During ice ages, polar regions expand and tropical regions shrink a little, but temperate regions almost vanish.

In the open oceans, however, the habitat is vast. Abundant plankton forms the basis of the food chain, and there are many animals grazing it and being hunted by carnivores. Shoals of herring — different populations, which may constitute distinct species, in the Atlantic and Pacific — feed on the young of other species by day, and at night continue to feed by filtering small particles from the water by means of their 'gill rakers'. There are shoals of carnivorous mackerel and, in the southern hemisphere, of anchoveta — relatives of the herring.

Not all the plankton-feeders are small and fast-moving. Blue (*Balaenoptera musculus*) and fin (*B. physalus*) whales graze the rich plankton of the southern tropics, for exam-

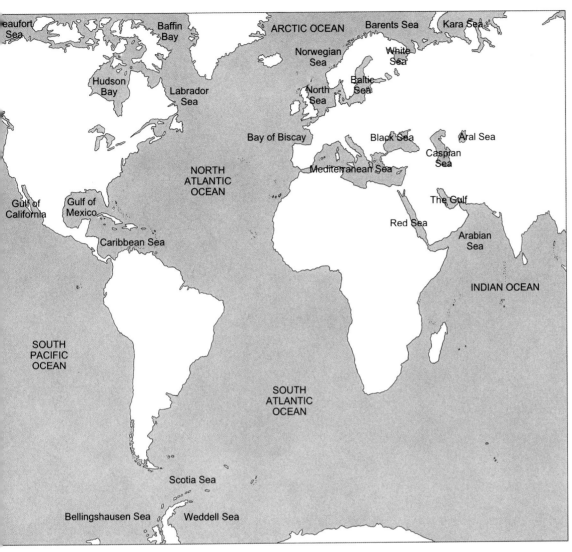

The seas and oceans of the world

ple, and in both hemispheres, in temperate as well as tropical waters, there are basking (*Cetorhinus maximus*) and whale (*Rhincodon typus*) sharks. These are the biggest fishes in the world. Basking sharks can grow to 50 feet (15 m) long and whale sharks to almost 60 feet (18 m).

Few predators will attack such large animals, but smaller prey are hunted by other species of sharks and by carnivorous bony fishes, such as the barracuda, of which there are about 20 species. These are solitary, watchful animals, which hunt by pursuing anything that moves, in much the same manner as the freshwater pike.

Not a great deal is known about the ocean sunfish (*Mola mola*), except that it swims slowly among the plankton, feeding on small animals, and avoids predators by its size and curious shape. It is almost spherical, up to 12 feet (3.7 m) in diameter, and weighs about two tons. Other animals have evolved camouflage. Sea horses, for exam-

ple, are difficult to see as they sway with the seaweed to which they cling with their tails. The sargassum fish (*Histrio histrio*) is even better hidden, for it matches almost perfectly the *Sargassum* weed among which it lives.

Mysterious eels

To the west of the central North Atlantic, ocean currents enclose an approximately elliptical area of relatively calm water. This region is called the Sargasso Sea. It is a place of legend, for its often windless conditions becalm sailing ships, and the Sea contains vast mats of *Sargassum* weed to foul rudders. It is from here, in the mysterious Sargasso Sea, that eels (*Anguilla anguilla*) voyage the 3500 miles (5600 km) to European and North African rivers.

The eel larva is called a 'leptocephalus', which means 'small head' and it was many years before scientists realized that these small, leaf-shaped animals are not a distinct species, but grow into familiar freshwater eels. To this day controversy surrounds the story of their migration. Adult eels are known to leave their rivers for the sea, and eels are known to spawn in the Sargasso Sea. The leptocephali are known to cross the Atlantic to Europe, but no adults make this crossing. What is not known is whether the larvae are the offspring of the European eels, which die after spawning, or whether all the adult eels die before reaching the Sargasso Sea, and the larvae are the offspring of American eels, which also spawn in the Sea and then die, but that have a much shorter journey to reach it. It seems unlikely, though not impossible, that the American eels breed so successfully that they provide the entire stock for both American and European and North African rivers. Eels certainly possess the navigational ability to cross the Atlantic. Tagged eels released far out at sea have returned to the rivers from which they were taken.

As they approach to within about 200 miles (322 km) of the European coast the leptocephali metamorphose to become small eels, called 'elvers'. They enter rivers, always swimming upstream by moving their bodies

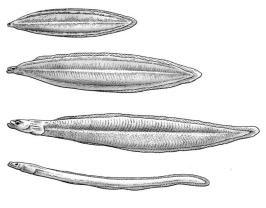

(Top) Eel larvae begin their lives in the Sargasso Sea from where they migrate, some to north-east America, others to north-western Europe and into the Mediterranean. (Bottom) The eel larva, or leptocephalus, begins its life shaped like a willow leaf but, before it metamorphoses into the adult form, it shrinks to the shape of a pencil.

so that the pressure on either side is equal, and by watching the river bed to check they are travelling in the right direction.

Migratory fishes

Eels are remarkable not only for the great distance they travel, but also for their ability to move from salt to fresh water. Very few fishes can tolerate such a change in salinity. Salmon (*Salmo salar*) and sturgeon (*Acipenser sturio*) are among the rather larger number of species that move in the opposite direction, from rivers to the sea.

Frank Buckland (1826-79), one of the most endearing of English eccentrics and a pioneer of salmon breeding, used to joke about the 30,000 salmon he said he had hatched in his own kitchen. He told audiences at his lectures that since 'salmon always returned to the places where they had hatched, they would see that he had a very cheering prospect before him'.

The Atlantic and Pacific salmon belong to different species and, although the Atlantic salmon travels far between the gravel beds in the shallow rivers where it spawns and the ocean where it matures and feeds, it is the Pacific species that may make the longest journey. The king (*Oncorhynchus tshawtyscha*) and humpback (*O. gorbuscha*) salmon are believed to cover 2000 miles (3200 km).

Such extremely long journeys are unusual, but many species of marine fish migrate between the areas in which they feed and those in which they spawn. Some are affected by the temperature of the water, moving into higher latitudes in summer in search of food. In the last century, the pilchard (*Sardina pilchardus*) used to visit Cornwall in its summer migration and formed the basis of a major local industry. Then, around the time of the First World War, the shoals failed to arrive and they have not returned since. No one knows why fish suddenly alter their migration routes, but they do.

Other species follow the migrations of their prey. Schools of tunny (*Thunnus thynnus*) enter the Mediterranean in early summer in pursuit of the smaller fish on which they feed. Mackerel (*Scomber scombrus*) also leave the open seas where they spend the winter and come close to shore in summer in their hunt for fish fry, but on the way, while still a long way from the coast, they pause to spawn.

Fishermen have an obvious interest in tracing the migrations of valuable species and, not surprisingly, those are the fishes whose movements are known best. North Sea cod (*Gadus morhua*), for example, spawn on the eastern side of the Sea and then disperse to feed, some of them pursuing the herring (*Clupea harengus*). One group of herring move north from the English Channel, and a second population moves around the northern North Sea in a counter-clockwise circle. Marine mammals also migrate between breeding and feeding grounds. Many whale species travel from polar regions to the tropics and back again. That is a long journey, but northern fur seals (*Callorhinus ursinus*) travel further. Two populations of them breed on islands in the Bering Strait. Then one population travels south to Japan and the other to California, a round trip of some 6000 miles (10,000 km).

Giants of the deep
If stories of ships becalmed in an ocean of seaweed were dismissed by educated people as mere travellers' tales, how much more readily must they have laughed at legends of huge marine monsters. Yet the Sargasso Sea certainly exists, and so do at least some of the monsters — although they do not make a habit of attacking ships.

Some of the monsters may have been whales, but whales are animals familiar to sailors. Giant squid, on the other hand, are far from familiar, but they exist. Now and then a dead one is washed ashore, but what we know of them we have learned partly from studying whales.

The sperm whale (*Physeter catodon*) is a large animal. Males grow to a length of about 60 feet (18.5 m), females to about half that size. Unlike the great baleen whales, which obtain their food by filtering small morsels from the water, sperm whales have very small teeth in the upper jaw and functional ones in the lower jaw, and are carnivores. They feed mainly on squid, hunting their prey at great depths — they are known to dive to more than 3300 feet (1000 m), and one was once detected on sonar nearly 7400 feet (2250 m) below the surface. Sometimes, the squid they hunt

The common eel (*Anguilla anguilla*) spawns in salt water and the elvers, seen here, return to fresh water.

(Above) Atlantic salmon *(Salmo salar)* spawn in rivers and spend most of their adult lives at sea. (Opposite) The existence of giant squids was first inferred from the sucker scars found on sperm whales, which feed on squid they catch at great depths. A few very large squid have also been washed ashore.

fight back, gripping the whale with their tentacles. The tentacles are equipped with suckers that have claws, like those of a cat, to help them grip more tightly and, in tearing itself free, the whale may suffer skin injuries that leave permanent scars. Measurements of those scars, and the distances between them, indicate the size of the animal that inflicted the injury. This is how we know that some of the deep-sea squids (*Architeuthis* species) are more than 50 feet (15 m) long.

The tales of such beasts attacking ships may have arisen by confusing the giant squid with the 'flying squids', which leap from the water and glide, probably as a means of escaping from or confusing predators. Squid have been seen to leap vertically from the water. There are many species of squid, and they include some of the fastest animals in the sea — they are literally jet-propelled, swimming by means of water they expel with great force. Some of the flying squids have been timed gliding at 16 miles per hour (26 km/h) and sometimes they

miscalculate their flight path and land on the decks of ships.

A giant squid will provide a substantial meal, even for an animal the size of a sperm whale, so it is not too difficult to understand why the whale should pursue it. Explaining how the whale manages to reach such depths, and remain below the surface for nearly one-and-a-half hours, is much more difficult.

If you try to hold your breath, eventually you will be compelled to release it. A part of your brain constantly monitors the pressure of carbon dioxide in your tissues and, when this exceeds a particular value, it overrides your conscious brain. A whale is much less sensitive to the accumulation of carbon dioxide, and probably its tissues are more tolerant of an oxygen deficiency than those of a land-dwelling animal. Its heart also helps, by undergoing 'bradycardia', or a slowing of its beat. Soon after the whale dives its heart beat slows at least to half its rate at the surface. This makes the oxygen last longer, and the animal may be able to

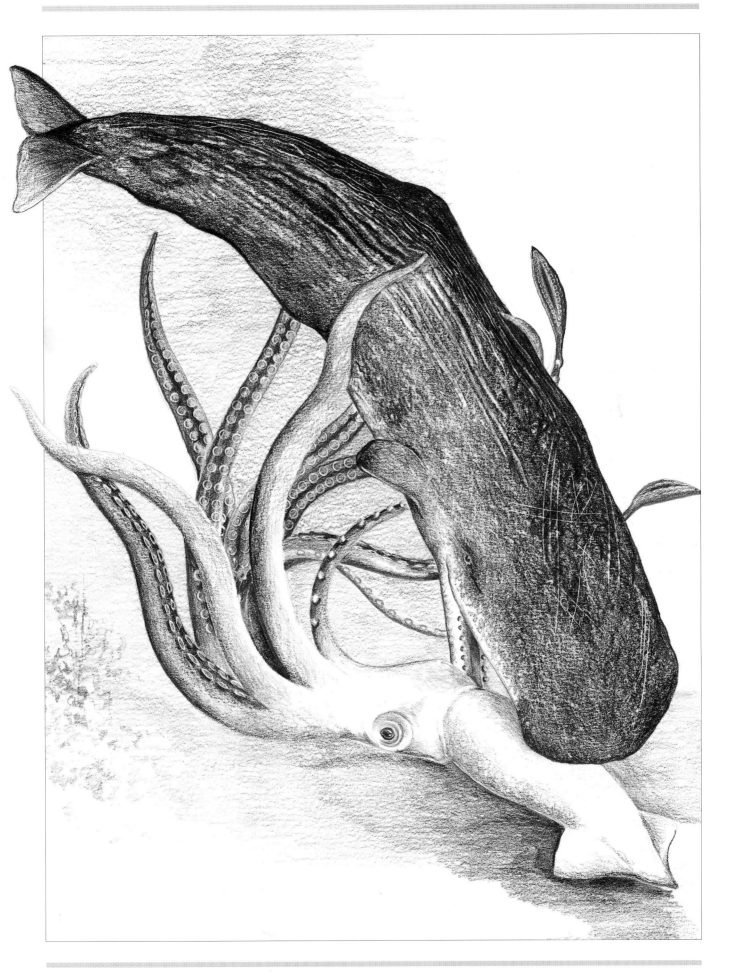

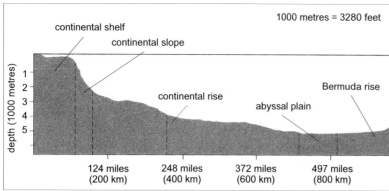

1000 metres = 3280 feet

continental shelf

continental slope

continental rise

abyssal plain

Bermuda rise

depth (1000 metres)

124 miles (200 km) 248 miles (400 km) 372 miles (600 km) 497 miles (800 km)

Beyond the coastline, the submerged outer margins of continents are divided into regions, the average dimensions of which conceal variations. This cross section is of the part of the eastern United States that extends beneath the Atlantic Ocean, from the coast to the abyssal plain, with the Bermuda rise beyond, and the horizontal distances and depths are somewhat different from the averages given in the text.

store oxygen in its tissues, as well as in its lungs. Even so, the mechanism by which it avoids asphyxiation is not well understood. Sperm whales always surface close to the place from which they dived, so it is possible that they move little while they are hunting, selecting prey from among large schools of giant squid.

To attain great depths, the sperm whale must overcome the buoyancy caused by its air-filled lungs. This may be achieved by the spermaceti, which fills the huge reservoir at the front of its head. Spermaceti is composed of tissue made up largely of vessels and filled with oil (sperm oil). This oil is liquid at warm temperatures, but solidifies if it is cooled below about 90 °F (32 °C) — about 5.4 °F (3 °C) below the whale's body temperature. As it dives, the whale may cool the spermaceti, perhaps by taking in water through one of its nostrils, or by increasing the blood flow near the skin. The oil cools and, as it solidifies, its volume decreases and its density increases. The head of the whale changes shape as the whole reservoir shrinks and becomes heavier. Calculations have shown that this would be sufficient to counteract the animal's buoyancy down to about 6500 feet (2000 m). When the whale wishes to surface it uses its body warmth to melt the oil, which expands again, 'inflating' the reservoir and restoring the lost buoyancy.

The sperm whale hunts in total darkness, for no daylight penetrates below about 3300 feet (1000 m). Like its relatives the dolphins and porpoises, it uses sound waves to locate its prey, and it may also use intense sound to stun or even kill it. As well as helping the whale to regulate its buoyancy, the spermaceti may serve some purpose connected with sound production.

It is the darkness deep below the surface that conditions the way marine animals must live. The plant growth on which they feed occurs only in the upper layers of the ocean, so animals which live at greater depths must depend on the organic wastes that fall from above like a constant rain. This 'rain' is utilized by animals which recycle it continuously and carry some of it — as part of themselves — back to the surface layers, so that only a proportion of it ever reaches the ocean floor. You might picture it as rain falling on a dense forest, dripping slowly from leaf to leaf and evaporating all the time so that the forest floor remains comparatively dry. Over much of the ocean, animals living at great depths inhabit a region where food is scarce, and many of them are equipped to survive on very occasional, but very large meals.

The oceans' profile
When you visit the coast it may seem that the boundary between land and sea is abrupt, and that you overlook the deep ocean. There may be high cliffs, for example, and beaches that shelve steeply so that when you bathe you are soon out of your depth. The appearance is misleading. The sea cliff is the remains of a hill whose seaward side has been eroded by the battering of waves, and the beach does not have to shelve far before the water is deeper than your height.

The continents are raised above the ocean floor, and beyond the region of dry land there is a large area covered by water. This is the 'continental shelf', and it extends to an average distance of about 45 miles (72 km) from the shore. The shelf slopes gently until, at its outer margin, the sea is about 500 feet (150 m) deep. Then the gradient increases, down the 'continental slope', though it averages no more than about 4 degrees. There are hills and valleys on the slope, and deep canyons that end in great, fan-shaped deposits of sediment. The sediment reduces the gradient, and the continental slope gives way to the gentler 'continental rise'. Eventually, the rise leads to the ocean floor, the place where the distinctive crustal rocks, from which continents are built, give way to the rocks of the oceanic crust. This is the 'continental margin', at a depth of about 6500 feet (2000 m), and it opens on to the 'abyssal plain'. International law now recognizes the territorial rights of coastal states to their share of the continental shelf, slope and rise, to an arbitrary distance of 200 miles (322 km) from the shore.

It is the shallowest region, where the depth is less than 650 feet (200 m) that supports life most abundantly. This is called the 'neritic zone'. Beyond it, at depths between 650 and 6500 feet (200-2000 m), lies the 'bathyal zone', and beyond that again, at depths of 6500 feet (2000 m) or more, lies the 'abyssal zone'. The deep abyssal plain has its own hills and valleys but also, in certain places, deep, wide trenches where one of the plates that comprise the crust is being subducted beneath another. The bottom of such trenches is often nearly 20,000 feet (6000 m) below the surface, and the deepest of them all, the Marianas Trench between the Pacific and Philippine Plates, is 36,000 feet (11,000 m) deep. This region, below 20,000 feet (6000 m), is the 'hadal zone', a very isolated habitat, inhabited by strange animals (see page 90ff).

The neritic zone occupies about 8 per cent of the ocean area and the abyssal zone, where the sperm whale hunts, about 75 per cent. The neritic zone is fed with a constant stream of nutrient compounds washed from the land. These sustain the photo-synthesizing phytoplankton, and the water is sufficiently shallow for significant amounts of nutrient to reach the sea bed. 'Pelagic' animals — those which range freely through open water — feed on the plankton and on one another, and 'benthic' — bottom-dwelling — invertebrate species, live permanently on or just below the sea bed, where they are prey to 'demersal' fishes — those which are free-swimming, but find their food on the sea bed.

Bottom dwellers

The demersal species include the flatfishes, such as plaice, flounder and turbot, which have adapted to a life spent cruising close to the bottom or lying, virtually invisibly, on the bed itself. Many flatfish species are able to expand or contract pigmented areas in their skin so they match the background and, if you have visited a marine aquarium, you will know how difficult it is to see them unless they move.

A fish that spends most of its time on the sea bottom will find ample food and can avoid predators by its camouflage, but it has two difficulties. A fish breathes by taking in water through its mouth, passing it across its gills, and expelling it through its gill slits. If its mouth is too close to the sea bed, its gills

may clog with mud and sand. The skates and rays, which are also bottom feeders, take in water not through their mouths but through an opening on the tops of their heads. The flatfishes, faced with the same problem, solve it by swimming on their sides, so at least part of the mouth is clear of the sediment.

This solves one problem only to create another. A fish that swims on its side may keep half its mouth clear of the mud, but one of its eyes will almost scrape through it. So the flatfishes carry both eyes on the same side of the body. Some, such as the turbot (*Scopthalmus maximus*) swim on their right side with their eyes on the left, and others, such as the plaice (*Pleuronectes platessa*), flounder (*Platichthys flesus*), and sole (*Solea solea* is the Dover sole, *Microstomus kitt* the lemon sole), swim on their left side with their eyes on the right. The flatfishes begin life the same torpedo shape as other fishes. As the time approaches for the growing larva to graduate from life among the plankton one of its eyes migrates across its head. Then, with both eyes on the same side, it settles on the bottom.

There would be little point in adopting such elaborate camouflage were the fish to live in total darkness. The extent to which sea water absorbs and scatters incoming radiation depends on its wavelength. Ultraviolet and infra-red radiation cannot penetrate to a depth of more than about 3 feet (1.0 m), and most red light is ab-sorbed in the upper 33 feet (10m). Some invertebrates, which live just below this level, are coloured red and, because red light cannot penetrate, they look almost black. At a depth of about 164 feet (50 m), 95 per cent of the light has been lost, even in the clearest water, but photosynthesis can continue to three times this depth, and a little light penetrates even deeper. The light does not give way to darkness suddenly, but fades gradually through an extensive twi-light zone which ends at around 4000 feet (1200 m), below which no sunlight ever reaches.

Deep-sea life

No sunlight penetrates, but many animals that live in the twilight, or complete darkness, emit light of their own — 'bioluminescence'. It usually takes the form of very faint flashes and probably serves mainly for camouflage. It may seem paradoxical that in dim light an animal can use its own light in order to hide but, in fact, it can use light to render itself invisible, and that is what many fishes do. In dim light, animals cast dim shadows and when seen from below they are only faintly silhouetted. Provided the light is of precisely the right wavelength and intensity, an animal that emits light downwards can compensate for the light blocked by its body — and its silhouette will vanish. In the same way, an animal that directs just the right amount of just the right wavelength of light in a direction that is towards a source of light will eliminate its own shadow. The trick does not work on land, or even in the brighter sunlight near the sea surface, because it is impossible to generate light that is sufficiently intense — although the pale underside of many fishes goes some way to producing a similar effect. Many fishes of deeper waters have silvery, reflective sides which work the same way — but it is very effective in the twilight, and the animals which use it are reluctant to leave the zone in which the level of light is the one in which they find safety. Other animals use light to make decoys, patches of light they can detach from themselves. The decoy holds the attention of a predator long enough for the potential prey to make its escape.

The ability to produce light biologically was acquired long ago, probably at about the time when the free oxygen released by photosynthesis began to accumulate. For most bacteria, oxygen was extremely poisonous, and they evolved various chemical means for making it safe. It seems likely that some of the complex reactions involved the synthesis of a compound called 'luciferin'. In the presence of an enzyme ('luciferase'), luciferin can be oxidized (thus absorbing oxygen) to produce two of the compounds from which it was synthesized in the first place, plus water and energy, the energy being released as light. The light-generating ability has been retained to this day by many bacteria and protozoons, and it has been passed to some other organisms, such as dinoflagellates — simple, single-celled plants — which have improved on it so they emit much more light than a bacterium. Larger animals, however, employ colonies of bacteria, of the genus *Photobacterium*, which they contain in special cavities

in their skin. On land, fireflies and glowworms also employ such bacteria, but for mating rather than for defensive purposes.

Anglerfishes and more

Not all luminescent fishes use their light for defence. The deep-sea anglerfishes use theirs to lure prey. There are 215 species of anglerfishes (comprising the order Lophiiformes). They are all bottom-dwellers, but *Lophius piscatorius* and *L. americanus*, of the eastern and western Atlantic respectively, are sometimes caught by fishermen and kept because they are edible. These two species occur at depths below about 1600 feet (500 m). Other anglers inhabit deeper waters. The angler has a huge mouth, with a large number of long, very sharp teeth, and its dorsal fin is modified into a flexible, rod-like structure, called an 'illicium', with a fleshy lure at the end of it. The shape of the lure varies from one species to another — in some it looks and moves just like a small fish — but its purpose remains the same. It attracts fish. As soon as a would-be predator is within range, the huge mouth opens and the angler draws in a rush of water, making a current that sweeps in the hapless victim. Where there is little light such a lure is of limited value, but in almost all deep-sea anglers the lure bears colonies of luminescent bacteria. The bacteria are perfectly safe, for no fish survives the mouth long enough to attack the lure!

The large mouth of the anglers is typical of deep-sea predators, and a mark of poverty rather than plenty. In the somewhat barren regions they inhabit, when food approaches they cannot afford mistakes, for it may be a long time before the next meal appears.

It may also be a long time before a possible mate appears, and these more or less sedentary animals might have died out long ago had their evolutionary development not found an ingenious solution to their difficulty. Most anglerfishes are females parasitized by males.

When anglerfish eggs hatch, among the plankton near the sea surface, the larvae look much like those of any other fish, but the females can be identified by the small bump on the snout that will grow into an illicium. Probably there are far more males than females. Both sexes pass through several metamorphoses, descending into deeper water as they approach maturity, but in some species the male becomes sexually mature, while in all other respects he is still a juvenile. He stops feeding, finds a female, attaches himself to her with his pincer-like jaws, and mating takes place. In other species, the male attaches himself in the same way, but then ceases to grow. His testes and the ovaries of his mate both develop, but his attachment becomes permanent so he can no longer live independently. He is a parasite, contributing only his sperm to the union, and the female is effectively a hermaphrodite. It is not unusual for a female to have two 'husbands' attached in this way.

The tripodfishes are true hermaphrodites. At least some of them may be able to fertilize themselves but, in general, they mate in a synchronized way, so that each partner is fertilized. Various species of tripodfishes live at depths from about 1500 to more than 18,000 feet (457-5500 m), and their fins are modified to form struts on which they rest on the sea bed.

The twilight region is inhabited mainly by shrimps, prawns, small squid, and the small fishes that feed on them. Here, and below in the bathyal zone, any fish longer than about 8 inches (20 cm) is considered large and most are much smaller. Lures, with lights, are common but, among fish that stalk their prey, rather than lying in wait for it like the anglers, lures usually consist of modified chin barbels.

Finding food

Many fish have barbels around their mouths — the catfishes earn their common name because some of them have barbels that are slightly reminiscent of a cat's whiskers. They are not whiskers, of course, but fleshy protuberances — fish have no hairs. Most species use them to feel the mud in which they find food, often in very cloudy water. The deep-sea species also use their barbels to find food, presumably by waving them until another fish comes close to investigate. The barbels vary in form. *Grammatostomias flagellibarba*, for example, has a barbel like an illuminated whip, several times the length of its body, and in *Chirostomias pliopterus* the barbel is quite short but, behind it, the pectoral fins are greatly modified into a branching shape that looks very like the root system of a plant — if you can imagine a root system covered in tiny lights. Both these fishes are about 8 inches (20 cm) long,

and have large jaws armed with long teeth. There is a further set of smaller teeth set in the throat (pharynx), which can work the food back into the gullet. Many carnivorous fishes possess two sets of teeth and, in some, the head can be raised so the end of the pharynx is open, like a second mouth. In the rat-trap or loosejaw fish (*Malacosteus niger*), the jaws are so large and mobile and the pharyngeal opening, with its teeth, so obvious that the fish really does look as though it possesses two sets of jaws.

These fishes hunt by stealth, and can deal with surprisingly large prey because of another adaptation they share with many deep-sea species — a distensible stomach that allows them to swallow an animal half their own length. This feature is most highly developed among the gulper eels (of the order Saccopharyngiformes) and giant swallowers (family Chiasmodontidae). *Saccopharynx harrisoni* — one of the larger deep-sea fishes, growing up to 6.5 feet (2 m) long — has immense jaws, fearsome teeth, and can take large prey. The black swallower (*Chiasmodon niger*) is able to swallow animals larger than itself.

A large mouth does not necessarily imply that an animal eats large prey. The gulper eel *Eurypharynx pelecanoides* has an immense gape, but probably swims along with its mouth open, scooping up nothing bigger than prawns.

Plankton

Many fish start life among the plankton and, like many planktonic animals, spend the day at around 660 feet (200 m) and feed close to the surface at night. Then, as they mature, they move to the depth where they will spend their adult lives and where they remain. Each level has its own population of animals adapted to its conditions.

The phytoplankton are green plants, most no more than one cell in size, that drift in great numbers near the sea surface. When the sea appears green it is because of the abundance of phytoplankton and, so far as living organisms are concerned, a green sea is a rich, nutritious sea.

Like other green plants, the phytoplankton use carbon dioxide and water to synthesize sugars, but they also need a range of other chemical nutrients, just as land plants do, and these they must obtain from the water itself. Because they photosynthesize, they need daylight and so they can live only above the depth to which light penetrates sufficiently strongly. This varies, but is about 330 feet (100 m).

Waste organic matter, consisting of the excrement of animals, the inedible parts of prey, and dead organisms themselves, drift down through the water to fall like rain on the sea bed. There it can provide food for bottom-dwelling organisms, but it is out of the reach of the phytoplankton. It is the availability of mineral nutrients that limits the growth of phytoplankton and, because they form the basis of the marine food chain, of the biological productivity of the ocean itself.

There are regions, however, where nutrients from the sea bed are carried back to the surface. Where this happens the results are dramatic. The most famous example is to be found off the western coast of northern Chile and Peru.

In each hemisphere of the Atlantic and Pacific there is a major gyre (see page 108) flowing anticlockwise in the southern hemisphere. The South Pacific gyre begins off the coast of Antarctica, where cold, saline water sinks beneath less dense water, carrying with it a load of organic matter from what is perhaps the most biologically productive of all oceans. Following the pattern of the prevailing winds, the cold water flows northwards, close to the South American coast, but far beneath the surface. As it approaches the equator, it enters a region where the prevailing trade winds create a surface current flowing westwards and carrying water warmed by the Sun (see page 135). The difference in temperature between the deep water and the surface water is no more than about 41 °F (5 °C), and the Humboldt, or Peru, Current wells up to the surface.

It still carries much of its original load of organic matter from Antarctica but, in its movement north, it has scoured more from the sea bed and collected more, falling as the 'rain' from above. This water, rich in nutrients and dissolved oxygen, reaches the warmth and intense tropical sunlight, the phytoplankton flourishes, and the entire community of animals that live on the plants and on one another prosper.

The upwelling Humboldt supports populations of fish, especially anchovetas, so large that at one time the Peruvian catch amounted to more than one-sixth of the entire world catch.

The fish are also eaten by birds that roost and nest on rocky coasts and islands where their droppings have accumulated over centuries to form huge deposits of guano that is collected for use as fertilizer.

Strange new animals
In 1900, in waters off Indonesia, a single specimen of an animal completely new to science was dredged from the sea bed. It was so different from any other known animal that it had to be classified in a phylum of its

own, the Pogonophora, or 'beardworms'. Today, we know there are many pogonophore species, and that they are very abundant in particular places. Most live in tubes they construct themselves, usually from chitin, the material from which the exoskeleton of an insect is made, and the tubes stand upright in the mud on the sea bed, often in colonies with up to 240 to the square yard (200 per sq mile). Others do not build tubes, but lie on the rocks, long, worm-like, translucent animals. Most pogonophores are 4-34 inches (10-85 cm) long, but there are others up to 6.5 feet (2 m) long. Each animal has a blood circulatory system, and a body cavity that continues into its tentacles. What makes it so different from other animals is that, although it is clearly not a simple community of semi-autonomous cells, like a sponge or Portuguese man-of-war, it has no mouth and no digestive system of any kind. It is believed to feed by absorbing nutrients directly into its cells.

Where seafood is abundant, rocky islands are likely to support vast populations of marine birds. Their accumulated droppings form guano, a valuable fertilizer. These are flightless cormorants on the Galápagos Islands.

Such an animal can live only in water that is rich in nutrients and, in some places, the deep ocean provides the conditions pogonophores — and many other animals — require. The animals of the abyssal plains are sustained only by the sparse rain of organic wastes from above, but the sediment on to which they fall tends to flow down gradients and to accumulate at the bottom of deep trenches, making the trenches much more hospitable than the open plain — although they are unstable because of sediment falls, sometimes caused by earthquakes, down the steep sides. The trenches support quite dense communities, mainly of beardworms, sea cucumbers, brittle stars, molluscs, worms and crustaceans.

Black smokers
There are also hydrothermal vents, or 'black smokers', fissures through which gases from the hot rocks below the solid crust leak to the surface, dissolve in the sea water, and rise in what look like clouds of black smoke. The water at the vents is at about 400 °F (204 °C). That is much too hot for any organism, but a little further off, where the temperature is around 63 °F (17 °C), conditions are ideal. The vents release a range of chemical elements, including sulphur, carbon and silicon, much of which accumulates as precipitates around the vents. It is believed that hydrogen sulphide nourishes bacteria, and the bacteria form the basis of the food chain.

Black smokers are associated with the mid-ocean ridges, where crustal plates are moving apart, and they are found at depths of about 8200-9800 feet (2500-3000 m). Around them, apart from the beardworms, there are colonies of translucent sea anemones, sea pens, crabs, squat lobsters, giant clams, mussels, limpets, sponges, corals and great shoals of shrimps, as well as what look like mats of bacteria and what may be colonies of protozoans. Octopuses and deep-sea fishes have also been seen hunting among vent communities.

Fishes of the coral reef
Keeping fish in aquaria is one of the most popular hobbies — understandably, because the fish sold by suppliers include many that are very attractively coloured. Only the more ambitious hobbyists attempt to keep tropical marine species, because it is difficult

to maintain the correct chemical balances in the water but, for those who do, the range of colours and body forms widens greatly. There are the pink-and-white striped anemone fish (*Amphiprion percula*), the Achilles tang (*Acanthurus achilles*), the imperial angelfish (*Pomacanthus imperator*), the Moorish idol (*Zanclus cornutus*), and the lionfish (*Pterois volitans*) with its bizarre shape and long, pretty, but poisonous spines. All of these species come from the Indo-Pacific area, but the aquarium might also contain the four-eye butterfly fish

(*Chaetodon capistratus*) and queen parrot fish (*Scarus vetula*), which come from the Atlantic.

All of these, and many more, are fishes of coral reefs, and their coloration and form equip them for life in that habitat. They live among brilliant colours, complex shapes, and sharp contrasts between bright light and deep shadow. They may appear highly conspicuous in an aquarium but, in their natural surroundings, they are well camouflaged — as they need to be, for there is no shortage of predators. Their body shapes may contribute to the camouflage or may enable them to enter small crevices in search of food or shelter. The shapes of their mouths allow them to graze on the coral surface, to snatch tiny morsels from the water, or to feed on larger prey. It is impossible for any aquarium to convey even an approximate idea of the abundance of species that live on and around a coral reef.

Oases in a marine desert
The Great Barrier Reef, off the north-east coast of Australia, is believed to support

The Marianas Trench is the deepest point on the Earth's surface. It is in places such as this that vents release smoke-like clouds of hot water, rich in minerals, the 'black smokers'.

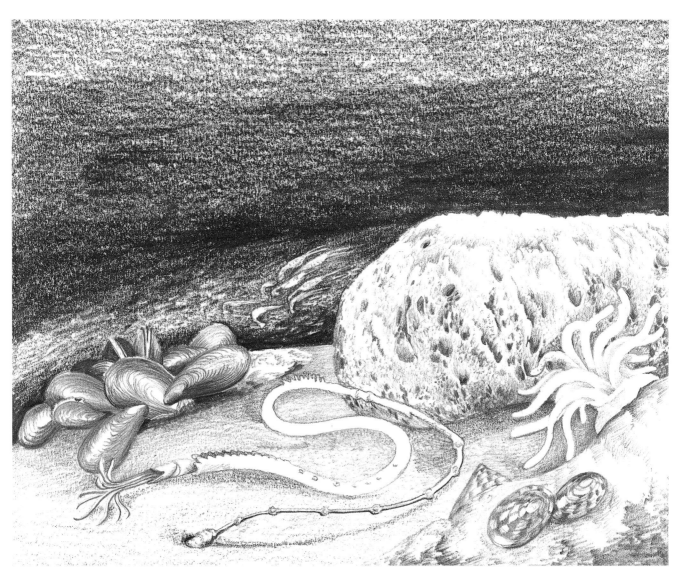

The deep ocean floor is home to more than 80 species of beardworms (Pogonophora), which are not closely related to any other animals. They often live in dense colonies, each individual inside a stiff tube it secretes around itself and, depending on the species, they can be from 4 inches (10 cm) to more than 6 feet (150 cm) long. Relatives of more common species, such as anemones, mussels and limpets also inhabit the ocean deeps.

3000 species. In the richness and diversity of the life on and around them, coral reefs are the equal of the tropical rain forests, and by far the most productive of any marine habitat.

This is curious, because coral reefs develop only in the aquatic equivalent of deserts. Their requirements are quite precise. The water temperature must not fall below 68 °F (20 °C), so they are found only in low latitudes, and they must have plenty of light, which means they are restricted to shallow water, between 33 and 200 feet (10-60 m), and to water that is very clear. Cloudy or even slightly muddy water can be enough to kill them, especially at the edges of their range. This is why they are so vulnerable to any human activity that stirs up the sea-bed sediment, or that increases the amount of silt discharged from rivers — there are no coral reefs around the mouths of the Amazon or Congo.

During the Second World War, an airstrip was built in Castle Harbour, Bermuda, projecting into the sea. It altered the flow of water currents, which stirred up sediment, making the water rather cloudy, and this caused considerable damage to the nearby patch reefs which have still not recovered. There are fears that oil exploration and exploitation off the Queensland coast may damage the Great Barrier Reef, not so much because there is a risk of spills — although they would have grave consequences and have seriously harmed other reefs — but because the installation of the platforms and pipelines would disturb the sea bed and water. The Australian federal government has provided some protection by establishing the Barrier Reef Marine Park. In various parts of the world, reefs have been damaged by nutrient-rich water running off adjacent farm land. They have also been damaged physically by dynamiting to stun fish, and by being quarried to make cement.

Water that is rich in nutrients usually supports large populations of phytoplankton, extremely small green plants that colour the water green and make it turbid. Clear, blue water contains few single-celled organisms, and perhaps none at all, because it has insufficient nutrient and, where the water supports little or no life, the sea bed below it will be similarly deficient. Yet it is only under these apparently harsh conditions that coral reefs can survive at all. The solution to the paradox lies in the fact that the reefs are entire unto themselves, closed systems that manufacture their own food and recycle their own wastes.

The reefs take several distinct forms. 'Fringing' reefs grow outwards from the coast to which they remain connected just below the sea surface. They may extend long distances along continental coasts, and some completely surround islands. They are the commonest type of reef.

Those which form parallel to a coast, but separated from it, are 'barrier' reefs, and the water between the reef and the coast is a 'lagoon'. The Great Barrier Reef is of this type and is the longest reef in the world. It extends from the Tropic of Capricorn in the south to the Torres Strait in the north, a distance of about 1250 miles (2010 km). The Reef follows the 100-fathom (183 m) contour, which is about 200 miles (320 km) from the shore in the south, and about 19 to 31 miles (30-50 km) from the shore in the north.

Coral reefs may also form around the summits of inactive submarine volcanoes. Such a reef, called an 'atoll', is roughly circular or oval in shape and encloses a lagoon. Its formation proceeds in stages. A volcano, projecting above the sea surface, becomes quiescent, as a small volcanic island, and a fringing reef forms around it. Over many years the weather erodes away the top of the volcano, so the volcano subsides, eventually to below the surface. Then the reef extends all the way across it. The volcano continues to subside and, although coral accumulates on top of it — in the case of Eniwetok Atoll to a thickness of a mile (1.6 km) — the central part is shaped like a basin. A small fall in sea level may now expose the higher parts of the reef, around the rim, leaving the centre covered by water, as a lagoon.

Coral reefs all form in the same way, but different types are distinguished by their locations. (Top) Where the summit of an inactive volcano protrudes above the sea surface, a reef may develop around it. Erosion removes the exposed summit, forming a shallow basin across which the coral extends below the surface. A fall in sea level may then expose the higher parts of the reef. The result is an atoll, consisting of the higher parts of the reef surrounding the former summit and enclosing a shallow lagoon, and higher parts of the interior reef projecting as patch reefs. (Middle) A fringing reef is attached to the coast and develops outwards from it. (Bottom) A barrier reef develops parallel to the coast, but separated from it, the water between the reef and the coast forming a lagoon.

A reef supports many species of coral living side by side.

Atolls

There are about 300 atolls in the Indian and Pacific Oceans, but only about 10 in the Atlantic. Gaps occur in the reef, permitting access to the lagoon, and parts of the reef may protrude above the surface as islands — the islands of Bermuda are part of an atoll. A reef of this type does not have to project above the surface to be called an atoll, and most atolls are submerged.

Small reefs, of irregular shape or sometimes circular, which occur inside lagoons are called 'patch' reefs, and small reefs, without lagoons, that occur in the open sea, are 'table' reefs.

A coral reef forms below the surface of the sea but, over long periods, the sea level changes as a result either of climate change or of movement in the crustal plates. Should the sea level rise, a reef can grow upwards, but, should the sea level fall, the uppermost parts of the reef may be exposed. The reef

organisms die and that part of the reef becomes dry land. If there is a supply of fresh water, eventually it will be colonized by land plants. If not, it will be a true desert island. It is the gradual rise in sea level since the end of the last ice age that has allowed reefs to grow to their present height, and the height of coral reefs is used as a measure of sea-level change. Test drilling has penetrated the Great Barrier Reef to a depth of more than 700 feet (210 m) without reaching bedrock.

On its seaward side, a reef has long 'fingers' projecting forwards and separated by 'valleys'. The gradient varies as the height of the reef increases to a crest, and behind the crest (the 'backreef'), it often slopes gently downwards, with water channels and small pools of calm water. The structure is complex and provides habitats of many kinds, supporting different types of coral.

The coral itself is constructed by animals related to, and not unlike, sea anemones, but usually much smaller. The phylum to which they belong (Cnidaria) comprises animals with life cycles that take them through two distinct forms — a medusa (like a jellyfish) which then settles in one place as a 'polyp'. Some members of the phylum have abandoned one or other stage in the life cycle. The familiar jellyfish never become polyps, and the animals that build coral live only as polyps. Each individual polyp is like a tube, enclosing the cavity in which food is digested, sealed at the lower end and having a mouth surrounded by tentacles — some of which sting — at the upper end. The body secretes a casing, made of calcium carbonate, in which the animal lives. Some coral polyps are solitary and up to 10 inches (25 cm) in diameter, but those which build reefs live in colonies of millions and are no more than 0.04 to 0.12 inches (1-3 mm) in diameter.

The 'skeleton' is secreted by the lower half of the body of the polyp and at its base, and each polyp is connected to its neighbours by a sheet of tissue across the top of the casing. Sometimes polyps reproduce sexually, and the progeny settle down to found new colonies. Within the colony, the polyps reproduce by budding — one individual divides into two, the way it does so varying from one species to another — and in many species the polyps lift themselves up from time to time and secrete a new base, sealing off a tiny, hollow area. This is how reefs grow. Scientists have estimated that coral reefs may grow thicker at a rate of about 0.6 inches (1.6 cm) a year, although erosion removes nearly as much calcium carbonate

Rarotonga Atoll, in Micronesia.

Coral polyps (*Zoantharia scleractinia*) feeding. The brown patches inside them are their symbiotic zooxanthellae.

as is added, and that reefs may occur where calcium, carried from the land by rivers, tends to accumulate.

Inside their body cavities, almost all reef-building polyps have colonies of single-celled algae called 'zooxanthellae'. These contain chlorophyll and other pigments which together give the corals a generally yellowish-brown colour. Photosynthesis by its zooxanthellae contributes nutrients to the coral polyp, and the polyp augments this with the food it catches with its tentacles — anything from plankton to small fishes depending on the size of the polyp. Wastes from the digestion of this food contain nitrogen and other elements, which are used by the zooxanthellae. The polyp and zooxanthellae cycle food back and forth between them and the system is very efficient indeed.

The activity of the zooxanthellae also stimulates the secretion of skeletal material, probably by removing carbon dioxide from the water. Calcium bicarbonate ($Ca(HCO_3)$) in the water breaks down into calcium carbonate ($CaCO_3$) and carbonic acid (H_2CO_3). The calcium carbonate is precipitated, and the carbonic acid breaks down into water (H_2O) and carbon dioxide (CO_2). The solubility of carbon dioxide is limited, and the reaction will cease when the water is saturated. By removing carbon dioxide, the zooxanthellae allow the reaction to continue — in effect they drive it — and this produces a steady supply of calcium carbonate.

The construction of a reef begins with the formation of the skeleton. As it grows, unevenly, the flow of water around it is altered and some areas are more sheltered than others. These differences provide suitable conditions for other coral species, including very small, delicate corals, which form secure links between larger blocks, cementing them together. A mature reef may comprise many coral species —

there are more than 200 forming the Great Barrier Reef. Some are massive, but others resemble fans, or form the most delicate traceries.

Coral as a producer

It is not only other corals that are attracted, however, and no sooner has a reef started to grow upwards (leaving lower regions that are no longer occupied by polyps and so consist of bare, exposed, calcium carbonate) than it comes under attack. Sponges and molluscs bore holes into it, sometimes from below so they undermine it but, as they bore, these organisms are constantly excavating fine material that accumulates around them and eventually may bury them. The crown-of-thorns starfish (*Acanthaster planci*), a Pacific species, feeds on polyps and from time to time its numbers increase dramatically. This damages the coral, but it also provides food for animals that feed on the starfish, such as a marine snail called the giant triton (*Charonia* species) and painted shrimp (*Hymenocera* species).

Exposed surfaces also provide sites on which other algae can grow, especially filamentous green algae so, in places, the living reef will be green because it is blanketed by plants. Fishes feed on the plants, and are hunted by other fishes, but it is the plants which make up most of the living material. The green algae are more abundant than the zooxanthellae, and altogether the mass of plant material is usually about three times that of the animal material. The total mass of living material ('biomass') of a reef comprises 25 per cent of animal and 4.5 per cent of plant (zooxanthellae) matter inside the polyps themselves, 26 per cent of plant material between the polyps, and 44 per cent of plant material in the region of the skeleton below that which is currently inhabited by polyps.

A relationship between two species in which each partner benefits from the other is called 'symbiotic', and the partnership between the coral polyps and their zooxanthellae is one of the clearest examples of a symbiosis. Because the zooxanthellae use photosynthesis to convert simple compounds into sugars, they form the base for a food chain similar to the base provided by green plants on land. In ecological terms they are 'primary producers' and, because they form an integral part of the coral, the coral itself may be regarded ecologically as a primary producer.

The coral ecosystem

As well as being a producer, the coral is also a 'primary consumer' — a herbivore, occupying the same position as, say, a rabbit on land — because it utilizes the sugars produced by its zooxanthellae — it digests the algae in its body cavity. An animal that obtains food by eating other animals is called a 'secondary consumer', and the coral is also a secondary consumer because, in addition to digesting algae, it feeds on zooplankton, the tiny animals living among the plankton. The polyps are usually inactive during the day, keeping their tentacles withdrawn, and feed on zooplankton at night. The zooxanthellae photosynthesize during the day and are inactive at night.

This complex system provides food for others. The algae on the coral surface, which in places grow to a large size and almost hide the coral beneath dense thickets of waving fronds, add to the primary production. The algae are grazed by other herbivores, including sea urchins, brittle stars, molluscs and some fishes. Other molluscs are carnivorous, and so are some groups of worms, such as the 'Christmas tree worms' (*Spirobranchus* species). These animals bore into the coral surface to make the tubes in which they live, and feed by filtering zooplankton from the water with their tentacles that are shaped very like the branches of a fir tree. Many of the fishes are also carnivorous. Apart from the pretty ones, the rich feeding grounds of a coral reef are patrolled by most species of sharks. At the end of the food chain there are the decomposers, the fish species such as the blennies (family Blenniidae) that live on the wastes suspended in the water, and bacteria, which break down large molecules into smaller, simpler ones, ready to be taken up again by the plants.

A coral reef is very stable and its natural lifespan is long. The Great Barrier Reef began growing some 10 million years ago, when part of the Australian continental shelf subsided. Other reefs, built by species long since extinct, are known to have existed about 500 million years ago. Reefs may be damaged naturally, by hurricanes or sequences of unusually low tides, but they recover. Whether they can survive human disturbance is less certain.

WATER IN MOTION

RIVERS, SEAS AND OCEANS

The hydrological (water) cycle by which water evaporates from the seas, lakes, rivers and wet ground, is transported by the air, condenses to form clouds, falls as precipitation and returns either to the air or from land back to the seas. Every day, a total of about 248.5 cubic miles (1035.8 cu km) of water evaporates. The values represent percentages of the average amount of precipitation falling over the world as a whole in one year.

100 units = mean annual global precipitation 33.8 inches (85.7 cm)

If all evaporation and transpiration were to cease suddenly, but rain and snow continued to fall normally, the amount of water held in the atmosphere would be sufficient to last about 10 days, during which it would deliver the equivalent of 1 inch (25 mm) of rain distributed over the entire surface of the planet. Almost all of the Earth's water is contained in the oceans, and a small amount as ice, but very little indeed exists in the gaseous phase or as the airborne droplets that comprise clouds.

At any time, 97 per cent of all water is in the oceans. Of the 3 per cent that exists as fresh water, 75 per cent (or approximately 2.25 per cent of the total) forms the polar ice sheets and glaciers. Between them, lakes and rivers contain about 0.33 per cent of the fresh water, the soil about 0.06 per cent, and the atmosphere contains only about 0.035 per cent.

That we receive a significant amount of rain and snow, that the sky is often completely covered by cloud, and that the air is often very humid indicate only the speed with which water is transferred between land and sea. Another way to describe the 10 days' supply of rain and snow in the atmosphere is to say that, on average, a water molecule that enters the atmosphere will remain there no longer than 10 days.

The movement of water from the oceans

and land surface into the air, and its return to the oceans by direct precipitation and from rivers, forms the 'hydrological cycle'. Over the world as a whole, each day about 210 cubic miles (875.3 cu km) of water evaporates from the oceans, and about 38.5 cubic miles (160.5 cu km) evaporates or is transpired by plants from the land surface. This is the water vapour that enters the atmosphere, a total of about 248.5 cubic miles (1035.8 cu km) a day. Of the water that evaporates from the oceans, about 24 cubic miles (100 cu km) is carried over land. Every day about 186 cubic miles (775.3 cu km) falls as precipitation over the oceans and about 62.5 cubic miles (260.5 cu km) over the land, and about 24 cubic miles (100 cu km) is returned to the oceans by rivers.

This is the cycle but, of course, it is much more variable than so general a description makes it sound. The amount of water involved varies according to the season, for example, because more water evaporates in summer than in winter. This means that in summer the air carries more water — even though the amount of rainfall may be less. The seasonal difference is considerable. In the northern hemisphere, the air in January contains, on average, water equivalent to 0.8 inches (19 mm) of rain and in July the equivalent of about 1.3 inches (34 mm).

The air carries rather less water in the

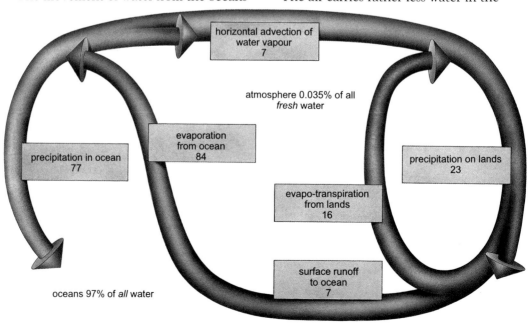

horizontal advection of water vapour
7

atmosphere 0.035% of all *fresh* water

precipitation in ocean
77

evaporation from ocean
84

precipitation on lands
23

evapo-transpiration from lands
16

surface runoff to ocean
7

oceans 97% of *all* water

southern hemisphere than in the northern [about 1 inch (25 mm) in January and about 0.8 inches (19 mm) in July]. This is because, at present, (the situation changes over a cycle of about 10,000 years) the Earth's orbit around the Sun makes the northern-hemisphere summer about five days longer than the southern-hemisphere summer, and the transfer of heat from the Equator to the poles makes it somewhat warmer (although northern-hemisphere winters are cooler).

Finally, the global average does not reflect the very uneven distribution of water. Evaporation is obviously much less from the interior of continents than it is over the open sea, and the amount of precipitation varies widely, from the humid tropics to the most arid deserts, and these two extremes often occur within a short distance of one another. In the interior of Sierra Leone, for example, at a latitude of about 8 degrees north, the annual rainfall averages more than 175 inches (4445 mm). At about 15 degrees north, and some 870 miles (1400 km) away, Tombouctou (formerly Timbuktu) has only 9 inches (229 mm) a year, and a little way north of that there are many years when no rain falls at all.

Vertical migration in the sea
The plankton drifts near the sea surface and, below it, the living organisms occupy distinct layers, down to those which live buried in the sand or mud of the sea bed. About 98 per cent of the estimated 160,000 species of marine organisms live on or in the bottom sediment.

This picture of the layering of marine species may give too rigid an impression. Pelagic organisms, after all, live in three dimensions, not the two to which land-dwellers are confined, and many of them make frequent and extensive journeys vertically as well as horizontally. Even members of the plankton do not spend all their time at the surface. If you wish to sample the marine zooplankton — the planktonic animals — the time to do so is at night. During the day they are well below the surface, some of them, depending on the species, at depths of up to nearly 5600 feet (1700 m), others at anything from 160 to 3000 feet (50-900 m). At nightfall they begin to move upwards to feed, and can be found very close to the surface. Such vertical migrations apparently occur at all levels.

In the tropics, the ground is warmed strongly by the Sun. Water evaporates into warmed air and is carried aloft by strong vertical air currents. As it rise, the air cools and its water vapour condenses, forming large cumulus and cumulonimbus storm clouds. The storms return the water to the surface close to the place from which it evaporated. This tropical rainstorm is in Nigeria.

The phytoplankton — the planktonic plants — form the base of the marine food chain and, of course, it can occur only where light is available for photosynthesis. This layer, where biological productivity occurs, is called the 'euphotic zone' and, although its lower boundary is not precise, in most oceans it is more or less limited to the uppermost 160 feet (50 m).

The animals that move between the euphotic zone and much deeper levels experience dramatic changes in temperature. Apart from the mammals, they have no means of regulating their body temperatures, but this does not seem to inhibit their migrations.

Thermal cycles

When water is warmed, it expands as its molecules gain energy and move further apart, and so it becomes less dense. The less dense the water the lighter it will be, and it will tend to float above cooler, and therefore denser, water. The surface of the oceans is warmed by solar radiation, which means that over most of the total area there is a layer of relatively warm water floating above

the cooler, denser, water mass. The thickness of this layer varies according to the latitude and season, as does its temperature, but it accounts for only a small part of the total volume of the oceans. In the tropics, the surface temperature — the water in which people bathe, and in which the zooplankton feeds at night — may be as high as 86 °F (30 °C), but at depths between 985 and 3300 feet (300-1000 m) the temperature is close to 40 °F (5 °C), and the average temperature of all the water in all the oceans of the world is only about 38 °F (3.5 °C).

There is little mixing of water between the warm surface layer and the underlying layer. Warm water tends to rise, and the heat is being applied from above, so the mechanism inhibits mixing — a situation opposite to that of the atmosphere, which is heated from below. This also suggests that the surface water forms but one of several layers, and that the oceans can be divided into approximately horizontal layers according to the water temperature.

Water in the surface layer itself is mixed, however, because of the action of the wind. This is called the 'mixed layer'. Its thickness is variable, but it is thicker in winter, when winds are generally stronger, than it is in summer. Off the Atlantic coast of North America, for example, the mixed layer is 33 to 200 feet (10-60 m) thick in summer and 130 to 395 feet (40-120 m) thick in winter.

The lower boundary of the mixed layer is marked by a region in which the temperature decreases rapidly with increasing depth. This boundary, called the 'seasonal thermocline', forms only in summer in middle latitudes but, despite the name, in the tropics it tends to persist throughout the year. A 'thermocline' is simply a region in which the temperature of water changes rapidly with changing depth. The existence of this thermocline greatly restricts the upward movement of any substances dissolved in water, because the water below the thermocline is markedly denser than that above it. In particular, this means that nutrients cannot move upwards, and it explains the relatively low biological productivity of many tropical waters and of waters in middle latitudes in summer.

At a depth of 980 to 3300 feet (300-1000 m), in both tropical and mid-latitude waters, there is a second, permanent, thermocline, where the temperature falls

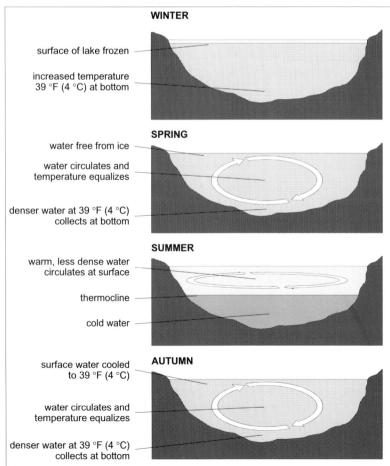

The annual thermal cycle and turnover pattern in a typical temperate lake

WINTER
surface of lake frozen
increased temperature 39 °F (4 °C) at bottom

SPRING
water free from ice
water circulates and temperature equalizes
denser water at 39 °F (4 °C) collects at bottom

SUMMER
warm, less dense water circulates at surface
thermocline
cold water

AUTUMN
surface water cooled to 39 °F (4 °C)
water circulates and temperature equalizes
denser water at 39 °F (4 °C) collects at bottom

Depth		Temperature		Density	Salinity	Sound speed		Pressure	
(ft)	*(m)*	*°F*	*°C*		*(ppt)*	*(ft/sec)*	*(m/sec)*	*(psi)*	*(kg/sq cm)*
1000	300	56	13	25.0	33.2	4900	1493	445	6327

Limit of light detectable by human eye — about 1500 feet (450 m) in clear water

2000	600	42	5	7.0	34.2	4850	1478	892	12 684

Limit of light detectable by instruments — about 3000 feet (900 m). Below 3000 feet pitch dark

THERMOCLINE

4000	1200	38	3	27.8	34.4	4860	1481	1788	25 425
6000	1800	37	2	27.8	34.5	4880	1487	2685	38 180
8000	2400	36	2	27.8	34.6	4910	1496	3586	50 992
10 000	3000	35	1	27.8	34.6	4940	1505	4488	63 819
12 000	3700	34	1	27.8	34.6	4970	1514	5388	76 617
14 000	4300	34	1	27.8	34.6	5020	1530	6288	89 415

rapidly to about 40 °F (5 °C). In very high latitudes, above about 50 degrees north and south, where the water is very cold throughout the year, the permanent thermocline lies close to the surface. Some scientists call the region of warm surface water the 'thermosphere' and the cold water beneath it the 'psychrosphere'. Like the seasonal thermocline, the permanent thermocline prevents the upward movement of substances dissolved in the water. At such depths the biological consequences are minor, but the human consequences could be significant, because it is virtually impossible for industrial wastes dumped below the thermocline to return to surface waters — from which fish are taken for human consumption — even if they leaked from their containers and dissolved.

A thermocline can also occur in a lake, but the form it takes depends on the climate. In regions where there is a marked difference between summer and winter temperatures, a thermocline may form in summer. During the winter the water is mixed thoroughly by the wind, and it is all at the same temperature. In summer, however, the surface water is warmed by the Sun and forms a distinct layer, called the 'epilimnion', that is separated by a thermocline from the colder 'hypolimnion' below it. As the summer ends, the surface water cools and the upper and lower waters mix once more. Depending on local conditions, the thermal stratification may be permanent, seasonal, or completely absent. In cold climates, the freezing over of lakes in winter can produce an inverted stratification, with cold water lying above warmer water. There are some lakes in which a normal stratification occurs in summer, and an inverted one in winter.

The salinity of the oceans

The salinity of the oceans varies only slightly, although that of the smaller seas can depart further from the oceanic average (see page 112). The constituents of sea water are present everywhere in precisely similar proportions, but the total quantity of dissolved substances can vary locally, depending on the extent to which fresh water is added to or removed from the sea water. Close to the Equator, where rainfall is high, the average salinity is about 34.5 parts per thousand. In the subtropics, around latitudes 20 degrees north and south, where rainfall is light, but evaporation intense —

In the deep oceans, the upper and lower waters are separated by the thermocline, below which the temperature, density and salinity remain constant all the way to the ocean floor. The overlying mass causes the pressure to increase steadily, and sound travels faster the denser the water.

on land, this is the belt that includes the major deserts — it rises to about 35.8 parts per thousand. At higher latitudes it falls again to around 34.0 parts per thousand.

The situation is much more complicated where rivers flow into the sea and fresh and salt water meet. The two bodies of water have different densities. Fresh water is less dense than salt water. In most estuaries it is also warmer in summer, but colder in winter. The fresh and salt waters are slow to mix, especially in summer. This is the basis of the controversy over the discharge of sewage into the sea. Were the two water bodies to mix readily, the sewage would vanish as it dispersed rapidly over a wide area. The sewage is essentially fresh water, however, and tends to rise to the surface, with very little mixing, and wind or tide may carry it back to the shore.

In some estuaries, the incoming tide forms a 'salt wedge' beneath the outgoing river water, allowing marine fishes to move upstream in the salt water. In others, distinct streams occur, moving in opposite directions as the river flows outwards and the tide inwards.

Waves, tides, and currents

The oceans and seas are in constant motion. Indeed, that is a main cause of their attraction for seaside holidaymakers. Surfing, bathing among the breakers or just watching as the waves lap or crash against the shore would be impossible were the waters still.

Breakers are waves that become unstable and collapse as they reach shallow water. Waves move at their own speeds and the distance between one crest and the next defines their wavelength. When they reach the shallow water of a shelving beach, however, they are slowed down and this reduces their wavelength because each incoming wave is moving faster than those ahead of it. The quantity of water involved remains the same, of course, and so the waves grow higher and steeper.

When the height of the wave reaches about 80 per cent of the water depth it becomes unstable and collapses.

The waves themselves are produced mainly by the wind but also by tides. Tidal movement is caused by the combined effect of the gravitational attractions of the Earth, Sun and Moon. The Earth's attraction acts vertically downwards but those of the Sun and Moon act upwards and sideways. The Moon's attraction has about twice the force of the Sun's, but variations in the amount of tidal movement are caused by the relative positions of the three bodies. When the Moon is new or full, for example, the three are all in the same plane, and the tidal movement is greatest, producing 'spring' tides. During the first and last quarter of the Moon, the Sun and Moon are at right angles to one another as seen from Earth and their attractions tend to cancel one another, producing small 'neap' tides. It is not only the oceans that experience tides. There are also atmospheric tides, and even Earth tides that can be measured in the rocks, but these are smaller and less evident than ocean tides.

Some coasts experience two complete tidal cycles a day — although a 'tidal day' is about 50 minutes longer than an ordinary day — some have only one, and the amount of tidal movement varies widely from place to place. The tidal range — the distance between the high and low tide lines — in the Bay of Fundy is about 50 feet (15.25 m) and in the Mediterranean and around many Pacific islands it is about 2 feet (60 cm). Some coasts experience no obvious tide at all. These differences are due to the volume of water affected, the shape of the basin in which it is held, and its geographical location in relation to the tidal forces acting on it.

As they ebb and flow, tides produce currents that seldom act precisely at right angles to the shore. Often, the current flows parallel to the coast, as a 'longshore' current that reverses direction when the tide turns. There are also other currents, however, not linked to tidal movements, and their effects on the way we live are much more profound.

The island of Newfoundland (the province also includes the Coast of Labrador, extending far to the north) is a cool place. The average July temperature is 60 °F (15.5 °C) and that is the only month which can be guaranteed to be free from frosts. It is also a damp place, famous for its fogs, especially in May and June, and for its annual precipitation of about 53 inches (1346 mm), which includes the 114 inches (2896 mm) of snow that falls in the capital, St John's, every winter. Despite being an island, Newfoundland has a mainly continental climate, strongly influenced by the huge North American land mass to its west, but this does not entirely explain the weather. St John's lies in latitude 47.34

(Above) Newfoundland is some distance south of the Isles of Scilly (right), yet the Scillies have much the milder climate because of the North Atlantic Drift.

Oceanic surface currents in the northern hemisphere winter (yearly average)

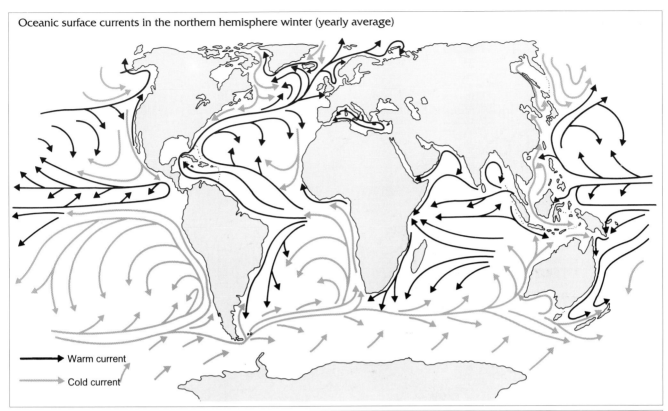

→ Warm current

→ Cold current

north, which places it just a little to the south of Paris, another continental city, and quite a long way south of the British Isles, which have a maritime climate.

At Poolewe, on the other hand, in the north-west of Scotland and a little south of 58 degrees north, summer visitors flock to see the gardens of subtropical plants. There are palm trees growing in sheltered spots in Sutherland, north of Poolewe.

The climatic differences between north-west Scotland and Newfoundland are due not to their latitudes, nor even to the fact that one is a mainly continental type and the other maritime. It is due to the Atlantic Ocean itself, which carries relatively warm water along the Scottish coast and relatively cold water along the Newfoundland coast. The ocean supplies one of the principal mechanisms for transferring heat from the Equator to the poles. The importance of this mechanism is only now coming to be appreciated, and much remains to be learned about it.

The effect of wind
In equatorial and subtropical regions the oceans are warmed by the Sun, and a surface layer of warm water lies above the seasonal thermocline (see page 102). You might suppose that this water would spread into higher latitudes, warming the cooler water

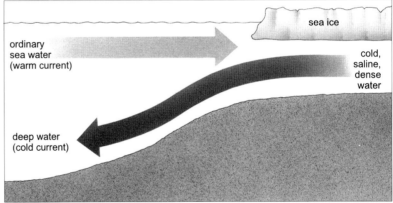

ordinary sea water (warm current)

sea ice

cold, saline, dense water

deep water (cold current)

with which it came into contact, and so bringing some warmth into regions where the Sun does not beat down so strongly. This is not at all what happens, for there is no reason why warm water, floating above cooler water, should move at all. Were the water being warmed from below — as the air is warmed by contact with the ground — its heat would be distributed by convection and might well warm the water in higher latitudes, but it is warmed from above, and convection does not occur. The movement of surface water is caused mainly by prevailing winds. If a wind blows steadily for long enough, friction between the moving air and the surface of the water will move the water in the same direction as the wind, but the Coriolis force, exerted by the rotation of the Earth, will then deflect the flow of water

The formation of North Atlantic deep water. The formation of sea ice removes fresh water from the sea surface. Immediately below the ice the water is therefore more saline, and is at a temperature of about 39 °F (4 °C). These factors combine to make the water more dense than the water below it. It sinks below the less dense water, moving away from the ice edge, and forms the deep water flowing towards the Equator. Its place is taken by water flowing polewards. This mechanism is believed to drive the oceanic current systems.

The South Pacific Gyre is a semi-closed current system of oceanic water which flows in an anti-clockwise direction, beginning off the coast of Antarctica and flowing northwards along the west coast of Chile.

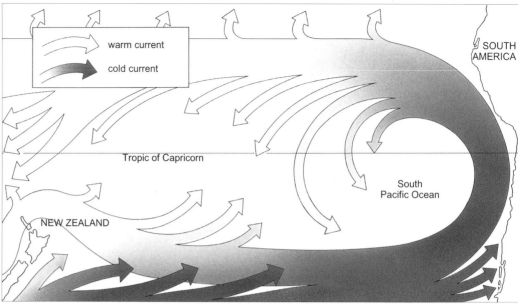

to the right in the northern hemisphere and to the left in the southern.

The Coriolis force, named after Gaspard Gustave de Coriolis (1792-1843), who discovered it in 1835, acts at right angles to the direction of flow — of air as well as water — and is proportional to the speed and latitude of the motion, so it is zero at the Equator and reaches a maximum at the poles. In fact, there is no real 'force' at all. If you picture any object at the Equator, it will be moving with the rotation of the Earth at a speed determined by the circumference of the Earth. At the Equator this gives the object a speed of about 1038 miles per hour (1670 km/h). If the object is moved to a higher latitude, but continues to move at its equatorial speed, its motion will seem to be deflected because the surface beneath the object is moving more slowly than it is, because the circumference is smaller. To complete one revolution in 24 hours, for example, Rome moves at about 833 miles per hour (1340 km/h).

Gyres

In each of the oceans, in both hemispheres, the wind system establishes a roughly circular system of currents, called a 'gyre'. The centre of the gyre lies at about 30 degrees latitude, but displaced to the western side of the ocean. The gyres flow in a clockwise direction in the northern hemisphere and anticlockwise in the southern. To either side of the Equator the prevailing winds are from the east — north-easterly in the northern hemisphere and south-easterly in the southern. These are

the 'trade winds' and they generate the north and south equatorial currents, which flow in a westerly direction. The constant 'pushing' of water westwards in low latitudes causes it to 'pile up' against the continental coasts, so that, in the tropics, the sea level is appreciably higher on the western side of an ocean than on the eastern side. Turning away from the Equator as they encounter the continents and flowing roughly parallel to the coasts as 'boundary' currents, the flow continues to circle the subtropics and so forms the gyres. The Gulf Stream is part of the North Atlantic gyre, and in the centre lies the Sargasso Sea.

The Gulf Stream

Its name gives the impression of a single, coherent movement of water, but the Gulf Stream comprises several currents and its motion is complex. It takes its name from the Gulf of Mexico but, when its northward movement reaches the tip of Florida, it becomes the Florida current, 30-45 miles (50-75 km) wide and flowing at 3-10 feet per second (1-3 m/s). At Cape Hatteras, North Carolina, the current moves away from the American coast to become the Gulf Stream proper, in fact a system of narrow, meandering streams. As the Stream approaches Newfoundland, it is deflected by the southward-flowing Labrador current, bringing cold water from the arctic. It is this confrontation, a little way to the south of the island, between warm and cold water that produces the fogs of Newfoundland, and it is the cold waters of the Labrador current, washing the shores of Newfound-

flows eastwards all around Antarctica, and the bottom water also flows in an easterly direction — although both waters occupy a very broad band. Above the Antarctic deep water there is yet another layer, of Antarctic intermediate water. This is chilled by the winds, sinks beneath the warmer water of lower latitudes that are being forced to rise as they encounter the Antarctic bottom water and, after some mixing with the warmer water, finds its own level at a depth of about 3300 feet (1000 m). It can be traced beyond the Equator, as far north as about 25 degrees in the North Atlantic — although the thermal Equator, the latitude where the temperature is highest, varies from 0 to about 10 degrees north of the geographical Equator so the 'migration' is not so surprising as it may seem.

This flow of very cold water in both hemispheres constantly 'pumps' water in the direction of the Equator. The water returns to high latitudes where it rises and is chilled again. Its movement accounts for the low temperature of the water below the permanent thermocline in all the oceans, and for the quite sharp separation between the waters above and below the thermocline.

The transport of heat

It is easy to see how the surface gyres and their currents transport heat. Close to the Equator the water is warmed directly by its exposure to solar radiation. It then warms the air in contact with it. Because both water and air are warm, the rate of evaporation is high. This has a cooling effect because latent heat of evaporation must be taken from the water-air system. As the warm, moist air rises and cools the water vapour condenses, releasing its latent heat of condensation, warming the air around it and creating unstable conditions in which towering cumulus and cumulonimbus clouds form. The warming of the air, and the evaporation and condensation of water, produce a region of low atmospheric pressure into which air is drawn. This is the source of the trade winds which drive the surface currents.

The winds drive the water which flows into higher latitudes, taking its stored heat with it. Its place at the Equator is taken by water flowing at much lower temperatures from high latitudes, and ultimately from polar regions. Cold water flows towards the Equator, is warmed, and returns to warm the

As it moves away from the continent, the flow of Antarctic bottom water comes under the influence of the most important ocean current in the southern hemisphere, the Antarctic circumpolar current, or west wind drift. It is the only current to flow all the way round the world and, as the name suggests, it is driven by westerly winds. It

high latitudes from which it came. Were it not for the oceanic surface currents, conditions in high latitudes would be a great deal cooler than they are. The corollary of this is that the transport of cool water to the Equator prevents tropical regions from being as hot as they would be otherwise.

Movement of deep water

The picture is clear and its climatic significance self-evident, but it is misleading. Although the surface currents are very important, the movement of deep water may be much more important. The water that flows at great depths is almost completely isolated from the surface, and so its influence is not obvious. Think, though, of the relative volumes of the two bodies of water. The surface currents, even those as deep as the Florida current — which is an exception — involve only about one-tenth of the total mass of ocean water. The remaining nine-tenths consists of water below the thermocline. This water is isolated, except in the regions where it forms — it forms, and is being formed constantly — at the surface.

About 500 to 800 years elapse between the time Atlantic water sinks from the edge of the sea ice to the time it returns to the surface, and the recycling of most Pacific water takes about twice that time, although the age of North Pacific deep water has been calculated at 3400 years. When, eventually, the water is forced to rise against the downward flow of cold, saline water, it is relatively warm. It reaches the surface and is chilled, which means it loses heat to the atmosphere. Paradoxically, the formation of sea ice is a major source of atmospheric warming — partly because of the released latent heat of freezing, but partly, and perhaps mainly, because of the heat transferred from the rising water. At the surface, water absorbs oxygen and carbon dioxide from the air. This supplies oxygen and carbon for deep-sea organisms and is an important 'sink' for carbon dioxide.

Should the present trend towards global warming continue, it is possible that the sea ice might melt altogether in the northern hemisphere during summer — it is very unlikely to do so in the colder Antarctic. Were this to happen, access to the carbon dioxide 'sink' would be restricted, accelerating the accumulation of carbon dioxide in

the air, but there are other possible, but less obvious, consequences. An interruption, even seasonally, in the formation of North Atlantic bottom water might alter the entire circulation system in high latitudes. One effect of this system is to draw into itself the northern branch of the North Atlantic Drift. This might then disappear, the entire gyre turning south in the latitude of Portugal. North-west Europe would lose its warm current and, although the world as a whole might be growing warmer, temperatures in that region would fall sharply. Britain, for example, might expect cool summers and very cold winters. Some scientists believe this happened twice as the last ice age was drawing to a close, plunging north-western Europe back into near-glacial conditions.

The Dead Sea

For centuries, wealthy Europeans have visited health resorts whose highly mineralized waters they found beneficial. To the east of Europe, the Dead Sea serves a similar purpose. Indeed, its water is so dense that total immersion presents difficulties because the human body pops to the surface like a cork. At the same time, of course, it is almost impossible to drown in the Dead Sea, and the relaxations it offers include floating easily on your back with no need for an inflatable mattress. The water contains an average of about 250 parts of salt to every thousand parts of water, with about 195.4 at the surface and 266.6 below a depth of 250 feet (76 m) — compared with about 35 parts per thousand for ocean water. Apart from the Great Salt Lake, Utah, with about 270 parts of salt per thousand, it is the saltiest natural water in the world and, at 1302 feet (397 m) below the level of the Mediterranean, it is the lowest of the world's seas.

The minerals, with the water itself, are supplied by hundreds of springs and other underground sources, by rain, and by the River Jordan. Rainfall is light in this arid region, rarely exceeding 5 inches (127 mm) in a year. The minerals are concentrated in the Sea because there is no outflow. Water is lost only by evaporation — at an average rate of about 0.4 inches (10 mm) a day. The evaporated water condenses quickly, to form a mist over the surface, and is carried away by the winds. It is called 'Dead' because few organisms can survive in it.

Clearly, there is a great difference between a sea, such as the Dead Sea, and an ocean and the difference is due to the relative isolation of a sea. This does not necessarily mean a sea is more saline than the ocean. The reverse is true of many seas. The salinity of the Caspian Sea, for example, is about 13 parts per thousand and, in the Gulf of Bothnia, the water of the Baltic contains only about two parts of salt per thousand of water, making it virtually a freshwater sea.

These seas are bordered by land, but the Sargasso Sea is not. Its boundaries are formed by the North Atlantic gyre (see page 108), water bounded by water, yet it is a sea in the true sense because its qualities are easily distinguished from those of the surrounding ocean. In particular, it is more saline than the Atlantic because of the high rate of evaporation, its water containing 36.5 to 37.0 parts of salt per thousand of water.

The Mediterranean

The most famous of the smaller seas is the Mediterranean. It is not so much a single sea as a system of seas that includes, in addition to the Mediterranean proper, several regions that are usually considered seas in their own right. The Tyrrhenian Sea lies in a deep basin bounded by Sardinia to the west, Italy to the east and Sicily to the south. The Adriatic Sea lies between Italy and Yugoslavia and Albania. The deep, large basin to its south, extending from Greece and southern Italy most of the way to Cyrenaica in Libya, and bordered by Sicily to the west and Crete to the east, forms the Ionian Sea, and the area, dotted with islands, between Greece, Turkey and Crete, is the Aegean Sea. Beyond the eastern end of the Mediterranean, but connected to it and so part of the system, there are the Sea of Marmara and the Black Sea.

The Mediterranean complex is all that remains of the Tethys Sea, which once separated the two supercontinents of Laurasia and Gondwana (see page 118). It was compressed as Africa moved northwards into Eurasia, sedimentary rocks from the bed of the Tethys being crumpled into the Alpine and Atlas mountain system of Europe and North Africa. The sea was confined to the folds in the system, and some regions enclosed by folds subsided to form five deep basins — apart from those containing the Tyrrhenian and Ionian Seas,

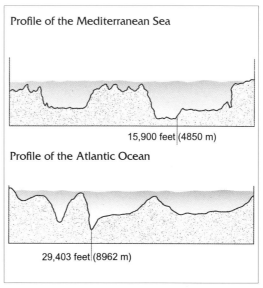

Profile of the Mediterranean Sea

15,900 feet (4850 m)

Profile of the Atlantic Ocean

29,403 feet (8962 m)

As this profile of its bed illustrates, the Mediterranean is a complex of basins, rather than a single sea, linked to the Atlantic Ocean only through the shallow Strait of Gibraltar. It is all that remains of the ancient Tethys Sea (see page 118) and much older than the Atlantic. The Atlantic now holds a much greater volume of water than the Mediterranean. Apart from its much larger surface area, its deepest point is at almost twice the depth of the deepest point in the Mediterranean.

there is a small basin south of Malaga, a very large one to its east, its northern and southern boundaries running parallel to the European and North African coasts, with a kind of shallow bay in which the Balearic Islands lie, and bordered to the east by Corsica and Sardinia. Another large basin lies to the north of Egypt, extending as far as Crete and almost to the Turkish coast, and the last small basin is between Cyprus and Lebanon.

More recently the two modern continents moved away from one another. This reduced the mountains between Greece and Turkey sufficiently to allow the sea to flood in, forming the Aegean, and at the same time opened the gap at the Dardanelles, which links the eastern Mediterranean to the Sea of Marmara and, through the Bosporus beyond, to the Black Sea. The volcanoes and earthquakes of the Mediterranean region supply evidence that this movement has not yet ended. At various times in its history, during the ice ages (see page 138), the Mediterranean has been reduced to a chain of lakes, but today it is filled and it is large. The Strait of Gibraltar is more than 2300 miles (3700 km) from the Syrian coast, and Trieste is almost 850 miles (1368 km) north of the Libyan coast. The total area of the Sea is about 965,000 square miles (2,500,000 sq km) and it holds rather more than 1 million cubic miles (4.38 million cu km) of water. It is also deep. Nearly one-third of the total sea floor lies 6500 feet (1982 m) or more below the surface, and the greatest depth recorded, off Cape Matapan, southern Greece, is 15,900 feet (4850 m).

The Mediterranean Sea fills six major basins and the shallower areas separating them. The Adriatic and Aegean Seas form part of the Mediterranean complex, which is also linked with the Black Sea through the Dardanelles, the small Sea of Marmara and the Bosporus.

Water enters the Sea as rainfall, and is fed from rivers and from the Atlantic and, to a much lesser extent, the Black Sea, as surface currents. The climate varies considerably from the European mountains to the Sahara, with rainfall ranging from 181 inches (4597 mm) a year on the coast of Yugoslavia to less than 1 inch (25 mm) near the desert. The rivers include some, such as the Nile, Rhône and Po, which are large, but the most important source of water is the Atlantic.

The surface water is warm. Its winter temperature is usually between 50 and 54 °F (10-12 °C) and in August it can rise in places to about 77 °F (25 °C) or even 84 °F (29 °C). Below the surface the temperature falls to about 55.4 °F (13 °C) and remains fairly constant throughout the year. The high surface temperature means that the rate of evaporation is also high and this, in turn, means that Mediterranean water is more saline than Atlantic water. Wind-driven surface currents tend to flow

Movement of water in the Mediterranean

There are only three ways for water to leave the Mediterranean. Much — about 57 inches (1440 mm) a year — is lost by evaporation, and some flows eastwards in to the Black Sea but, beneath the surface current that flows inwards through the Strait of Gibraltar, there is also a deep current flowing in the opposite direction, returning warm, but relatively saline, water to the Atlantic at a depth of just over 900 feet (275 m). Once it has crossed the Gibraltar sill into the Atlantic it sinks to about 3300 feet (1000 m). It takes about 80 years for Mediterranean water to be renewed by exchange with Atlantic water — and much longer than that to renew the more isolated waters of the Black Sea.

Other seas

The Black Sea, with the Sea of Azov linked to it by the Kerch Strait to form an extension to the north-east, was a brackish lake until the opening of the Bosporus connected it with the Mediterranean. Now its salinity is low, mainly because it is fed water principally from rivers, including the Danube, Dnieper and the Don — which flows into the Sea of Azov. It loses water by surface currents flowing into the Mediterranean, but also gains water in currents flowing in the opposite direction at depths below about 65 feet (20 m).

The Caspian Sea is more saline, with about 13 parts per thousand of salt — it is more saline in the south than in the north, where the Volga feeds in fresh water — but the mineral content of the water is different from that of sea water. The rivers, especially the Volga which supplies about 80 per cent of the fresh water entering the Sea, deliver relatively large amounts of sulphates, and small amounts of chloride. Water is lost from the Sea only by evaporation, and it used to have its own natural evaporation basins, the largest of which was a large, shallow inlet called the Kara-Bogaz-Gol on the eastern side, separated by a sand bar from the main body of water. A strong current used to carry water into the basin where it evaporated, leaving mineral deposits — especially Glauber's salt — that were mined. Since about 1930, the abstraction of water for irrigation and industry has lowered the level of the Caspian and separated the Kara-Bogaz-Gol.

anticlockwise around the entire Sea, and also around smaller parts of it, but the overall flow of surface water is from west to east. Evaporation continues all the way, and so the salinity of the water increases from about 37 parts per thousand in the west, to about about 39 parts per thousand in the east, with an overall average of about 38 parts per thousand. The salinity is not constant, however. It decreases during the winter rains and when the Nile floods, and it is lower in the vicinity of river mouths.

The Caribbean Sea is sometimes called the 'American Mediterranean', because it consists of a series of basins separated by ridges, but it formed in a quite different way.

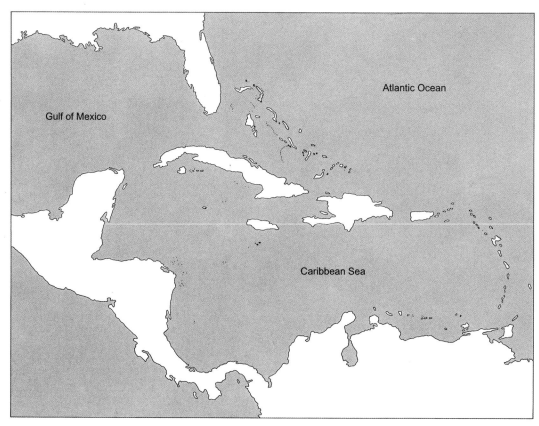

It is shrinking, and the other, smaller inlets are now reduced to salt pans.

On the opposite side of the Atlantic, the Caribbean Sea is composed of a series of ocean basins separated by ridges, making it in some respects much like the Mediterranean. Indeed, some geographers include the Gulf of Mexico to its north, and refer to the resulting sea as the 'American Mediterranean' — with a total area of about 1.7 million square miles (4.36 million sq km) and a volume of about 2.26 million cubic miles (9.43 million cu km).

The Sea was not formed in the same way as the Mediterranean, however, but is much more like an ocean basin, the configuration of which is determined by adjustments of the underlying oceanic crust. It is smaller than the Mediterranean — nowhere more than about 1500 miles (2400 km) from west to east, and 700 miles (1126 km) from north to south, with a total area of about 1.05 million square miles (2.72 million sq km) — but deeper. Its deepest point, between Cuba and Jamaica, is 23,750 feet (7244 m) below the sea surface. Water flows into the Sea from the Atlantic and leaves mainly through the Yucatan Channel, between Cuba and the Yucatan Peninsula of Mexico, in the north, but the sill formed by the Straits of Florida trap water at depths of

more than about 2500 feet (763 m), so the exchange with the ocean is almost wholly confined to the surface water and there is a sharp thermocline separating the two parts of the Sea.

The North Sea and Baltic form another complex not unlike the Mediterranean and Caribbean. The North Sea, covering about 220,000 square miles (570,000 sq km), is shallow — in the south some areas are barely covered at low tide — and its volume is about 12,000 cubic miles (50,000 cu km). Indeed, at one time much of what is now sea was forested (see page 138). The Sea is linked to the Atlantic through the Straits of Dover and between Norway and the Shetlands, and it is fed by several major rivers — principally the Thames, Rhine and Elbe — which reduce its salinity. It also exchanges water with the Baltic.

The Baltic, with a surface area of about 163,000 square miles (422,000 sq km) and a volume of about 5000 cubic miles (20,000 cu km), is fed by rivers, including the Vistula, Oder and Neva. Baltic water is brackish rather than truly saline, and the saltier North Sea water tends to sink beneath the Baltic water. The highest salinity, in the Kattegat where it joins the North Sea, is only 30 parts per thousand. The sea surface is actually higher in the

Baltic than in the North Sea — even in the Kattegat there is a 4 inches (100 mm) difference and it increases further east. This is due partly to the lower density of the Baltic water, and partly to the volume of water supplied by its rivers, which drain a land area of more than 640,000 square miles (1.66 million sq km), with only small losses by evaporation. The low salinity means the Baltic ports are closed by ice in winter.

There are many such large areas of water that are more or less isolated from oceanic water. The Irish Sea, for example, has an area of about 39,000 square miles (100,000 sq km), the Red Sea 174,000 square miles (450,000 sq km), the Persian Gulf 93,000 square miles (240,000 sq km), and the Bering Sea 872,000 square miles (2.26 million sq km). Together such seas occupy about 7 per cent of the world's total sea area.

Life cycles of seas and oceans

The Red Sea is one of those almost land-locked seas, and its waters, at about 36.5 parts per thousand in the south and about 41 parts per thousand in the north, are more saline than those of the Indian Ocean, to which is is linked through the Gulf of Aden. We tend to think of the seas as eternal, but until about 20 million years ago the Red Sea probably did not exist. Seas, and oceans, have life cycles. They are born, grow, age, and eventually they disappear. The Red Sea is very young, and it is still growing. One day, a long time in the future, it will rank as an ocean, separating the Arabian peninsula from the continent of Africa.

According to Tuzo Wilson, Professor of Geophysics at the University of Toronto and one of the leading authorities on the subject, the life cycle of an ocean — known as the Wilson cycle — has several distinct stages. It begins when great blocks of the Earth's crust are lifted up and moved apart, forming a 'rift' valley between them into which water will enter if there is a link to an ocean. The base of the valley then subsides and widens further, forming a narrow sea with parallel sides — like the Red Sea. A valley of this kind often has a 'triple junction' — a place where one valley divides into three. Two of these smaller valleys may widen, like the Gulf of Suez and the Gulf of Aqaba, while the third forms a long extension called an 'aulacogen', like

the Ethiopian Rift, which continues all the way to the great lakes of East Africa.

The sea continues to widen, forming an ocean basin bounded by continents, until it becomes unstable. When that happens, part of the basin, well away from the centre, sinks back into the Earth's mantle. This produces a deep ocean trench and, associated with it, an arc of islands. This process continues as, little by little, the ocean floor sinks — is 'subducted' — back into the mantle. Finally, the entire floor disappears and the continents to either side collide.

The Red Sea is at an early stage in its life cycle, and only about 20 million years old. The Atlantic Ocean is about 200 million years old, and still growing, and the Pacific Ocean is now distinctly elderly, and shrinking.

These ages, measured in millions or even hundreds of millions of years, sound immense and so far beyond ordinary human experience as to be unimaginable. In the history of the planet, though, which is measured in thousands of millions of years, they are brief and oceans are emerging, changing shape, and disappearing at a quite remarkable speed. Even on the human scale, the rate of movement is considerable. The North Atlantic, for example, is growing wider by about 1inch (25 mm) a year — by a curious coincidence, exactly the rate at which human toenails and fingernails grow. When next you trim your nails, the amount of nail you remove is equal to the distance Europe and North America have separated since you last trimmed your nails! Over the course of 200 million years, the Atlantic has widened to about 3000 miles (4800 km) at this apparently slow rate.

Fit of the continents

Francis Bacon (1561-1626) is said to have been the first person to notice that South America and Africa look as though they should fit together, suggesting they might once have been joined. It would not have been possible to make such an observation earlier because maps of the world were insufficiently detailed and accurate. In later centuries other scientists were drawn to the curious coincidence of the shapes of continents, and Eduard Suess (1831-1914), Professor of Geology at the University of Vienna, found such a close correspondence among the southern continents that he proposed they had once

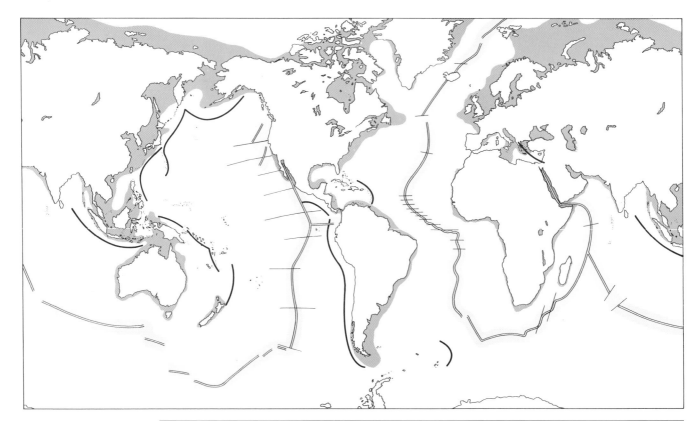

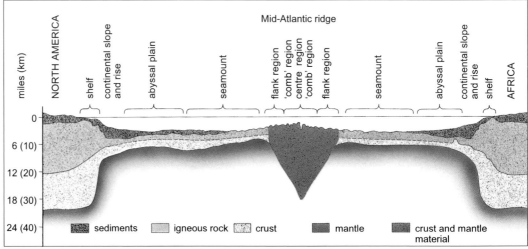

(Above) The mid-ocean ridges (parallel lines) and principal deep-sea trenches (solid lines). The ridges are at regions from which the sea floors are spreading. The lines crossing the ridges and trenches mark major transform faults, where sections of crust are moving past one another. (Right) A cross-section of the North Atlantic Ocean, showing the submerged parts of the North American and African continents, the Mid-Atlantic ridge, where new material is being added and the ocean floor is spreading, flanked by mountain ranges (seamounts). The diagram also shows the material from which the upper part of the sea floor is made. The scale on the left shows the depth below the sea surface.

been joined in a supercontinent, which he called Gondwanaland. South America, rotated a little, fits against the western side of Africa, Antarctica fits around the tip of South Africa and against the south-eastern side of the continent, and Australia fits against the eastern side of Antarctica. If the fit is based on the edges of the continental shelves, rather than the present coastlines, it is even better. What are now the northern continents were also joined, forming a supercontinent called Laurasia, separated from Gondwanaland by the Tethys Sea.

No one could imagine how continents might be joined together at one time, but not at another, but the evidence that this was the case continued to accumulate as biologists and geologists pursued their explorations of the world. Coal measures, in both Europe and North America, were found to be the remains of vast swamp forests that grew during the Carboniferous Period, around 300 million years ago. Plant fossils, found in the coal, were identified as species now extinct which, in Carboniferous times, had occurred there — in Europe and North America — but nowhere else. Living plants were identified that grow wild only in New Zealand, Australia and South America — lands separated by thousands of miles of ocean.

Continental drift

By early in this century it was being proposed that continents can indeed move, in a process called 'continental drift'. A principal proponent of this hypothesis was Alfred Wegener (1880-1930), a German meteorologist and physicist, who gathered evidence from fossils, past climates, and rock types and formations. In 1915, he published his arguments in a book, *Die Entstehung der Kontinente und Ozeane* (it was first published in English in 1924, as *The Origin of Continents and Oceans*). Wegener went further than Suess, suggesting that all the present continents were once joined in a single supercontinent he called Pangaea, surrounded by a single world ocean, Panthalassa. A small arm of this ocean later became the Tethys Sea. Pangaea formed during the Permian Period, about 240 million years ago and, therefore, after the Carboniferous, by the joining of even older continents, of which we know nothing, and it broke into two parts some 40 million years later.

Wegener is now recognized as the first person to have presented this concept in the form of a sound, scientific argument, but he found little support. No one could suggest any mechanism by which continents might move. The first step in the discovery of such a mechanism came a little later, with the theory of sea-floor spreading. This holds that the floor of an ocean grows wider from a central ridge. New rock from the underlying mantle emerges molten at the ridge, flows to either side, and cools, pushing the adjacent, older rock ever further from the ridge. In other places, or other oceans, rock is being returned to the mantle at precisely the same rate — which it must do if the surface area of the planet is to remain constant.

This theory was reinforced by the discovery that the rocks from which continents are made are much older than those found on the ocean floors. So far, the oldest oceanic crust to be discovered, in the western Pacific and the North Atlantic, is about 200 million years old. The oldest known continental crust, on the other hand, is more than 3500 million years old. The theory explains this stark difference in ages, since new crust is being formed constantly at the mid-ocean ridges, older oceanic crust is removed by being subducted back into the mantle, and continental crust is left unchanged for long periods.

Further, somewhat indirect, confirmation came from the discovery that oceanic crust forms bands, to either side of the ridges and more or less parallel with them, that record reversals in the polarity of the Earth's magnetic field. While rocks remain molten, certain molecules within them — such as iron — align themselves, like compass needles, with the magnetic field around them. As the rock solidifies, the molecules are locked into the positions they hold at the time, and are unable to move further. The bands of crustal rocks contain aligned molecules whose polarity changes from one band to the next. The rocks, therefore, record changes in the polarity of the magnetic field, but because these changes must have occurred at particular times, and in sequence, the rocks themselves must have formed in sequence, their age increasing with distance from the ridge.

Plate tectonics

Today, the theory of continental drift has been abandoned in its original form although, of course, there is no doubt that continents move. The theory of sea-floor spreading survives, as an integral part of the broader, unifying theory, of plate tectonics, which provides a satisfactory explanation of the controlling mechanism — although many details remain to be discovered.

The modern theory holds that below the crust the rocks of the mantle, although much denser than crustal rocks, are plastic. They behave in some respects like a liquid, and heat is transported through them by convection which causes currents to flow — though very slowly. Above the mantle, the crustal rocks have cooled and solidified, but not as a single, continuous covering. The crust is in the form of discrete blocks that, together with a layer of shattered rock at their bases, form the 'lithosphere'. This lies above the rocks of the upper mantle — the 'asthenosphere' — and the boundary between the two is called the 'Mohorovičić discontinuity', or 'Moho' for short, after Andrija Mohorovičić (1857-1936), the Croatian scientist who discovered it. The discrete blocks, or plates, from which the crust is made are able to move in relation to one another as though they were floating on the surface of a liquid, the speed and direction of their movements being related to the convection currents in the mantle.

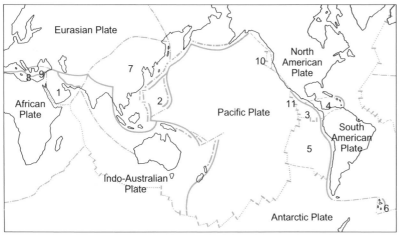

The crust of the Earth comprises plates of material that move slowly in relation to one another. There are seven large plates and a number of smaller ones, of which 11 are shown here. At their boundaries, plates may be spreading apart, one may be moving beneath the other (the process is called 'subduction') or they may be moving past one another along transform faults. Volcanic islands are believed to form at particular points on plate margins and to be carried by their plates. Another island forms in the same place in relation to the underlying mantle, but behind the earlier one in relation to the plate motion, so that an arc of islands develops.

'Tectonic' means 'pertaining to building' or, to a geologist, 'pertaining to deformations of the Earth's crust', and so the theory was named 'plate tectonics'. Continents and oceans can exist on the same plate, but continental crust and oceanic crust are of different composition and different thickness. Oceanic crust, everywhere in the world, is about 7 miles (11 km) thick. Most continental crust is 18.5-25 miles (30-40 km) thick, but up to 43.5 miles (70 km) thick in places, like the Himalayas, where mountains have formed fairly recently by the crumpling that occurs when continents collide.

Although the rocks of the ocean crust are different from those of continental crust, they do not remain exposed for long before they are covered by sediments. A cross-section of the Atlantic sea floor, for example, shows sediment, and sedimentary rocks formed from it, accumulated on the continental slope and rise on both sides of the ocean, and the rocks of the continental crust projecting much deeper into the mantle than those of the oceanic crust. The layer of sediment becomes thinner with increasing distance from the continents. The sea floor slopes gently upwards to the centre of the ocean where, at the Mid-Atlantic Ridge, new mantle material is being added. The Ridge marks the 'constructive' margin between two crustal plates.

A constructive margin is one where the addition of new material means the plates are moving apart, but margins may also be 'destructive', marked by a system of 'transform faults', or inactive. At a destructive margin one plate is subducting beneath the other, and the combined area of the two plates is decreasing, and at transform faults the two plates are moving past one another

in opposite directions. An inactive margin is one where the plates are not moving in relation to one another. Inactive margins may eventually form sutures, binding the two plates together securely.

The major plates

There are seven major plates — the African, Antarctic, Eurasian, Indo-Australian, North American, Pacific and South American — and several minor ones. The African Plate comprises the continent of Africa, extending westwards to the Mid-Atlantic Ridge, bounded to the east by the Indo-Australian Plate, to the south by the Antarctic Plate, and to the north by the Eurasian Plate, with which it has collided, one consequence of the collision being the formation of two minor plates, the Aegean and Turkish. The sea floor is spreading along the boundary between the African and Indo-Australian Plates — the boundary runs through the Red Sea, separating the Arabian peninsula from the African mainland.

The Antarctic Plate, comprising the continent of Antarctica and the surrounding oceans, is also bounded by margins, many of which are spreading, although the character of its margin with the African Plate is uncertain.

The Eurasian Plate is bounded to the south by the African Plate — the collision zone runs through the Mediterranean Basin — and the Indo-Pacific Plate, which is also moving northwards. Starting some 200 million years ago, but reaching its climax about 25 million years ago, the collisions with the Africa and Indo-Pacific Plates raised both the Alpine and Himalayan mountain ranges. The Eurasian Plate is bounded to the west by the Mid-Atlantic Ridge, and to the east by the North American Plate.

The Indo-Australian Plate is bounded by the Eurasian Plate to its north, is being subducted in the region from Malaysia to New Guinea, at its boundary with the Pacific Plate, and is also bounded by the Pacific Plate, at a margin running north to south through New Zealand. Material is being added to it along its southern boundary with the Antarctic Plate.

The North American Plate extends from the Mid-Atlantic Ridge in the east, to a very complex system of boundaries with the Pacific Plate and a number of smaller plates, close to the western coast of the continent. The volcanoes of western North America are associated with the subduction of the quite small Juan de Fuca and Gorda Plates beneath the North American Plate and, off the Central American coast, the Cocos Plate, which is disappearing beneath the North American Plate and another minor plate, the Caribbean, to its east.

The Pacific Plate carries no continent, and is the only plate to consist entirely of oceanic crust. It is also the largest plate, but it is shrinking because it is being subducted at its margins with the Eurasian and Indo-Australian Plates in the north and west. The Marianas Trench, at the margin between the Pacific and Philippine Plates, is the deepest of all ocean trenches. The Trench is just to the west of the Marianas Islands, some 1700 miles (2730 km) west of Manila — and the Philippine Plate itself is splitting through the Marianas Islands, the two sections moving apart at about 2.4 inches (60 mm) a year. The Aleutian Islands, which almost enclose the Bering Sea, mark part of the margin with the Eurasian Plate. They are of volcanic origin and a continuation of the mountains of Alaska. The eastern boundary, with the North American Plate, is marked by faults — which are still active, and produce earthquakes — and the Plate is growing only at its southern margin with the Antarctic Plate.

The South American Plate extends from the Mid-Atlantic Ridge, westwards to the minor Nazca Plate, which is subducting beneath it along the Peru-Chile Trench, north to its boundaries with the Caribbean and North American Plates, and south to the Antarctic Plate.

Continents are made from continental crust, and so are most offshore islands which stand on the continental shelf. Geologically, they are part of the mainland, no more than hills or areas of high ground standing to the seaward side of lower ground that has been inundated. From time to time, when the sea level falls (see pages 141-42), such islands are rejoined to their mainlands. The British Isles, Newfoundland and the Falkland Islands (Malvinas) are of this type.

Other islands, much further removed from any continent, are usually volcanic. Iceland, for example, lying on the Mid-Atlantic Ridge, is formed entirely from mantle material derived from the Ridge, and none of its rocks is more than 65 million years old. New volcanic islands can appear at any time, and suddenly. The most recent example was Surtsey, just south of Iceland. It emerged in 1963, following a series of dramatic volcanic eruptions that were recorded by film and television cameras. The violence of the eruptions was due to the fact that sea water flowed into an open vent in the Ridge, and came into direct contact with the mantle. It was the rapid expansion of the water as it was heated that caused the explosions. Ascension Island, St Helena and Tristan da Cunha are also volcanic islands that formed above the Mid-Atlantic Ridge.

Volcanic islands sometimes form as chains, and the longest chain of all is the Hawaiian-Emperor chain. It stretches from Kamchatka, the peninsula forming the eastern boundary of the Sea of Okhotsk, where there is a seamount — an isolated mountain on the sea floor — all the way to an active submarine volcano south-east of Hawaii.

The volcanic activity that forms such chains is believed to be associated with 'hot spots' and 'mantle plumes', phenomena that are related, in turn, to a particular kind of convection current flowing through the plastic rocks of the asthenosphere. The currents seem to originate very deep in the mantle, close to its boundary with the Earth's core. Being convection currents, they tend to form 'cells' in which hot material rises more or less vertically, loses its heat, and sinks again. Just beneath the crust, the currents deliver hot, buoyant material — the mantle plume — that may produce a dome, like a blister, in the crust. Should the dome then become a chamber filled with magma — a hot spot — and only weakly sealed, it may develop into a volcano. The erupting volcano builds into a mountain, and if it is on the ocean floor, and high enough, its uppermost part will project above the ocean surface, as an island. The plumes and hot spots occur in particular places, where they remain, and the location of those places is fixed in relation to the core, not to the crustal plates. The crust, together with local weaknesses in it, moves over the hot spot. As a volcano is carried away from its hot spot it becomes inactive. Some time later a new crustal weakness will be carried over the hot spot and a new volcano forms. Island chains result from the repetition of this process.

WATER AND CLIMATE

Hurricanes

If it begins over the Caribbean, or in Australia, it is called a 'hurricane', but in other parts of the world it has different names. They know it as a 'tornado' in the central parts of the United States, as a 'cyclone' if it begins over the Bay of Bengal, and as a 'typhoon' in the western Pacific. A 'hurricane' is also the name given to a fierce gale, with a wind speed of at least 64 knots (118 km/h), and a 'cyclone' is also a particular type of weather system, which is not necessarily violent. Used in their other sense, however, these words describe a quite distinct, and extremely violent, indeed terrifying, kind of storm — and one that has a great deal to do with the subject of this book — water.

Call them what you will, hurricanes are common. About 80 of them occur every year in the world as a whole, most of them (70 per cent) in the northern hemisphere. Of the total, 40 occur in the North Pacific, nine in the North Atlantic, and six or seven in the northern Indian Ocean. They develop mainly in the late summer and autumn — September is a peak month for them in the Atlantic — although they can occur at other times of year.

They are also confined to particular latitudes. They very rarely begin close to the Equator, because there the Coriolis force is insufficient to set them twisting, and it is unusual for them to form more than about 15 degrees north or south of the Equator, because in these higher latitudes there is often a very strong wind at high altitude — a 'jet stream' — which sweeps away the rising hot air on which they feed. Once they are established, however, hurricanes may travel long distances on tracks that take them far from the latitudes in which they form. They are weakening all the time, but they are so fierce at the height of their powers that even a dying hurricane can bring severe gales and wild, dangerous seas. It is not unknown for them to move as far north as Europe, even to Britain, still with sufficient energy to cause serious damage.

For a hurricane to establish itself, the first requirement is a large area of very warm sea — which confines hurricanes to low lati-

tudes. The surface temperature must be not less than 80 °F (27 °C). Air, warmed by its contact with the sea surface, expands, and rises because it is then less dense than the air above it. This causes an area of low atmospheric pressure to form over the warm sea, and air from an adjacent area of relatively higher pressure flows towards the low-pressure area to fill it.

The Earth, turning on its axis, moves beneath the rising air, producing an apparent deflection — the Coriolis force — in the incoming air so that instead of flowing directly, and rapidly equalizing the pressures of the two bodies of air, the air spirals inwards. This establishes the necessary twisting motion and, because the Coriolis force has no effect at the Equator, it means such systems can form only some degrees away from the Equator. In the northern hemisphere, the winds blow in an anticlockwise direction (and clockwise in the southern hemisphere) around the centre of the low-pressure area. Winds blow in the opposite direction around regions of high pressure, called 'anticyclones'. (In fact, the direction of rotation in both hemispheres carries the wind in the direction of the Earth's rotation — to the east — around anticyclones and in the opposite direction — to the west — around low-pressure areas as air moves away from the Equator.)

At this stage, only a very ordinary low-pressure weather system has formed — a 'depression', known to meteorologists as a 'cyclone'.

Very warm, very humid air is rising rapidly. Cloud forms and, as the water vapour condenses into liquid droplets, the latent heat of condensation is released. This warms the surrounding air, accelerating its upward movement. Huge, towering cumulus and cumulonimbus — 'anvil' — clouds develop, up to 40,000 feet (12,000 m) high, and it starts to rain. Surface air is drawn in from outside the system to replenish the supply.

Ordinarily, this will lead to an intense tropical rainstorm that dissipates the excess warmth, but, in very warm conditions, the low atmospheric pressure at low levels may be accompanied by high pressure at high altitude, and in this situation the outcome is

(Opposite) Although they lie in similar latitudes, the climates of Ireland (top) and the North American prairies (bottom) are strikingly different because of the influence of the oceans.

very different. The warm, rising air is added to the high-pressure, upper-level air, tending to increase its pressure still further. As it rises, the warm air cools, and cool air sinks from the top back into the centre of the system. As it sinks, the air is warmed — descending air warms, just as rising air cools — so adding to the supply of warm air.

Low pressure system

The system now consists of an area of intensely low pressure, about 400 miles (650 km) in diameter, formed above sea that has a high surface temperature, and containing some cumulus, but also between 100 and 200 large cumulonimbus storm clouds. At the centre there is a region of calm weather, 200 to 300 miles (300-500 km) across, and surrounding this 'eye' a region where wind speeds may exceed 120 miles per hour (193 km/h). The system is self-sustaining, fed by air drawn in from outside and sinking at the centre, and provided with energy initially from the warm sea, but then from the latent heat of condensation, and the warming of the sinking air. It has become a hurricane, and the entire system moves at around 10 to 15 miles per hour (16-24 km/h) until, usually after two or three days, it enters the middle-latitude region of prevailing westerly winds and begins to break down, although a dying hurricane can continue to generate storm-force winds and waves for some time.

Clouds are essential, of course, but they do not form automatically when air becomes saturated with water vapour. It is quite common for air to be supersaturated — with a relative humidity greater than 100 per cent. In saturated air, cloud will form only if there are suitable surfaces on to which water vapour can condense. Such surfaces are provided by very small solid particles, called 'cloud condensation nuclei' or 'CCN'. Over land, dust particles are the most common CCN, but as dust produced on land is carried by the winds over the sea, the particles settle into the sea, or are captured by surface spray, or are washed down with the raindrops that have condensed on to them. Over the open ocean the air contains almost no dust — so how is it possible for clouds to form?

Formation of clouds

As spray is whipped up by the wind, some of its water droplets fall back into the sea, but some evaporate. This leaves behind very small, airborne, salt crystals. These crystals are of a size and shape suitable for water condensation, and they provide some CCN, but nothing like enough to account for the amount of cloud over the ocean. The other source, and probably the principal one, is the marine phytoplankton. For reasons that are not really understood, but which may be connected with the regulation of salt levels inside cells, many species of plankton excrete a compound called dimethyl sulphide, $(CH_3)_2S$. Some of this enters the air and is oxidized in a series of reactions, and one of the reaction products is sulphate, SO_3, which exists as small crystals. Sulphate crystals are also effective CCN. In recent years there has been a marked increase in the amount of phytoplankton in the seas and oceans — the algal blooms that have caused concern in the North and Adriatic Seas are part of this phenomenon, but there are also large blooms in the Atlantic. Raindrops that have condensed on to sulphate crystals are acid because, when sulphate reacts with water, it becomes sulphuric acid (H_2SO_4). Marine plankton are one of the major causes of 'acid rain'.

Sulphate crystals also occur over land, as a result of burning fuels that contain sulphur, and the consequent release of sulphur dioxide (SO_2). Some climatologists who are calculating the consequences of 'greenhouse effect' warming have warned that reducing the amount of carbon-based fuel we burn and, therefore, the amount of carbon dioxide we release into the air, may have less effect than we suppose because it will also reduce the quantity of sulphur dioxide emitted. This, they suggest, will reduce the amount of cloud and precipitation, which probably have a cooling effect, while increasing the average humidity of the air — and water vapour is a 'greenhouse gas'.

A hurricane is an extreme type of tropical depression. Others are more benign, and include the monsoons of southern Asia. These summer rains begin in May in the south and move northwards to reach the belt from Afghanistan, across northern China, to southern Korea by the middle of July. They are caused by complex seasonal changes in the circulation of air in the upper atmosphere, linked to the topography of Asia, that draw warm, very humid air mainly from the Pacific and the Arabian Sea.

(Opposite, top) Glaciers carve valleys with a very distinctive shape. This is in North Wales. When permafrost thaws briefly in summer, the surface becomes wet mud in which large boulders slide downhill until the autumn freeze halts their progress. (Opposite, bottom) The permafrost here in Dartmoor, England, melted at the end of the last ice age, leaving a periglacial landscape, frozen in time.

Cumulus cloud forming over the English Channel.

When warm air passes over the ocean water evaporates into it. If the air continues to move, when it passes over dry land, it may release some of its moisture as precipitation. It is not difficult to understand the way in which water is transported from sea to land. At least, it would not be difficult were this the whole story, but it is not. It does not explain why the air should move in the first place, and that is a little more complicated.

Rotation of the Earth's atmosphere and oceans

The Earth's atmosphere and oceans rotate as the Earth itself rotates on its axis, and at the same rate. This gives them all an 'angular momentum', which has a value that can be calculated by multiplying together the mass of the body of air or water being considered, the radius of its orbit (that is, its distance from the axis of rotation, linking the North and South Poles through the centre of the Earth), and the square of the rate of spin (known as the 'angular velocity'). The total angular momentum must remain constant (it must be conserved), if the system as a whole is to maintain a constant angular velocity, so, if one component of angular momentum changes, the other components must compensate. If, for example, the radius of the orbit of a part of the overall system is

ing as media for its transport, that move as discrete entities, cannot do so in a straight line. The further they move from the Equator, the more strongly they will move eastward.

At high altitudes, in the subtropics and again in middle latitudes, sharp differences in temperature between air masses generate jet streams, irregular, fast-moving, westerly streams of air, with speeds of 100 to 150 miles per hour (160-240 km/h) and in winter sometimes reaching 300 miles per hour (480 km/h). The middle-latitude jet streams tend to drive low-level depressions in an easterly direction, and this is another reason for the tendency of weather systems to move from west to east. It accounts for the different climates that are encountered on either side of an ocean. The eastern coast of North America, for example, usually receives weather that has travelled across the continent, while in the same latitudes the western coast of Europe receives weather that has crossed the Atlantic.

It is not simply the humidity of the air that is conditioned by its contact with the oceans or dry land, but also its temperature. Water has a much greater capacity than dry land for storing heat. This quality has nothing to do with the fact that water occupies a much larger surface area of the planet than does dry land, although this obviously determines the magnitude of the effect. The quality belongs to water itself and derives from its specific heat.

Specific heat and albedo
The specific heat of a substance is the quantity of heat that is required to raise the temperature of 1 gram of the substance by 1 degree Celsius at a constant, sea-level, atmospheric pressure. At one time, the unit of heat was the calorie, which was defined as the amount of heat required to raise the temperature of 1 gram of liquid water by 1 degree Celsius, and so the specific heat of water was given a value of 1. In practice, this value varies according to the temperature of the water and so the calorie, and specific heat, had to be defined more precisely. The 'mean calorie', for example, is one-hundredth of the heat needed to raise the temperature of 1 gram of water from 0 °C to 100 °C. Today, the joule is the standard scientific unit, and the specific heat of water is, less conveniently, approximately 4.18 joules per gram. No matter

reduced, while its mass remains unaltered, the angular velocity of that part will increase. It is why a pirouette accelerates if the dancer starts with her arms extended, and then draws them to the sides of her body. The orbital radius of a mass of air or water will decrease if the air or water moves to a higher latitude, because its distance from the axis is reduced. This will accelerate its motion in an easterly direction — easterly because the Earth, and everything upon or connected to its surface, spins in a west-to-east direction (the Sun rises in the east and sets in the west).

As heat is transferred from low to high latitudes, bodies of air and water, function-

which unit is used, compared with most other substances, the specific heat of water is high. It is about five times higher than that of dry sand.

Its high specific heat means that water must absorb a great deal of heat for only a small increase in its temperature. That is why the ocean warms so slowly in summer. Dry soil, on the other hand, with a specific heat about one-fifth that of water, responds much more quickly. By the middle of the afternoon, on a really hot, sunny day, the dry sand on a beach may be so hot that walking on it in bare feet is uncomfortable or even painful. The sea adjoining the beach, and receiving a similar amount of solar heat, is pleasantly cool or even cold.

The heat of the beach may be moderated by a sea breeze. This is caused by the strong heating of the air over the land. The heated air rises and is replaced by cooler air drawn from over the sea. At night, when the land cools much more quickly than the sea, the wind blows in the opposite direction, as a land breeze, because the air over the sea is warmer and less dense than the cool air which is subsiding over the land.

If you dig into the beach sand, however, you will find it much cooler below the surface. Indeed, the difference has been measured in Japan, and it was found that where the temperature of the sand was 104 °F (40 °C) at the surface, 2 inches (50 mm) below the surface it was only 68 °F (20 °C), and 6 inches (150 mm) below the surface it was 45 °F (7 °C). The temperatures in other types of soil were also measured and in them, too, the temperature was found to fall rapidly with increasing depth. There are several reasons for this. Soil particles are opaque, so radiant energy cannot penetrate through them. Depending on the type of particle, they are more or less light in colour, and light colours reflect radiation without absorbing it. In dry soil, the spaces between particles are filled by air, and air is a poor conductor of heat. These factors combine to trap heat close to the surface. The temperature falls more slowly with increasing depth in wet soil, because water is a better conductor of heat than air. If the soil is very wet, however, the high specific heat of water becomes more significant than the low specific heat of the soil itself, and more heat is needed to warm the soil.

Bathing water, on the other hand, may be cool, but you will feel little difference in its temperature as you dive beneath the surface — you are not likely to swim all the way down to the thermocline! Except when the Sun is low in the sky so that much of its radiation is reflected, water is dark and absorbs most of the radiation falling on it. The degree of reflectivity of a surface, called its 'albedo', can be given a value, in which 1.00 represents the reflection of all incident radiation and 0 represents total absorption. Sand has an albedo of 0.30 to 0.35 but, depending on the angle at which the radiation strikes it, the albedo of water is 0.06 to 0.10. It is a big difference. Water is also transparent, so radiation can penetrate further into it than it can into soil, and the mixing in the surface layer, caused by waves, helps maintain its constant temperature.

Translate these observations to a scale of entire continents and oceans, and the climatic consequences become apparent. Over a continent, the summer warmth heats the soil rapidly. Contact with the warm ground heats the air, and a mass of warm, dry air forms — dry because it is far inland. This air mass moves across the ocean and is cooled from below by its contact with the relatively cold water, and water evaporates into it. This, too, cools the air, because it is from the air that the latent heat of evaporation must be extracted.

The cooling effect is not strong, because it increases the density of the air close to the surface, preventing it from rising — the air becomes more stable. By the time it reaches the continent on the opposite side of the ocean, what began as hot, dry air has become somewhat cooler, but still warm, moist air. For those who live on either side of the ocean, the temperature difference is not great. The average temperature in late July in Winnipeg, Manitoba, is about 68 °F (20 °C) and that at Stornoway, on the Isle of Lewis in the Outer Hebrides, is about 55 °F (13 °C) — but Winnipeg is at 50 degrees north and Stornoway at 58 degrees north.

In winter, the opposite occurs. Both land and sea grow cooler, but with its low specific heat, and the shallow depth to which it has warmed, the land cools very rapidly and releases little heat, for it has stored very little. The sea cools much more slowly and, because of its high specific heat, its cooling releases a much larger amount of heat — volume for volume, five times more heat than the land. A cooling of the upper layer of the ocean by as little as one-tenth of a degree Fahrenheit (0.05 °C) will release enough heat to raise the temperature of a layer of air above it 30 times thicker than the layer of water by 9 °F (5 °C).

Air over the continent becomes extremely cold, but it is warmed by its passage over the sea. In Winnipeg the average January temperature is about 0 °F (-18 °C), and in Stornoway — 8 degrees further north — it is about 40 °F (4.5 °C).

On a global scale, the climatic effect of the oceans is to moderate temperatures. The water prevents the world from becoming too hot in summer, or too cold in winter.

Trade winds and Hadley cells

In 1735, G. Hadley attempted an explanation of the reason for the easterly trade winds that blow in the tropics. They were called 'trade' winds by seafarers, who made much use of them, and they became famous, as did the belt of low winds — the 'doldrums' — lying between the northern-hemisphere north-easterlies and the southern-hemisphere south-easterlies. Hadley suggested that equatorial air is heated strongly by its contact with the surface, rises vertically, and is replaced at low levels by cooler air, which is drawn in from higher latitudes.

The rising air is very humid. The line of the Equator lies mainly over sea areas and where it crosses land, in South America, Africa and south-east Asia, the natural vegetation cover consists of rain forest, area for area releasing at least as much water vapour into the atmosphere by transpiration than the oceans do by evaporation. As the warm, moist air rises it also cools to below its saturation temperature. Clouds form and the rainfall is intense. Around the Equator, therefore, the climate is warm and humid.

The rising air reaches the tropopause — the upper boundary of the lower part of the atmosphere — and can rise no further. It spreads away from the Equator, cools — the temperature at the tropopause is usually -56.5 °F (-49 °C) — and sinks, to replace the low-level air flowing towards the Equator. The sinking air is very dry, for its severe chilling has wrung all the water from it very effectively. As it sinks, it grows warmer. It reaches the ground in the subtropics, the belt around the world in which the major deserts are located. This belt is also the

The convection of air between the Equator and the subtropics forms vertical cells — Hadley cells. A second system of cells is believed to exist at high latitudes. These two systems drive a third system that lies between them, in middle latitudes.

region from which air is drawn towards the Equator.

The movement of air forms a convection cell, called a 'Hadley cell' after the man who first suggested it, and the permanent flow of air towards the Equator at low level is what we know as the trade winds. This was Hadley's explanation and, in general, it is accepted to this day, although in the real world matters are rather more complicated than his description makes them sound. The trade winds do not blow everywhere around the world, for example, the heating of the world is not concentrated evenly around the Equator, as Hadley's explanation requires, and we know now that the movement of air away from the Equator, and its subsequent sinking, is a much more complex process than Hadley supposed. Hadley believed that the trade winds blow from the east, because of the effect of the Earth's rotation on the poleward-moving air — the effect that came to be known later as the Coriolis force. It is more likely, however, that the poleward-moving mass of air is accelerated to the east because of the need to conserve its angular momentum — the motion is real, not the result of the Earth rotating beneath it.

Nevertheless, with all the qualifications and amendments that have been added to it, the Hadley theory does explain the transport of heat from the tropics to the subtropics. There are several cells, rather than the single one in each hemisphere which he proposed, and they are much more important in winter than in summer — although they are involved in producing the monsoons. The easterly winds are balanced elsewhere by westerlies. If they were not, friction between the winds and the surface would gradually slow the Earth's rate of rotation. Not all of the descending air of the Hadley cells returns as the trade winds.

Equatorial air rises to the tropopause, losing its water as it does so, then descends into the subtropics, where its dryness produces deserts.

Some escapes to produce rather unreliable westerlies in middle latitudes. In Equatorial regions, westerly winds prevail in summer over Africa, much of southern Asia and northern Australia, and western South America.

At the poles there may be — it is not known for certain — another, smaller system of convection cells in which air is warmed, rises, moves polewards, and is replaced by cold air flowing away from the poles. Between them, the tropical Hadley cells, and polar cells, 'drive' a system of middle-latitude cells in which low-latitude descending air is drawn down with the subtropical air that flows back into the tropical cells, and is replaced at high level by rising air drawn upwards with the middle-latitude rising air of the polar cells.

The transport of heat away from the Equator creates a region of low atmospheric pressure, extending as a 'trough' right around the world. This trough tends to move with the thermal Equator, so it is further north in the northern-hemisphere summer, and further south in the southern-hemisphere summer.

Beyond it, in the subtropics, the descending air of the Hadley cells creates generally high pressure, but not in a continuous band. The high-pressure areas form cells over the Sahara, over the Atlantic, roughly between Bermuda and the Azores, over the western United States, and over the North Pacific. In the southern hemisphere, the high-pressure cells form over the oceans and, in summer, over Australia. The high pressure gives way to generally low pressure in the middle latitudes, which gives way, in turn, to generally high pressure around both poles.

Air masses and fronts

In summer, as the tropical low-pressure trough moves away from the Equator, the subtropical high-pressure system moves with it. Tropical air brings summer rains to the subtropics and, in temperate latitudes, the weather becomes more or less dominated by the subtropical highs. Yet again, though, the real world is much more complicated than any brief description makes it seem. Weather systems continue their constant eastward migration through the middle latitudes, among other things bringing chains of depressions to north-western Europe. If the subtropical high-pressure area over the Azores establishes itself firmly, extending as far north as about 50 degrees, it will dominate the weather. Depressions travelling east will move around the high, to its north or south, and north-west Europe will enjoy sunny, dry, warm weather which will last for as long as the Azores high remains stationary and stable. Should it weaken, on the other hand, or should it fail to extend far enough north, the march of the depressions will not be interrupted, and north-western Europe will have a summer of cool, overcast weather with much rain.

Since air is heated from below, its character is determined by that of the surface across which it moves. A large body of air, in which the temperature, pressure and humidity are fairly constant horizontally over hundreds of miles, is called an 'air mass'. At the boundary where two air masses of different types meet, there is a 'front'. At a front, warm, less dense air is either riding up over colder, denser air, or, more usually, the denser air is undercutting the less dense air because it is moving faster and overtaking it. The warm air is made to rise, and such moisture as it contains forms clouds, so 'weather' is often associated with a front. The cooler, denser air has a shape rather like a hill, the surface of which is the front. The leading edge, marking the transition between warm air in front and cool air behind, is called 'cold', and the trailing edge, marking the transition from the cool air into warm air, is called 'warm'. These terms are only relative. Warm air is warm only by comparison with the adjacent cold air, and it may still be distinctly cool, and cold air may feel warm because it is cool only by comparison with the warm air next to it.

Monsoon rain falling over Celebes, Indonesia.

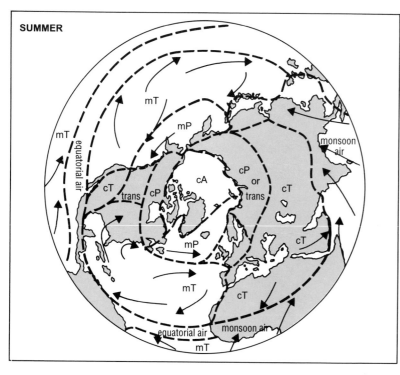

SUMMER

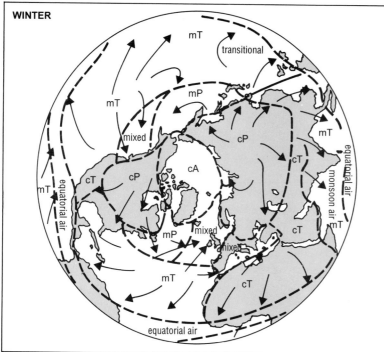

WINTER

Air masses in the northern hemisphere

mA = maritime arctic
mT = maritime tropical
mP = maritime polar
cT = continental tropical
cP = continental polar
cA = continental arctic
trans = transitional

The origins of air masses

Air masses are given names based on the regions in which they originate. The first distinction is between 'continental' and 'maritime' air. This reflects the moisture content of the air, which strongly conditions the kind of weather associated with it. The second distinction relates to latitude, and air may be designated as 'arctic', 'polar' or 'tropical'. Equatorial air is not usually counted because, by the time it moves away from the Equator, its character has changed sufficiently for it to fall within one of the 'tropical' categories.

At ground level there is no real difference between arctic and polar air. The distinction really refers to conditions at high altitudes where, in winter, arctic air is much colder than polar air. The northern-hemisphere source area for arctic air is quite small, and this type of air is of interest mainly over Antarctica. In the northern hemisphere, the principal sources of polar air are North America and Siberia, in an area that expands southwards in winter to cover most of North America, and most of Europe and Asia north of the Himalayas. Southern-hemisphere polar air forms over and around Antarctica. Tropical air is formed to the south of the northern-hemisphere polar air, in the southern United States, Africa, Arabia and southern Asia in winter, but in a larger area, encompassing southern Europe and most of central Asia, in summer. In the southern hemisphere, tropical air forms over Australia and southern Africa in both summer and winter, and in summer a small amount also forms over southern South America.

Arctic, polar and tropical air may be either continental or maritime. Continental polar air, for example, forms over areas that are covered in ice and snow. The air is exceedingly cold and, being so cold, it is very dry. It is the kind of air that brings the still air, clear, pale-blue skies, and extremely low temperatures, of winter, modified from time to time by the formation of cumulus clouds and squally showers due to local warming of the ground. Air of this type often crosses the Atlantic, from Canada, and the Pacific, from Asia. As it does so, its title changes, and it becomes known as maritime polar air, and the change of name refers to the way it is altered by its encounter with the ocean.

The lower layers are warmed, especially as the air mass crosses the Gulf Stream. As it warms, water evaporates into it and the air mass becomes unstable. The warmer, moister, lower air rises, air is drawn in to replace it, and surface winds blow more strongly. The moisture in the rising air condenses to form clouds and, long before it reaches the far shores of the ocean, the intensely cold, dry, stable air mass has become one composed of cool, moist, unstable air. As what has become maritime polar air crosses a large continent, little by little it will lose its moisture, until it is once more of the continental type.

Sometimes, continental polar air moves over land rather than the ocean. As it does so, it is likely to cross warmer ground. This will make it more unstable, as the warmed air rises, but it remains dry, because the interior of continents have insufficient surface water to make much difference.

Continental tropical air is hot, dry, and often unstable because of intense surface heating. The gusty winds caused by this instability may cause dust storms. If such air crosses a large expanse of water — as happens when air from the Sahara moves over the Mediterranean — it acquires moisture rapidly, becomes even more unstable, and may produce thunderstorms. Warm, moist, maritime tropical air may move into a higher latitude, bringing it into contact with cooler water. This causes the rapid condensation of moisture at very low levels, producing fog or, if there is sufficient wind to lift the condensing water to a higher level, cloud of the stratus type.

Monitoring the weather

Weather stations throughout the world monitor their local conditions constantly. Every few hours they report them to a central facility where, using a system of conventional symbols, they are written on a map to make a synoptic chart of a large area. ('Synoptic', from the Greek *sun*, 'with', and *opsis*, 'seeing', means 'having a brief, general view'.) Stations reporting the same atmospheric pressure are joined by lines — 'isobars' — and so a picture is compiled, and frequently updated, of the type, location, and speed and direction of movement of air masses, and of the weather associated with them and with the fronts at which they meet. The synoptic charts, these days augmented by satellite observations and photographs, provide the basis for weather reports and forecasts. In a simplified form, they also appear on television and in newspapers.

El Niño

In 1988, and continuing into 1989, there was a severe drought in North America. Crop yields were reduced, and the water level in navigable rivers fell to such an extent that cargo-carrying river vessels were marooned — sometimes literally stuck in

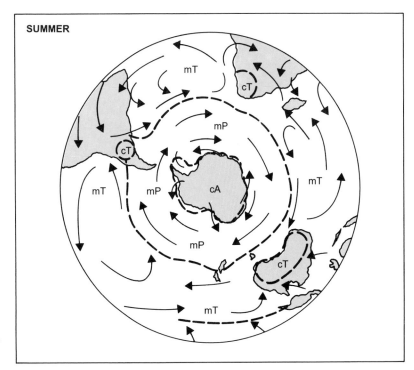

SUMMER

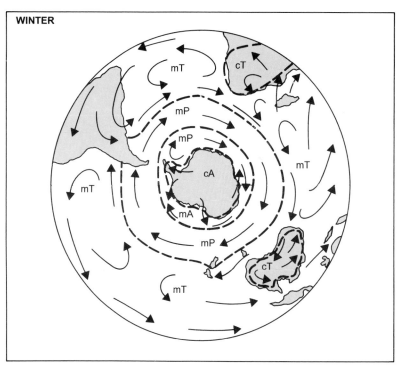

WINTER

the mud. In Kansas, dust storms closed interstate highways. The western USSR suffered a drought, and 1988 was also the year in which there were unusually heavy rains in Australia and serious flooding in Bangladesh, southern China and Sudan. In India, the monsoon, which failed in 1987, returned to bring the heaviest rains for 70 years. Some people believed the freak weather was a manifestation of the 'greenhouse effect', but a thorough investigation

Air masses in the southern hemisphere

mA = maritime arctic
mT = maritime tropical
mP = maritime polar
cT = continental tropical
cP = continental polar
cA = continental arctic

of the weather in that year, and of the climatic events which preceded it, drew scientists very firmly to a different conclusion. The weather of 1988 was caused, at least partly, by 'La Niña'.

Early in 1989, and based on certain observations made late in 1988, it was predicted that Britain would enjoy a fine summer. Indeed, in 1989 there was a drought in Britain. This, too, was associated with 'La Niña'.

'La Niña' is the opposite of 'El Niño' (and sometimes it is called an 'anti-El Niño'). El Niño is linked to world-wide climatic aberrations, its opposite to an intensification of the kind of weather that occurs normally. The severity of these events varies, and so does the weather associated with them. The most intense El Niño of this century occurred in 1982-3, but there were also major El Niños in 1925, 1941, 1957, 1965 and 1972.

'El Niño' is the Spanish for 'the (male) child', and this climatic phenomenon earned its name in South America because it occurs at around Christmas. The reference is to the Christ child. 'La Niña', meaning 'the (female) child', is a name invented by some climatologists, and not one that is used by ordinary people in South America. More technically, El Niño is known as an 'El Niño-Southern Oscillation Event', or 'ENSO', and it is only in recent years that it has received the full attention of scientists. Much remains to be learned about it, but what is known demonstrates rather dramatically the extent to which changes in the

surface waters of one part of one ocean — although a big part of a big ocean — can produce climatic effects over many thousands of miles.

Intertropical Convergence Zone

If the speed and precise direction of the trade winds are monitored over a prolonged period, in many places on both sides of the Equator, the speeds at each place averaged, and the resulting winds plotted on a map, the prevailing winds of the two hemispheres are seen to converge in the Equatorial trough of low atmospheric pressure. The procedure is complicated, because the trade winds are much more variable than their reputation might suggest. The region in which they converge is usually known as the 'Intertropical Convergence Zone', or ITCZ, although some scientists prefer to call it the 'Intertropical Confluence', ITC. This slightly pedantic insistence on an alternative name refers to the fact that the convergence of the trade winds is discontinuous and far from constant — its strength varies from day to day.

The ITCZ and the Equatorial low-pressure trough lie along the thermal equator, rather than the geographical Equator. Because of the great size of Antarctica, and the greater proportion of ocean to land, summers in the southern hemisphere are, on average, cooler than those in the northern hemisphere. Over a whole year this makes the northern hemisphere somewhat warmer than the southern, and so the thermal equator is usually located at about 5 degrees north — although it does not form a straight line like the geographic Equator, and its position moves with the seasons, though not in a simple fashion. To the south of the thermal equator, between it and the geographic Equator, there are regions of light and variable winds — the doldrums.

The trade winds of the southern hemisphere are intensified by a latitudinal cell (involving the movement of air approximately parallel with the Equator) which augments the effect of the meridional Hadley cells — in which the net movement of air is approximately at right-angles to the Equator. In both summer and winter there is usually a region of high atmospheric pressure near the surface in the eastern Pacific, close to the western coast of South America, and a region of low pressure in the Indian Ocean, around Indonesia. The

The 'doldrums' are predominantly windless areas occurring to either side of the Equator where the prevailing easterly (trade) winds meet. The broken lines enclose the areas affected by the trade winds in July, the solid lines the areas affected in January and the arrows show the wind direction.

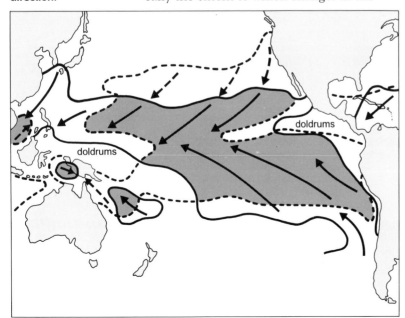

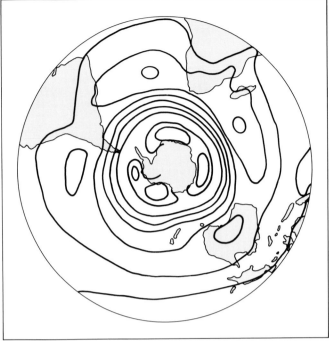

surface trade winds blow across the Pacific in a westerly direction at low level, from the region of high pressure to the region of low pressure. Once arrived in the low-pressure system, the air rises and moves eastwards at high altitude, to descend once more over the eastern Pacific. This movement of air reinforces the high and low pressure systems, and the overall regime is self-sustaining.

The regime is echoed in the movement of water in the Pacific. The prevailing surface winds generate a surface current flowing westwards, from South America to Indonesia. This is the South Equatorial Current, part of the Pacific gyre, and it is complemented by a deeper current, the Equatorial Undercurrent. This flows in the opposite direction, at a depth of between 230 and 660 feet (70-200 m), in a broad ribbon about 660 feet (200 m) thick and 186 miles (300 km) wide, straddling the Equator between about 2 degrees north and 2 degrees south. In its core it moves at about 5 feet (1.5 m) per second.

Because of the intense warming of the Equatorial surface waters, the South Equatorial Current carries warm water westwards. The deeper water of the Equatorial Undercurrent is much cooler. The result is that warm water is constantly being moved towards the west, so the depth of warm water is much greater around Indonesia than it is near the South American coast. The Peru (or Humboldt) Current, another component of the Pacific gyre, flows north-

wards, parallel to the South American coast, carrying water from the Antarctic. By the time it reaches the tropics, the water of the Peru Current is some 9 to 11 °F (5-6 °C) cooler than the water of the South Equatorial Current. It wells up to the surface, contributing to the relatively low temperature of the surface waters, but also bringing oxygen and a rich load of nutrients close to the surface. The upwellings stimulate vigorous biological activity. The vast shoals of fish (mainly anchovies), associated with upwellings of the Peru Current, used to sustain one of the largest commercial fisheries in the world, and the fish fed a large population of marine birds. The birds' droppings formed guano, which was the raw material for a large nineteenth-century fertilizer industry in Peru and Chile.

No one knows why, but from time to time, apparently at intervals of between two and seven years, the atmospheric pressure regime changes. The difference in pressure between the eastern Pacific and Indian Oceans decreases, and the ITCZ moves south. This is a 'southern oscillation'. It is associated with — and perhaps causes — a slackening of the southern trade winds and, because it is these winds which drive the South Equatorial Current, a slackening in the westward movement of warm water. In effect, the warm water accumulated around Indonesia flows back towards South America. The depth of warm surface water increases off the South American coast, and

The usual distribution of pressure over the South Pacific and Indian Oceans. Changes in this distribution are associated with ENSO events.

(Opposite) Abnormal weather is often caused by ENSO events in the Equatorial Pacific. It can bring severe drought to the interior of North America.

the cold upwellings of the Peru Current cease to reach the surface waters. This, or rather its climatic consequences, is 'El Niño'. The two together comprise an ENSO event.

An ENSO event brings unseasonally heavy rain and storms to coastal regions of Peru and Chile. These often cause flooding and damage crops, but offshore the effect is no less severe. With the disappearance of the rich upwelling, the biological productivity of that part of the ocean declines rapidly. The fish disappear — starved or migrated — and this brings real hardship to communities whose livelihoods depend on fishing. The popular name for the phenomenon, linking it to a season for Christian rejoicing, is ironic for there is little rejoicing when this 'child' is the Christmas visitor. In 1970, Peruvian fishermen caught more than 12 million tonnes of fish — about 17 per cent of the total world catch in that year. In 1972, an El Niño year, they caught less than five million tonnes and, in 1973, the catch was still lower.

Further afield, the strange weather, and sometimes the suffering, continue. The start of an ENSO event was detected late in 1986

and intensified into 1987. In southern Alaska, western Canada and the north-western United States, the period from December to April was unusually mild, and parts of the United States enjoyed the mildest winter and spring for more than 50 years. Parts of South America had very wet weather, but in the Philippines and Australia, on the other hand, the weather — summer and early fall in Australia, of course — was extremely dry, and in India and Pakistan the monsoon largely failed.

During a La Niña episode, the distribution of pressure in the Pacific and Indian Oceans intensifies, the southern trade winds blow more strongly, and more warm water flows westwards across the Pacific. The climatic effect is generally to exaggerate the normal weather — if rainfall is customary, there will be more of it, and if fine weather is usual, it will be warmer and last longer. It is impossible to do more than generalize, however, because, like all climatic phenomena, El Niño and its opposite develop in a non-linear (chaotic) fashion, so that very small differences in the conditions at their start lead to very different outcomes.

ENSO events bring unusually heavy rain to the western coast of the United States.

ICE AGES AND SEA LEVELS

Raised beaches

Walk along the sea shore, anywhere north of about 50 degrees north, and you may come across a 'raised beach'. You should look for it behind a sandy beach — cliffs made from hard rock do not provide the evidence you are seeking. Find places where, at the back of the beach, the sea and weather have made a low cliff by eroding the edge of ground the surface of which lies well above the high-tide line. Look carefully at the soil which is exposed on the face of the cliff. If you find sea shells embedded in it, in large numbers and probably somewhere near the top, you may find yourself puzzling over how they came to be there. Wild storms might throw a few shells a considerable distance, but they could hardly embed large quantities of them in the soil. What you have found is an ancient beach, its shells recording still the height to which the tides once reached. On the top of the cliff, if you are lucky and the site has not been destroyed by farming or building, you may find an almost level stretch of ground, parallel to the modern beach, with higher or more broken ground to its landward side. This may have been the beach itself. Today, it will most probably be covered with vegetation, but once it lay bare, at the very edge of the sea. It is a raised beach — clear proof that at some time in the past the sea level was much higher than it is today.

It is more difficult to see clear evidence of former sea levels that were lower than those of today, for the obvious reason that what was then dry land now lies beneath the sea. The evidence exists, all the same. It exists in some places in the form of what were clearly woodlands — the species composing them have been identified in some cases — but that are now as much as a mile or two from the shore, on the sea bed. There are places where, at very low tides and especially when recent storms have disturbed the sediment covering them, fragments of such submerged forests are exposed.

U-shaped valleys

If you live far from any sea coast, there is other evidence you may find to convince you that the waters of the world — fresh as well as salt — were not always distributed as

they are now. Valleys and waterfalls are good places to begin. If you look directly up or down a valley, so you can see it in cross-section, usually it will have more or less the shape of the letter V. The river at the bottom made the valley by washing away the material from its bed, so that, little by little over thousands of years, it cut down to the level at which it now flows. As it wore its way vertically downwards, the very steep sides of the valley it cut would become unstable and from time to time during its history they would collapse into the river, for there is a critical angle of slope beyond

which river banks and valley sides will slip. The cutting would begin again, but the overall effect was to widen the valley at the same time as it deepened. This, then, is an ordinary valley, made by its river.

It may be, though, that instead of a V shape, the valley is more rounded, making a shape like a letter U. There is no way a river can cut a valley of this shape. U-shaped valleys are often occupied by rivers, but they were cut by glaciers — vast streams of ice, moving down the slope at an imperceptibly slow pace, scouring away all traces of soil, all loose rocks, and grinding the surface of the underlying bedrock. Somewhere near the foot of such a valley you might even find evidence of piles of rocks — a 'moraine' — that the glacier pushed ahead of itself. Some

of them may well be 'erratics', rocks quite unlike the other rocks of the neighbourhood, and their presence can be accounted for only by assuming that the glacier moved them far from their original locations.

A glacial valley may have a waterfall, where a river spills over the side, the waters from its own, small valley at the top of the main valley falling to the floor, where they join the main river. This is a 'hanging valley', and there is no way in which it could form were liquid water the only agent involved.

At the junction where one river joins another, and both flow through valleys they themselves have made, the beds of the two are at the same level. They must be, because each of them seeks the lowest ground, and

In a previous interglacial the sea level was higher than it is today. When the level fell, new beaches formed and the original beaches remained, above the new beach, as raised beaches. This one is in south-west England.

the lowest ground is found at the bed of the main stream. Glaciers also have tributaries, but they join the main stream at the top of the ice rather than the bottom, because the tributary has insufficient energy to displace or cut through the much larger mass of the main glacier — which it would need to do were it to join at the bottom. A river that flows into a glacier has even less power to move the huge mass of ice and, therefore, the tributary never has an opportunity to deepen its bed. Should the glacier retreat, vacating its valley, the tributary will be left 'in the air', entering high on the valley side. A hanging valley can occur only on the side of a main valley that was made by a glacier.

As its waters fall from the hanging valley, the river cuts its own channel deeper and deeper. Eventually it will make its own 'proper' valley and join the main stream like an ordinary tributary, at the valley bottom. That it has not yet achieved this can only be because it has had insufficient time to complete the process. That, in turn, suggests that not only was the valley made by a glacier, but that the glacier occupied it quite recently.

Solifluction

Should you visit and explore Dartmoor, in south-west England, there is further evidence for you to discover. Here and there you will see huge granite boulders, scattered on sloping ground, apparently at random. Study them more closely, however, and you will see that they look as though they have been halted as they were sliding down the slope — and this is precisely what did happen.

The process is called 'solifluction', and it has now ceased on Dartmoor, but there are other parts of the world where it continues — in landscapes where, below the surface, the soil is permanently frozen, as 'permafrost'. In summer, the warmth of the Sun thaws the surface. As the ice melts, the frozen soil turns into a layer of mud a few inches thick. The mud is very wet because of the amount of ice — and probably overlying snow — that has melted into it and because the solid permafrost below it prevents water draining vertically downwards, as it would do in ordinary soil. The drainage occurs as surface run-off, and the almost liquid mud slides down hillsides. Large, heavy objects, such as boulders, their bases lubricated by the mud, travel with it.

The movement is not rapid and before they have moved very far the winter returns, the ground freezes once more, and they are locked in the ice until their gentle slide is resumed the next summer. Solifluction can occur only where the seasonal thaw produces a thin layer of very wet mud. It is characteristic of permafrost conditions, and these are found only in very high latitudes, not far from the edge of the permanent ice that covers the lands of the polar regions.

Periglacial landscapes and refugia

On Dartmoor the process came to an end when the permafrost also thawed, allowing the ground to drain. The surface layer ceased to become fluid each summer, and the boulders ceased to move. They are too large, and the land is too poor, for it to have been worth the while of any farmer to clear them, and so there they remain to this day, in what is called a 'periglacial' (meaning 'around a glacier') landscape. They demonstrate that once, not so long ago perhaps, Dartmoor lay close to the edge of the polar ice sheet. Dartmoor is not unique in this respect, but, because its granite tends to fracture into large blocks, its evidence is particularly well displayed.

There are also 'refugia', small, usually isolated areas where the plant life is typical of a climate different from that of the region as a whole. In parts of Europe there are pockets of this kind, often in the highlands, where some of the plants are more typical of tundra. Elsewhere, there are isolated plant communities typical of much warmer climates. Some plants which grow in sheltered parts of southern Ireland and the Lizard Peninsula of Cornwall in south-west Britain, for example, form a community that is found nowhere else north of Portugal. It is difficult to see how such communities can have developed in isolation, but their presence can be explained if their isolation has allowed them to survive from a time when they were much more widespread — a time when the climate was much colder or warmer than it is now.

The evidence for glaciers

The first person to draw widespread attention to evidence of this kind was the Swiss-born geologist Louis Agassiz (1807-73). He recognized that certain glaciers in his native Switzerland had once extended much further down their valleys. We know now that glaciers leave many traces because of the manner by which they disappear. We are used to ice melting — on ponds and rivers in spring, for example — and so it is tempting to suppose that a glacier shrinks in the same way, simply by turning into water. This is not quite what happens. The ice does melt, of course, but only at its lower margin, where conditions are at their warmest, and it ceases to advance beyond that point. Little by little, increasing warmth may erode it further. It does not melt all at once, but diminishes slowly — its lower edge retreats, quite gently.

At its lower edge, a glacier usually has a 'snout'. This is a kind of upturned bulge where the ice presses against the load of material it pushes ahead of itself. When the glacier retreats, the debris at the snout is left behind, and an experienced geographer can easily recognize it for what it is.

Agassiz published his findings in 1837, and in 1840 he visited Scotland, where he found further evidence of a glacial past. In 1846 he moved to the United States, to become Professor of Geology and Zoology at Harvard University, where he made further studies, but not before, in the year he arrived in the country, he had delivered a series of public lectures in Boston. These popularized his ideas and aroused a storm of controversy, because the 'orthodox' view of the day was that the deposits and landscapes Agassiz examined were the result of the Biblical flood. It was 30 years before his 'glacial theory' was fully accepted by scientists.

Agassiz was also a zoologist — he founded the Museum of Comparative Zoology at Harvard (in 1859) — and the distribution of animals provides further evidence in his support. Consider, for example, stoats and weasels. They are close relatives and widely distributed, but weasels do not occur naturally in Ireland. Ireland has stoats, but no weasels. Nor are any snakes native to Ireland. All these animals are able to swim, but none is capable of crossing the Irish Sea. They can have reached Ireland only by land. This suggests there was a time when mainland Britain and Ireland were joined — and also that Britain was joined to the mainland of Europe, for all the British animals, apart from those which fly, must have travelled overland. Stoats, it would seem, travelled ahead of the weasels. They

During the ice ages, the western isles of Scotland were joined to the mainland, rising as hills above the low-lying ground.

reached Ireland. The weasels reached Britain but, by the time they had extended their range to its western coasts, the link with Ireland had disappeared beneath the sea. The most likely explanation, and the one accepted by modern scientists, is that a rise in the sea level inundated what had been a bridge. A similar bridge, which once linked Asia and Alaska across the Bering Strait, allowed many species, including humans, to migrate between what are now separate continents. It, too, disappeared as the sea level rose.

Formation of ice sheets

An ice sheet forms by the accumulation of snow, and not by the freezing of water at the surface. As snow falls on top of snow, the weight gradually compresses the lower layers until the loose crystals are packed together tightly to make solid ice. The process is similar to that by which sediments begin to

Glaciers, like this one in Antarctica, have helped shape the landscape over much of the northern hemisphere.

be converted into sedimentary rock — and quite unlike the process by which we freeze water to make ice in a refrigerator. Today, the largest ice sheets are in Antarctica, and they contain about 90 per cent of all the ice in the world. The ice sheets are not continuous, and there are ice-free areas, but the average thickness of the ice is about 6900 feet (2.1 km), and its total volume is about 7.2 million cubic miles (30 million cu km). Were all of that ice to melt, the sea level

throughout the world would rise by some 250 feet (76 m). At various times in the past, the Antarctic ice sheets are estimated to have been 1000 to 2000 feet (300-600 m) thicker than they are now. The only substantial ice sheet in the northern hemisphere is that which covers about 85 per cent of the land area of Greenland. With a total area of just over 708,000 square miles (1.8 million sq km), and an average thickness of about 5000 feet (1525 m) it represents a volume of about 670,500 cubic miles (2.8 million cu km) of water. Large though it is, its melting would have only a minor effect on sea levels.

Although ice is clearly a solid, when it exists on this scale the pressures, to which its own weight subject it, cause it to behave like a very viscous liquid. It can be squeezed from the base of the sheet into any suitable rock fissure, and where it is squeezed into a structure that can be made into a valley, it becomes a moving glacier. The glaciers of Greenland flow to the sea, like rivers, where the ice melts or breaks off in large pieces — icebergs. Glaciers flow slowly, but some of those in Greenland move at up to 100 feet (30.5 m) in 24 hours, which is considered very fast — at 0.8 inches (22 mm) per minute, the ice moves at about the same speed as the tip of the minute hand on a clock that has a face about 16 inches (40 cm) in diameter.

When you see around you the evidence of former ice sheets, and wonder what the countryside looked like under glacial conditions, modern Greenland is an excellent example. Europe and Asia, to about as far south as Prague, once lay beneath the Siberian ice sheet, and North America, south to about St Louis, lay beneath the Laurentide ice sheet. These lands looked as Greenland looks today, with ice 5000 feet (1525 m) thick — and there is reason to suppose that in some places it was twice that thickness. The regions bordering the ice sheets to the south supported only tundra vegetation. Still further south lay great coniferous forests, like those of modern Canada and Scandinavia. The ice sheets of the southern hemisphere were also much larger once than they are now, although their expansion was smaller than that which occurred in the northern hemisphere.

The formation of an ice sheet involves the removal of water from the oceans, by evaporation, and its precipitation as snow.

Once precipitated, it accumulates because its rate of return to the ocean and atmosphere is much slower than the rate at which it is delivered. Some does return to the ocean, by the melting or 'calving' of glaciers to produce icebergs, and to the atmosphere, by 'ablation', the evaporation of surface ice melted by solar warmth, or by its direct change from the solid to gaseous phase (called 'sublimation'). The steady transport of water from the ocean to the ice sheet causes the sea level to fall. When the ice sheet melts, the water returns to the oceans and the sea level rises again. The theory explaining the process is called 'glacioeustasy'. A major episode of this kind may alter the sea level by up to 330 feet (100 m).

This is a fairly rapid process, in the sense that the sea level responds at once to the removal or addition of water, but there is a second process at work, called 'glacioisostasy', which is much slower and has an opposite effect. The weight of a large ice sheet depresses that part of the lithosphere on which it rests, so that while the removal of water from the oceans causes the sea level to fall everywhere, the land beneath the ice is sinking. This will not be immediately evident, because the thickness of the ice is growing, raising its surface, but its effects are felt when the ice finally melts, because then, fairly slowly, the land rises again, eventually to its former level. It is estimated that Scandinavia sank by about 3300 feet (1000 m) under the weight of its ice sheet and since the ice melted it has risen by about 1700 feet (520 m). It is still rising, and so is Scotland.

In high latitudes, where snow falls every winter and melts for a short time every summer, a slight fall in summer temperatures might prevent the seasonal thaw. Were this to happen, the snow from one winter would persist until the next. Freshly fallen snow has a high albedo — it reflects almost all of the sunlight falling on it. This allows it to absorb little warmth, so it tends to endure, and by chilling the air in contact with it, the air temperature is reduced around its margins, so it tends to spread. Under these conditions snow would accumulate, and a continuation of the process would lead to the formation of an ice sheet. This is what is believed to happen at the onset of an 'ice age', and many scientists believe it can happen rapidly once it begins because of the strong element of positive feedback — where each step encourages the next. It has been suggested, by supporters of

During ice ages, tundra landscapes, like this one in Norway, occurred widely across central Europe and North America.

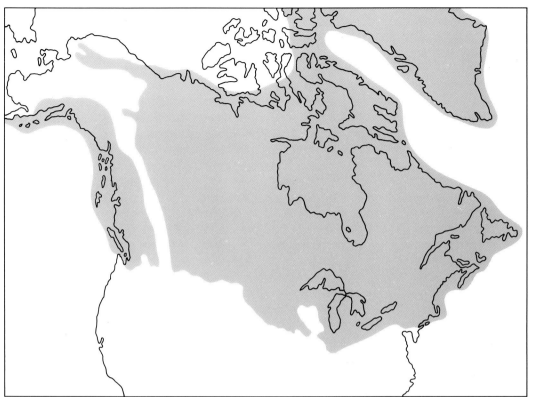

During the most recent (Wisconsinian) glaciation, permanent ice covered almost all of North America north of the Great Lakes, although, for some of the time, a belt of ice-free tundra may have extended along the eastern side of the Rockies and over most of Alaska. The climatic vegetation zones were shifted southwards.

century might be needed for a full-blown ice age to take the place of conditions like those we enjoy today.

The Pleistocene Epoch

The recognition that the polar ice sheets had once extended, and later retreated, was followed by the dating of these events. The period during which they occurred was named the Pleistocene Epoch. It began about two million years ago (although this date may need to be revised in the light of more recent discoveries), and ended about 10,000 years ago. It was followed by the Holocene, or Recent, Epoch in which we live today.

The names may suggest that for almost two million years substantial parts of Europe, Asia and North America lay buried deep and silent, sleeping beneath the ice, and that the ice has now departed for ever from all but the polar regions. Excavations for the foundations of new buildings in London revealed more information, however, and information that confuses so simple a picture.

The ground beneath Trafalgar Square in London, is made mainly from ancient deposits left by the River Thames, whose course subsequently shifted to the south. These deposits were found to contain remains of plants which no longer grow so

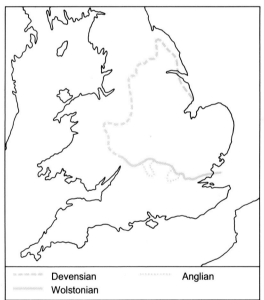

| - - - - - Devensian | .... Anglian |
| ――――― Wolstonian | |

The edges of the ice sheets in Britain during the three most recent ice ages: the Anglian (or Mindel or Elsterian), Wolstonian (or Riss or Saalian) and Devensian (or Weichselian or Würm).

far north. There was *Trapa natans*, for example, which is the water chestnut (not the same as the Chinese water chestnut, but edible), and *Acer monspessulanum*, the Montpellier maple, neither of which now grows any further north than central and southern Europe.

If these discoveries were startling, the animal remains were even more so. They included hippopotamus, rhinoceros, and a species of large elephant that is now extinct — animals that live today in climates much warmer than London can offer. The remains

During part of the Ipswichian Interglacial, the area around what is now Trafalgar Square, London, was inhabited by animals, including large cats and elephants, that are typical of a warm climate.

were dated as being about 100,000 years old. This made them older than some glacial features, but younger than others.

It was evidence of this kind that supplied the proof that during the Pleistocene there was not one, single glacial episode, or 'ice age', but several, and they were interrupted by much warmer periods, called 'interglacials'. The interglacial in which these tropical remains were discovered is known in Britain as the Trafalgar Square, or

more usually (because of other deposits found in East Anglia) the Ipswichian Interglacial.

Temperatures during the Ipswichian must have been higher than those of today if hippopotamus, rhinoceros and elephants could thrive in what is now central London. In fact, the average summer was probably 3.5 to 5.5 °F (2-3 °C) warmer. This is not much different from the temperature increase which is forecast for the end of the next century as a result of the 'greenhouse effect', so our meddling with the climate may benefit certain endangered species!

The ice ages which marked the beginning of the Pleistocene were not the first the world has experienced, although they followed a long ice-free period, which lasted more than 240 million years. There is some evidence of an ice age about 2300 million years ago in what are now North America, South Africa and Australia. There were more ice ages between about 950 and 615 million years ago affecting Africa, Australia and Europe, and about 440 million years ago an ice age affected what is now North Africa. There was widespread glaciation in India and much of the southern hemisphere around 250 million years ago, during what was probably the last ice age until the Pleistocene.

The two million years of the Pleistocene, then, comprise not one uninterrupted ice age but a sequence, in which the ice advanced and then retreated several times. The advances and retreats are named, with names derived from those of the places where traces of them have been found. Unfortunately, this has produced different names, in different parts of the world, for what may have been the same events.

In North America, there were four Pleistocene ice ages and three interglacials, all of them named after places in the upper valley of the Mississippi River. The earliest glaciation is called the Nebraskan. It ended about 1.3 million years ago and was followed by the Aftonian Interglacial. About 900,000 years ago this gave way to the Kansan Glacial, less extreme than the Nebraskan although it extended further south. The Kansan lasted until about 700,000 years ago, and was followed by the Yarmouth Interglacial. About 550,000 years ago the Illinoian Glacial began, when ice advanced from the north-east and average temperatures were 3.5 to 5.5 °F (2-3 °C) cooler than they are today. The Sangamon Interglacial followed, some 400,000 years ago, and was followed by the final, Wisconsinian, Glaciation, which began about 80,000 years ago and ended about 10,000 years ago. It was a cold time, when average temperatures were about 11 °F (6 °C) lower than they are now.

There were five glaciations in Europe. The Donau occurred at the beginning of the Pleistocene and is probably equivalent to the North American Nebraskan. It gave way to the Donau-Günz Interglacial and was followed by the Günz Glaciation, which began about 900,000 years ago and lasted about 100,000 years, and which may be the equivalent of the Kansan. The Günz is a river in the European Alps, and further north this ice age is known as the Menapian. It was followed by the Günz-Mindel (the Mindel is another Alpine river) Interglacial, known as the Cromerian (after Cromer, England) in northern Europe, which lasted from about 800,000 to about 500,000 years ago. The Mindel Glaciation, known in northern Europe as the Elsterian and in Britain as the Anglian, followed it, from about 500,000 to about 300,000 years ago. The Mindel-Riss (the Riss, too, is an Alpine river), or Great, Interglacial followed, from about 300,000 to 250,000 years ago. It is known as the Holsteinian in northern Europe and the Hoxnian in Britain — a time when the sea level along the Sussex coast was 100 feet (30 m) higher than it is today. It was followed by the Riss Glaciation, known as the Saalian in northern Europe and the Wolstonian in Britain, which lasted from about 250,000 to 100,000 years ago. The Mindel and Riss, together, may be equivalent to the Illinoian of North America. The Riss was followed by the Ipswichian, or Last, Interglacial, named after the English town of Ipswich (but also called the Trafalgar Square Interglacial), and known elsewhere in north-west Europe as the Eemian. It lasted from about 100,000 to about 70,000 years ago, and was followed by the most recent ice age, known in Britain as the Devensian, in northern Europe as the Weichselian, and in the Alps as the Würm. It is approximately equivalent to the North American Wisconsinian. The last 10,000 years are known as the Flandrian Interglacial, in which we are still living today.

It was during the Ipswichian that the hippopotamuses wallowed in Trafalgar Square, and humans were also living in the area at that time. Humans probably came and went as the climate changed, but those early Londoners were certainly not the first human inhabitants of Britain.

The earliest evidence of human occupation in Britain dates from the Hoxnian, named after Hoxne, near Diss in Suffolk. In 1797, John Frere presented a paper to the Royal Society of London in which he described tools that had been found at

Hoxne, about 12 feet (3.7 m) below the surface, in pits dug to obtain clay for brick-making. The tools were clearly of great age, and Frere suggested they were made by people with no knowledge of how to make metal tools. Similar tools have also been found at Clacton-on-Sea, and other sites. They may well be the oldest tools in Britain and are attributed to the Lower Palaeolithic Acheulian culture. The Acheulian industrialists left traces of their tool-making in many parts of the world. What is especially interesting about them is that, although they were undoubtedly humans, they were not modern *Homo sapiens*, but their ancestors, *Homo erectus*.

Glacials and interglacials

The glaciations varied in their extent. During the most recent, the Devensian, the ice sheet covered Britain approximately to a line linking the Thames and Severn valleys and, in the United States, the Wisconsinian ice sheet came as far as southern Indiana and Illinois. Complicated though it may seem, even this picture of glaciations and interglacials simplifies greatly what really happened, for during those long periods, lasting tens or hundreds of thousands of years, there were relatively warmer episodes, called 'interstadials', which interrupted glaciations and lasted a few centuries. These were briefer than a full interglacial, and probably cooler, but during some of them conditions were markedly warmer than they are now.

There were also cooler episodes. As the Devensian Glaciation was ending, and the glaciers retreating, north-west Europe was plunged almost into ice-age conditions for about 1000 years. Then the climate began to warm again, but only to regress into a second cold period, for another 1000 years. These two cold periods are known as the Older Dryas and Younger Dryas because they were identified by the discovery of the pollen of mountain avens (*Dryas octopetala*), a small alpine herb, in regions that are now much too warm for it.

No one can be sure just why the two Dryas episodes happened, but almost certainly they were caused by changes in the Atlantic. One theory holds that the rapid melting of the ice released vast quantities of fresh water. This flowed into the sea in high latitudes and, because there was so much, it took some time for it to mix with the sea water. It was carried south, floating on the sea, until it covered a large area in the North Atlantic. Then, one rather cold winter, it froze — fresh water freezing at a higher temperature than sea water. This chilled the air crossing the ocean and triggered the general fall in European temperatures. Alternatively, the retreat of the margin of sea ice altered, or even inhibited for a time, the formation of Atlantic Bottom Water. This, in turn, altered the track of the North Atlantic Drift, and north-western Europe lost its warm coastal current. Whatever the explanation, it is an undoubted fact that, probably because of its effect on the ocean, a very rapid climatic warming twice induced long periods of intensely cold conditions. Perhaps this should temper the confidence with which we predict the climate resulting from a possible 'greenhouse' warming.

What was once believed to be a single great ice age is now known to have been a complicated cycle of cold and warm periods, the transitions from one to another triggered by quite small changes in the average temperature. We live now in the Flandrian Interglacial, whose name suggests it is but another episode and that, one day, the ice will return. This, indeed, is what scientists believe will happen, and some maintain that the next ice age, predicted to be a relatively minor one, but an ice age for all that, may begin at any time.

It was a Yugoslavian physicist and mathematician, Milutin Milankovich (1879-1958), who discovered a close correspondence between ice ages, interglacials, and cyclical changes in the amount of solar radiation reaching the Earth. These are due to certain characteristics of the planet's rotation and orbit. The Earth's axis is tilted — because of the gravitational attraction of the Moon — but the angle of tilt varies over a cycle lasting about 42,000 years, which causes the dates of the equinoxes to change over a cycle of 21,000 years, and the distance between the Earth and Sun at their closest varies over a cycle of 95,000 years. Taken together, Milankovich calculated that, from time to time during these cycles, solar radiation was at a minimum, and found that these minima coincided with the onset of ice ages. At present the Earth is close to the position in this complex of cycles which, in the past, it has occupied at the commencement of a glaciation.

THE USES OF WATER

Some scientists believe that at one stage in human evolution our ancestors were semi-aquatic. They lived beside water — rivers, lakes, or the sea — and spent a great deal of time in the water seeking the fish and shellfish that formed a major part of their diet. This, the scientists maintain, explains such features as our almost complete lack of body hair and the thick layer of insulating fat just below our skins, as well as the ease with which young children learn to swim. These are characteristics we do not share with the other primates to which we are closely related — the chimpanzees and gorillas — but they are possessed by aquatic mammals, such as seals.

The idea is controversial, and most biologists reject it, but there is no doubt that humans show a preference for living close to water. A glance at a map is enough to demonstrate how many of our major cities lie beside rivers or a sea coast. Water is essential to life, of course, but it is perfectly possible to obtain enough for our biological needs from natural springs, or by conserving rain water.

A more obvious explanation refers to our social, rather than biological, needs. We live as members of societies and each human society is in contact with its neighbours. Very early in our history such contacts brought the realization that most societies produce surpluses of some goods, are deficient in others, and that trade is possible. People made encampments beside rivers partly to drink from their waters and to wash in them, and partly to fish them, but mainly to ride on them. It was from this need for communication that some of the riverside encampments grew into villages, then towns, and eventually into great cities.

At a time when pack animals and foot travellers could move overland only by roads and paths that led them slowly through dense forest, across deserts, or over mountain passes, over territory that was often dangerous physically or because of the risk of attack by robbers, river journeys were to be preferred. Though not without risk, river travel was generally safer and certainly less arduous than land travel.

Life on a river bank is not always secure, however, for the river may flood, and floods provide a recurring theme in the ancient myths of many peoples. A flood is often used as an instrument of divine retribution against people who offend. Zeus once inundated Greece as a punishment, for example, sending floods from which a few people escaped by climbing to mountain tops. A king, Deucalion survived, and saved his queen, Pyrrha, by building an ark — the gods had given advance warning.

The story of the Biblical flood — another punishment — is based on a tradition from the eighth century BC, but the story was already ancient. The earliest of many accounts of it was written in Sumerian, probably more than 4000 years ago, and geological evidence suggests it may recall a particularly devastating flood of the Tigris and Euphrates, rivers which occasionally cause serious flooding to this day.

If the flood is a recurring theme, so is the ark by which one particularly favoured individual is permitted to escape, taking his (it is always a male) family and possessions with him. The ark, of course, was a boat, and its occurrence in such ancient myths demonstrates the antiquity of this means of transport.

Transport by water

Once people were living beside rivers and lakes it was inevitable that they would discover ways to travel on the surface of the water. All it required was the imagination and technical ingenuity to transform plant material, like that which could be seen every day floating downstream, into a craft that would carry a human occupant without sinking or turning upside-down. The boat was invented not once but countless times, in every part of the inhabited world.

The technology called for the barest minimum of tools, and a wide range of building materials was available. In parts of Africa and the Middle East there were extensive reed swamps, and so reeds were used — and still are, in a few places. Apart from the skill derived from experience, all you need to build a reed boat is a knife — and a flint-bladed one is perfectly adequate — and a plentiful supply of tall reeds. The reeds are cut with the knife, stacked to dry, and then tied into tight bundles. The

Where reeds grow abundantly they have been used for thousands of years for making boats. These reed boats are on the shore of Lake Titicaca, Peru.

bundles are lashed together securely into the required shape, the ends trimmed and tucked inside, and the boat will float. Indeed, if it has been well made, such a boat is capable of long journeys, and it can be built large enough to carry a useful amount of cargo.

The need is for a vessel that floats, and plant material is not the only possible source. Inflatable dinghies were developed primarily for emergency use and modern versions serve as inshore lifeboats, but some of the earliest boats were inflatables, made from animal skins, sometimes of several fastened together.

Reeds and animal skins are not the raw materials of first choice, and boats made from them are found only in parts of the world where trees are scarce. Wood is much

stronger, no less buoyant and, where it is available, it is likely to be plentiful and easily obtained by people accustomed to clearing forests to provide pasture or crop land. Wooden boats may well have begun their history as rafts.

Made from logs lashed or pegged together, wooden rafts are clumsy, but capable of improvement. Fitted with a shaped bow and a centreboard for better control, and a raised cabin to hold passengers or cargo well clear of the water, they can be comfortable and efficient. Rafts of this kind survived into modern times in parts of Brazil and Sri Lanka — and until quite recently in the timber-producing regions of North America, where logs were floated by river from the forest to the sawmills with a supervisor, there to look out for and try to clear log

out the brittle charcoal and cinders. The technique sounds crude, but skilled workers can produce a finished craft that is elegant, efficient, and sometimes large. The American Museum of Natural History in New York has a Canadian canoe that is 63 feet (19 m) long, more than 8 feet (2.4 m) wide, and 5 feet (1.5 m) deep, made from a single tree trunk. Where trees grow tall but slender, a simple dugout may prove unstable. It can be made safer by adding an outrigger, or by linking two dugouts to make a single, twin-hulled canoe — the catamaran.

It may be that a relic of the dugout survives in modern vessels. When tools were available for making planks, these were added to raise the sides of the canoe and so provide more space. As the sides grew higher, a frame was devised to support them, and the dugout was progressively reduced until it formed no more than the centre of the keel. If this accounts for one strand in the evolution of modern boats, however, a convergent strand ran in parallel to it, for the dugout was but one of two methods for building a canoe.

For many people, the word 'canoe' conjures up a picture of either the open craft of the North American Indians or the Eskimo hunting boat, the 'kayak'. Modern canoes are descended from both, for they share a common method of construction. They are made from a frame covered with a skin. The main members of the frame are curved, giving them resilience and, therefore, great strength in relation to their weight, and they are light enough to be carried overland.

In Polynesia, the traditional vessel is narrow-hulled and uses an outrigger for stability. These boats are beside Lake Taal, Philippines.

jams, who sailed on a raft with a cabin. As a means of transport, the method may have been slow, but it cost nothing and used no fuel.

Canoes and kayaks

The dugout canoe was developed along the banks of many rivers, perhaps as an improvement on the raft. A 'canoe' is usually defined as a boat which is pointed at both ends and is propelled by paddles, rather than oars, the difference being that oars are pivoted on a fulcrum (the rowlock) and paddles are not. More elaborate boats and ships are believed to have evolved from canoes.

The dugout is made by hollowing out a single log, often by carefully burning away the wood, a little at a time, then chipping

(Opposite) Smaller waterways have found new, recreational uses. Canal boats, of a traditional design, are hired by holidaymakers. This scene is on the Trent and Mersey Canal, England.

The coracle, or currach, made from waterproof fabric stretched over a frame, is a substantial and reliable craft. This one is Irish.

A canoe is open, and propelled by single-bladed paddles, the kayak has a deck, with a cockpit in which its occupant sits, and is propelled by a double-bladed paddle.

The birchbark canoe, as its name suggests, was covered with the bark of *Betula papyrifera*, the canoe or paper birch, which was chosen because it is very waterproof. This is a North American species, different from the silver or European birch. The bark was softened and then stretched very tightly over thin planks so as to hold them firmly against the ribs forming the frame, the whole structure being locked together by the gunwale. Eskimos used the same technique, but with animal skins rather than bark. The birchbark canoe was still being used early in this century, but gradually the bark skin was replaced by one made from canvas. The basic frame design for most traditional craft of this type is very similar to that of early planked boats — overlapping planks are easily fixed to a frame designed for a different covering — which suggests an evolutionary link between such framed canoes and more advanced vessels. The

popularity of the modern sport of canoeing began more than a century ago in Britain, after the Scottish traveller John MacGregor wrote describing his journeys in a kayak of his own design he called the *Rob Roy*.

Canvas, planking, plywood, fibreglass, rubberized cloth, and plastic are just some of the materials from which canoe skins have been made. Canoe-making is now an industry of substantial size, and the original birchbark canoe and kayak must be the most successful boat designs the world has ever seen.

The early development of such vessels was not confined to North America. Celtic peoples also made them in the British Isles, and they are still used in some places, especially in Ireland. In Wales such a craft is known as a 'coracle', in Ireland as a 'currach' or 'curragh', but these are merely variants of the Celtic word for 'boat'. The frame is made from wicker, and canvas has replaced animal skins once used for the covering. Apart from its economical use of materials, a coracle, like a birchbark canoe, is light. It is easily carried from the water and so it

requires no permanent berth, far less a harbour.

Early exploitation of inland waters

It was among the great civilizations of the world that inland waters were exploited fully — and not only for serious business, for the modern floating restaurant and bar has an ancestry no less distinguished than the inflatable and the canoe. In the late thirteenth century, Marco Polo visited Hangchow — the city he knew as Kinsai. He reported that on the southern side of the town there was a large lake, and on its shores and on two islands there were splendid houses, palaces and monasteries. 'The lake', he wrote, 'is provided with a great number of boats or barges, big and small, in which people take pleasure-trips for the sake of recreation. These will hold ten, fifteen, twenty, or more persons, as they range from fifteen to twenty paces in length and are flat-bottomed and broad in the beam, so as to float without rocking.' He went on to explain that the boats were equipped with everything needed for a party. Passengers sat below deck, in sumptuous surroundings, and were propelled by poles worked by men standing on the deck. 'Indeed a voyage on this lake offers more refreshment and delectation than any other experience on earth.'

In modern times, the increasing use of rivers and canals for recreation and pleasure should delight a modern Marco Polo. He would marvel at the American riverboats, and might enjoy a package-holiday trip along the Rhine or Danube. No doubt the wealthy lakeshore residents of Hangchow had more than a passing interest in the serious business of commerce, and commerce made much use of less glamorous barges, plying the great rivers. A difficulty with river transport, of course, is that although the river may provide communication for those living close to its shores, it is isolated from similar communities living beside other rivers which drain other basins. River water had been used to irrigate crops since soon after the introduction of farming, and it was usually carried by means of canals, dug for the purpose. Sooner or later someone was bound to propose the linking of two rivers, or even seas, by canals that were like irrigation canals, only large enough to be used by cargo vessels.

Chinese canals

The earliest Chinese canal may have been the Ling Ch'ü, in Kwangsi, built in the third century BC. Another, linking the old capital, Sian (Hsi-an), with the Yellow River (Hwang Ho) was built in 133 BC and, by the time of Marco Polo's visit, sections of the Yün Ho (Grand Canal) had been in use for some 500 years. The Yün Ho linked the Yellow, Yangtze and Hai rivers.

Ancient though they are, these were far from being the first navigable canals in the world. Nearly 4000 years ago, the Egyptians, perhaps during the reign of the pharaoh Sesostris I, linked the River Nile to the Red Sea at a point somewhere close to Suez. This first Suez Canal fell into disrepair. Restoration began around 600 BC and was completed during the reign of King Darius the Great of Persia (522-486 BC) when Egypt became part of his empire. The freshwater canal continued to be used, abandoned, and restored again for centuries under Egyptian, Roman and Arab rulers. The Arabs used it mainly to transport grain from the farms along the Nile to Mecca. Eventually it was blocked permanently, for military reasons, in the eighth century AD, by the Arab Caliph Al-Mansur. More recently, but still long before the time of Marco Polo, the Romans built canals in various parts of their empire, and many canals were built in the Middle Ages, in Europe but also in India.

Anyone who attempts to link the waters of two rivers is likely to face a further difficulty. The rivers are usually at different levels. Simply link them and water will flow freely from the higher to the lower, flooding the lower ground and making the upper river into a tributary of the lower. This sometimes happens naturally, where two river channels are separated by soft, easily eroded ground. Appropriately enough, the process is called 'river capture'. The Chinese found a solution to the problem, and were the first people to use locks. The invention of locks made it possible to build much longer canals, including most of the great canal systems that played such an important part in the industrial development of Europe, and that are still in use today.

Canal locks

The canal which is to link two bodies of water at different levels is built as a series of terraces, with a 'step' between each level section and the next. At each of these steps, two watertight barriers are constructed, one at the edge of the upper side, the other in the lower section at a distance far enough apart to accommodate one vessel between the barriers. Both barriers can be opened and closed independently of one another. As a vessel approaches the lock, the barrier nearest to it is opened and the other is closed. The vessel enters and the barrier behind it is closed, so it floats in a pool of water isolated from both sections of canal. The barrier ahead of it is then partly opened, allowing water to flow at a controlled rate into or from the pool, depending on whether the open barrier is on the upper or lower side. The vessel floats up or down until the water level is equal on either side of the partly open barrier, then the barrier is opened fully and the vessel can continue its journey at the new level. Obviously, the method constantly transfers water from the upper level to the lower, but it does so in a controlled fashion and reduces, to a minimum, the amount of water involved. Some locks incorporate ponds into which some of the lock water drains and which can be returned to the lock, and in some places water is pumped from a lower to a higher level. Lifts are also used in some canals, in which the entire container of water and vessel is raised or lowered and no water is lost.

Linking major rivers

The installation of locks made it possible to establish major links between rivers. In 1642, for example, the Briare Canal was completed. It was 34 miles (55 km) long and linked the Loire and the Seine. In addition to this, engineers were now able to incorporate stretches of natural rivers into waterway systems linking sea ports. The Languedoc Canal from the coast to the River Garonne, built between 1666 and 1681, provided a route from the Mediterranean to the Atlantic coast, on the Bay of Biscay. Until then, ships had to sail all the way around the Iberian Peninsula.

It is one thing to build a canal that opens into the almost tideless Mediterranean, but it is rather more difficult to design one that is connected directly to a sea with a large tidal range, because the locks must accommodate the changing water levels caused by tidal movements. The solution is to use the mean high-tide level as a datum. This provides the level for which the lowest stretch of the canal is designed, and its locks can be opened to the sea only at high tide. Further inland, locks can be used to regulate the water level, so the tidal influence is removed. This ability to compensate for the effect of tidal movements made it possible for sea-going ships to deliver their cargoes directly to the inland cities where they were needed, and major ports, with warehousing, and dry dock and ship-repairing facilities, could be developed away from the coast and close to manufacturing centres. One of the first cities to benefit was Manchester. The Manchester Ship Canal, opened in 1894, provided 36 miles (58 km) of navigable waterway to Eastham, on the south bank of the estuary of the River Mersey. Cargoes intended for destinations further inland could be transferred to canal barges, and continue their journey along the Bridgewater Canal to Worsley — opened in 1761 — and from there to the River Trent, near Burton-on-Trent, along the Trent and Mersey Canal, and from Burton-on-Trent along the Staffordshire and Worcestershire Canal to Stourport, on the River Severn — and the Severn flows to Bristol, along the coast of South Wales — not far from the coalfields, and so into the Atlantic. Nor was it only cargoes that were carried. The inland waterways retained their traditional role, and continued to transport passengers until the establishment of the rail networks offered a faster service.

Rivers drain basins that are separated by hills. This elementary geographical fact presented a fresh challenge to the engineers designing long-distance canals, for a canal linking two adjacent drainage basins had to cross hills and valleys. Tunnels were excavated through hills and architecturally splendid aqueducts strode over valleys. Today, canal barges are powered by their own engines, but for many years they were drawn by horses, moving at a leisurely pace along the towpath. The towpath usually ended at the entrance to a tunnel, and the barge was propelled by its crew, lying on their backs and 'walking' along the tunnel roof.

Britain enjoyed a 'canal boom', a period during which investment in a canal company was safe and certain to bring good dividends. By the time the boom ended, around 1830, the country had some 4250 miles (6840 km) of navigable waterways.

The achievement was impressive, but geographically limited, for Britain has few navigable rivers. The navigable inland waterway system on the continent of Europe is much more extensive, and many of the canals themselves are much wider and deeper, so they can accommodate much larger barges. The principal rivers are connected to one another, and it is possible to sail from the North Sea or Baltic to the Adriatic or Mediterranean, from Le Havre to Prague, and from Amsterdam to Venice — two cities on opposite sides of the continent, both built around canals, and linked by water.

North America is well supplied with large, navigable rivers augmented by stretches of rivers that have been made navigable by 'canalization' — the installation of weirs or locks to regulate the water flow, or the construction of canals to by-pass difficult stretches of river. These are mainly in the United States, which has almost 29,000 miles (46,670 km) of navigable inland waterways, but some of the longest canals are in Canada. The Trent Canal, from Trenton on the shores of Lake Ontario to Georgian Bay on Lake Huron, is 275.5 miles (443 km) long.

In Britain, and to a lesser extent in the United States, canal systems declined as the railway networks expanded — in Britain because the railway companies bought up the canal companies and closed the canals. Elsewhere, the canals survived and new canals continued to be built. The Trent Canal was opened in 1918, for example, and the much more important St Lawrence Seaway, linking the St Lawrence River and the Great Lakes, was completed as recently as 1959. It allows ocean-going ships to sail as far as the southern shores of Lake Michigan — with access to Detroit and Chicago — and to the eastern end of Lake Superior, where they are 1370 miles (2200 km) from the Atlantic.

Suez and Panama Canals

The world's most famous canals are the Suez and Panama, both of which link seas and both of which were built at immense financial and human cost. The advantages were always obvious of a link between the Gulf of Suez on the Red Sea and the Mediterranean, and a Suez Canal had existed in the past, but the story of the modern Canal began with surveys conducted during the

Napoleonic occupation of Egypt. The idea was abandoned for some years because surveying errors made it seem impractical. The actual building of the Canal began in 1859. It was estimated to take six years, but took 10, and to cost F200 million, but cost F433 million. At one stage 25,000 Egyptian labourers were employed in the excavation. The Suez Canal is 101 miles (162.5 km) long, 179 feet (55 m) wide at its narrowest, and nowhere is the shipping channel less than 40 feet (12 m) deep at low tide.

It was a French diplomat, Ferdinand, Vicomte de Lesseps (1805-94) who inspired and drove the Suez Canal project and at the age of 74, with the Canal now open, he turned his attention to Central America, and the possibility of a link between the Atlantic and Pacific. In 1879, he proposed a sea-level canal across the isthmus at Panama, but the political complications of the task delayed the commencement of the work until 1904. At first, conditions were appalling and workers were provided with no proper accommodation or sanitation. The chief engineer resigned in 1905 and was replaced by John F. Stevens. Stevens had vast experience of large projects, having built and managed railroads in the Rocky Mountains and mines in Minnesota, and he understood well the ecological risks entailed in cutting a major canal through mountainous terrain. He improved working conditions, and also changed the plans. It was decided that the Canal should cross at high level, connecting natural rivers and lakes by a system of locks. The completed Canal runs from the northwest to the south-east, a distance of 40.27 miles (64.79 km) from shore to shore, and at Gatun Lake it is 85 feet (25.9 m) above sea level. The waterway was opened to shipping in 1914.

At the time the Suez and Panama Canals were built there was little concern about the possible environmental consequences of connecting the waters of two seas. There has been some migration between the Red Sea and Mediterranean, of species that can tolerate a passage through the freshwater sections, but the much greater possible hazard, of allowing migration between the tropical Pacific and Atlantic, was avoided. The high-level route, with its locks and the use of rivers and lakes, preserves the isolation of the two oceans and there is no migration between them.

(Opposite, top) Major waterways, such as the Rhine, are still of great commercial importance for the transport of goods. (Opposite, bottom) The traditional way of moving logs from forest to sawmill is to roll them into a river and let them float with the current. These logs are being rafted in Finland.

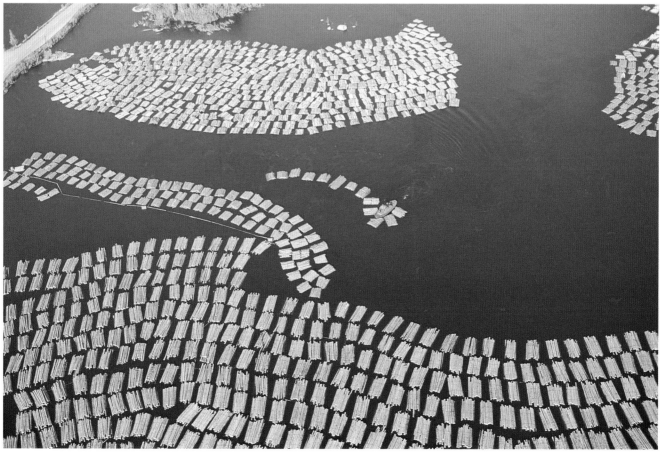

Greek triremes

A few years ago, a team of enthusiasts set about reconstructing a Greek warship that was known only from a few illustrations and references in ancient texts. Long and sleek, in its day it was the fastest vessel on the high seas. It carried a sail but was not dependent on it, for its power was provided by the three banks of oarsmen that gave this type of ship its name — a trireme. Its bow was extended to a projecting point at the water line and plated with metal to form a battering ram, so that any ship it attacked could be charged and holed so that it took in water and sank. Two and a half thousand years ago, when it plied the Mediterranean and Aegean, no rival could out-run it, and its appearance over the horizon must have struck terror into the crew of any ship the trireme captain considered hostile.

When eventually the reconstruction was completed and their crews learned, by trial and error, how to sail them, the new triremes — several were built — were found to be extremely sophisticated and capable of sustaining a high speed over quite long distances. In due course, the triremes were commissioned into the Greek navy.

The *Argo* — the name means 'the swift' — in which Jason and his band of heroes sailed through the dangerous waters of the Bosporus and so gained access to the Black Sea in their search for the golden fleece (although the legend is certainly much older than the actual Greek discovery of the Black Sea), was a direct ancestor of the trireme. The Argonauts sailed in a 'penteconter', a ship rowed by 50 oarsmen, as did the Greeks who invaded Troy. In the days when oars provided the principal method of propulsion, the only way to increase power was to add more rowers. The addition of banks of oars allowed more rowers to be accommodated without increasing the length of the ship. This was essential, because very long ships were liable to sag in the middle, and might break. In later, classical, times the trireme was succeeded by vessels with still more banks of oarsmen — ancestors of the medieval galleys.

Advanced ships of these kinds were the product of a long evolutionary process whose beginning is lost in antiquity. No one can know when, where, or by whom the first sea-going ship was launched. The ancient Egyptian hieroglyph for sailing up the Nile depicts a ship with a mast and raised sail, and the hieroglyph for sailing downstream shows a ship with no sail, but these were river craft and it is impossible to say when they or their descendants began to venture upon the open sea. Probably it was more than 5500 years ago.

For people living near the coast of a continent, with natural harbours to provide safe anchorage, the sea provided an obvious route to other coastal places. Their long experience of sailing on rivers would have provided them with the basis of an adequate technology, and their knowledge of seamanship probably began with fishing excursions into coastal waters.

Sea-going ships

There is a reference to the building of sea-going ships, 150 feet (45.75 m) long, in Egyptian records from about 2720 BC. It seems they were designed to sail to Lebanon and into the Red Sea, and by about 2300 BC, or possibly earlier, Egyptian mariners were visiting a land they called 'Pwnt' (or 'Punt'), a place renowned for its aromatic herbs and spices that is believed to have been in what is now the northern province of the Somali Republic, on the southern side of the Gulf of Aden.

Such voyages were undertaken for trade, and to establish the political alliances that would permit trade to be conducted peacefully. Travellers returned with cargoes of exotic goods — and they had been doing so for a long time. Orders for the building of some of those early Egyptian ships, inscribed in stone (literally) during the reign of the pharaoh Snofru, around 2720 BC, specify that the ships were to be made from cedar wood. Cedar did not grow in Egypt. It had to be imported from Lebanon by vessels travelling along the eastern coast of the Mediterranean to the mouth of the Nile — and those vessels may not have been Egyptian. It is quite possible that they belonged to the Phoenicians, the people who went on to become the dominant maritime power in the region — a role they assumed following the decline of their predecessors, the Minoans of Crete.

Phoenician supremacy did not go unchallenged, for it is clear that quite early in the development of their trading empire they distinguished between cargo-carrying ships and the warships they needed to combat rivals and pirates. Some of their warships

(Opposite, top) Sailing barges move more freely than those relying on draught animals and can sail in coastal waters between one river mouth and the next. This one is in Holland. (Opposite, bottom) Modern river barges, however, are large and have powerful engines. This one is at Rotterdam.

159

had battering-ram bows, like the later triremes, and the Phoenicians may have acquired this item of technology from the Egyptians. Clearly, as early as 3500 years ago the eastern Mediterranean and Red Sea were busy places.

As every modern amateur sailor knows, there is a great difference between a river journey and a voyage on the open sea, and although the Red Sea is relatively calm, the Mediterranean is treacherous and subject to sudden, violent storms. So far as anyone knows, Egyptian ships consisted of no more than a skin of planks built up from a base made from a hollowed log — essentially they were dugout canoes whose sides were raised by the addition of timbers. The

Egyptians sailed in the Red Sea but, apart from voyages to Lebanon, following the coast so they were never out of sight of land, it is doubtful whether they ventured far into the Mediterranean.

Greek ships, and probably those of the Phoenicians, were built quite differently. They had keels, which made them more stable and easier to handle, and the outer skin was attached to a strong frame. These were robust craft, and when Odysseus rode before a storm that carried him between the southern tip of Greece and Crete, out of the familiar Aegean and into the Mediterranean, he found himself in a fabulous world — but his strong, Greek ship survived.

In time, the Greeks and Phoenicians

Powered by three banks of oars, in its day the Greek trireme was the most formidable warship sailing the Mediterranean. This modern reconstruction was built with traditional materials and techniques to the original pattern.

explored the western Mediterranean and passed beyond it, through the Straits of Gibraltar — past the Pillars of Hercules — and into the Atlantic. The Egyptians were familiar with the Red Sea coasts, and around 600 BC the pharaoh Necho had the idea of sending an expedition manned by Phoenicians down the Red Sea, right around Africa to Gibraltar, and back to Egypt through the Mediterranean. The accepted wisdom at the time held that the world was a flat disc, with the Mediterranean at its centre surrounded by lands which projected more or less symmetrically on all sides, and beyond them an uninterrupted expanse of ocean, extending to the rim of the world. Necho had been dead for

more than two centuries before Aristotle demonstrated conclusively that the Earth is a sphere. Herodotus records accounts he heard of the voyage, and it seems likely that it really took place.

It was fortunate for the Phoenicians that the pharaoh decided they should sail southwards along the east coast of Africa and northwards along the west coast. Excellent though their ships were, it was difficult to sail them into the wind, and almost impossible to propel them against a strong current, but on the route they took wind and currents would have favoured them for most of the way.

The Kon-Tiki

The maritime history of Europe and North America began in the Mediterranean, Aegean and Red Seas, but it is not the only history. In 1947, a team of Norwegian explorers led by Thor Heyerdahl sailed the *Kon-Tiki*, a balsawood raft, from Callao, Peru, some 5000 miles (8000 km) across the Pacific to demonstrate that such craft could have carried people between the Pacific islands and the South American mainland. Among the islands, and sometimes for long voyages that took them far from land, Pacific peoples relied mainly on large dugouts, stabilized by outriggers.

It is perfectly natural that people living on small islands should build craft to carry them across the water to adjacent islands which they could see from the shore, and as they approached one new island others might become visible. It is certain that most island groups have been colonized in this way, but some longer journeys are more difficult to explain. Coastal navigation is one thing, but once out of sight of land the mariner must find other features by which to steer. The stars can be used — but only at night and only then when they are not obscured by cloud. The Sun is of some use, but by itself it provides only a very general idea of direction. Modern navigators employ a wide range of instruments, augmented by information from orbiting satellites, but none of these were available to the early voyagers.

Polynesian navigators

Studies of Polynesian methods suggest that the pre-technological navigators relied on keen observation and what, today, we would call a very high standard of seamanship.

They used all the information to which they had access. Where familiar land was in sight they orientated themselves in relation to it. They were intimately familiar with weather patterns, and the winds associated with them, they could recognize areas of the sea by their appearance, including their colour. This can reveal much to those who know how to interpret its changes. It is determined mainly by the level of biological activity and suspended matter. Green water may indicate changes in surface temperature due to cool ocean currents. Blue water supports little plant life and is most likely to be found far from land and the cool currents — where the direction of flow is constant, and would be well known. Brown water may suggest the proximity of major rivers. The colour and general appearance of the surface might alter as the craft sailed into shallow water. The navigators used the Sun, Moon and stars and, when there were no features to guide them, they used 'dead reckoning'.

With this method, the navigator extrapolates the known direction and speed of travel for the length of time that is known to have elapsed since the last sighting of features that allowed a position to be calculated, making due allowance for wind, tide and current. Ships and aircraft continued to navigate by dead-reckoning until radio beacons, and then more advanced aids, rendered the technique unnecessary.

Information regarding position, track and destination has meaning only in relation to a chart or map. The Polynesians carried their charts in their heads, as mental images built up by observation over generations and transmitted verbally, by a version of story-telling. They demonstrated that it is possible to cross the ocean without instruments and if they could do it, so, presumably, could others.

It would not have been difficult for them to calculate their position north or south of the Equator, at least approximately. A fixed star, or the Sun at noon, can be used — provided the navigator knows when it is noon, because at noon the Sun is directly overhead to an observer at the Equator, due south to an observer north of the Equator, and due north to an observer in the southern hemisphere. When Herodotus recounted the story of the voyage around Africa, which he heard from the Phoenician sailors who made it, he repeated their observation that for a time the ships sailed westwards with the Sun on their right. He found this incredible because the Mediterranean peoples knew that the Sun is always on the left side of a person facing west. This is invariably true in the northern hemisphere, and in his day the concept of the world as a sphere that can be regarded as two hemispheres was completely unknown. The report can have come only from people who had visited the southern hemisphere. Such a curious and otherwise pointless report is unlikely to have been a fabrication, and it gives credence to the general account. The latitude can be calculated from the angle between the star (the Pole Star is most commonly used in the northern hemisphere) or Sun and the horizon.

The magnetic compass

The first navigational instrument was the magnetic compass, which was nothing more than a magnetized needle or bar — sometimes fish-shaped — in its earliest form. No one can be certain when or where it was discovered, but the first references to its use occur around AD 1100 in China, 1220 in Arabia, and 1227 in Scandinavia. Quite possibly it was discovered independently in all these places. It was not until the fifteenth century that people realized that magnetic compasses do not point to the geographic (or true) north. Some of the compasses carried by Columbus had needles mounted on their cards in such a way as to compensate for this deviation. A compass indicates direction but that is all and, useful though it is, a navigator needs more. The accurate measurement of the longitude of an observer is possible only with the added help of an accurate clock — a chronometer.

Gemma Frisius, a Flemish astronomer, pointed out in 1530 that since the Earth turns on its axis at a constant speed, and noon is defined as the time when the Sun is directly overhead for someone at the Equator and due south or north for someone in the northern or southern hemisphere, the time that elapses between noon as this is observed in two different places can be used to calculate the longitudinal distance between those places.

To apply the principle, all you need to do is choose any line of longitude as a base, and set a clock to the time at that line. Use a compass to determine when it is noon, so the Sun is precisely to the south or north, note the time on the clock, and a set of tables will allow you to convert the time difference into an angular distance (the calculation does not determine the distance in units of length, of course, because lines of longitude converge at the poles). The method is very simple, but it can work only if the mariner possesses an extremely accurate clock. It must be accurate because one second of time represents 15 seconds of longitude, and close to the Equator 15 seconds of longitude are equal to about 1522 yards (1.39 km). So, although the principle was well known, it could not be applied until the eighteenth century, when John Harrison, a Yorkshire carpenter, won the £20,000 prize that had been offered by the British Government for a sufficiently accurate chronometer. Even then, it was not until 1765 that Pierre Le Roy, in Paris, invented a chronometer cheap and robust enough for general use. A ship's chronometer is usually accurate to within one second a day over a period of six months. Such accuracy is not difficult to achieve using quartz crystals, but to attain it with a system of weights, springs and cogwheels was a considerable engineering feat.

The accurate calculation of longitude also required an international agreement on the baseline. This was needed not for the calculation of position — for which any baseline will serve — but for its reporting. A longitude that is so many degrees east or west, must be east or west of somewhere. The lack of an agreed baseline was inconvenient for mariners and still more inconvenient for cartographers, for without it they had no standard by which to calibrate the lines of longitude shown on their maps. It was not until 1884, however, that the baseline which the British had been using for many years was accepted throughout the world. Since then, the zero line of longitude is the one which passes through what used to be (it has been moved since) the Royal Observatory at Greenwich, to the east of London. You can still see it at Greenwich, marked on the floor of what is now a museum. Time is also calculated with reference to 'Greenwich Mean Time' (GMT or, in navigational use, 'z').

Invention of the sextant

It was in 1731 that the British inventor John Hadley first described the sextant he had designed. This was the optical instrument used to measure angular distances, and

it increased greatly the accuracy with which latitude could be calculated. If it is known that a particular astronomical object appears to be directly overhead at a known point on the Earth's surface, the angle between that object and the horizon seen by an observer somewhere else on the surface can be used (in practice by reference to tables in an almanac) to calculate the latitude. Equipped with compass, chronometer and sextant (literally, the word means 'one-sixth of a circle', which is 60 degrees, although Hadley's original sextant actually measured 45 degrees, or one-eighth of a circle, so it was really an 'octant') ships could sail long distances, far from land, and their crews could know at all times where they were on the Earth's surface and, as their maps and charts improved, where they were in relation to particular places.

Until the introduction of the compass, few mariners dared to sail far from the sight of land, yet this limitation did not prevent them from making long journeys. Around 330 BC, Pytheus, a citizen of the Greek colony at Massilia — the modern city of Marseilles — travelled northwards along the Atlantic coast of Europe, described a visit to Britain, reached the Orkney Islands, and heard tales of ice-covered lands still further north. It is likely that on another voyage Pytheus entered the Baltic. Nearchus, a general in the army of Alexander the Great (356-23 BC), commanded a fleet which sailed from the mouth of the Indus river to the Persian Gulf — the first voyage by Europeans across the Indian Ocean. During the fourteenth century, when ships were equipped with compasses, exploration accelerated. The Azores, 800 miles (1287 km) from land, were colonized by the Portuguese in 1432, the Equator was crossed in 1481, for the first time since the Necho expedition and Columbus visited Iceland before he embarked on his trans-Atlantic voyage to the West Indies in 1492.

By the middle of the fifteenth century, European sea-going ships were built to a general design that changed little until modern times. In earlier designs, back to the Greeks and Phoenicians, and used later by such northern peoples as the Vikings, ships were essentially double-ended. The bow and stern were of similar shape and steering was provided by a large oar on the starboard side — the word 'starboard' comes from the Old English *steorbord*, and *steor* means 'rudder'

— which was often linked to a tiller. Early in the thirteenth century, it became the custom to fix a permanent rudder to the stern of the ship. The rudder had to be held firmly to a post — the sternpost — and this gave the stern of a ship a different shape from the bow. In time, the upper part of the stern was widened, to either side of the sternpost, by the addition of timbers laid across the ship — the transom — and this provided the foundation on which a stern castle was built. In the medieval galleon, the ram, built at or just below water level as an extension of the bow, was raised well clear of the water, extended into a long beak, and a large forecastle was built above and behind it.

This basic design is capable of many variations. In the eighteenth and nineteenth centuries the raised castles were abandoned, for example, and bigger ships were built — although Nelson's flagship the *Victory*, built in 1765 and at the time the biggest of all British ships (though a few French and Spanish ships were somewhat larger), was much the same size as the galleon *Grace Dieu*, built for Henry V in 1418. The *Victory* was 186 feet (57 m) long and this is close to the greatest possible length for a ship built entirely from wood — especially a warship, carrying heavy armament — because of the risk of sagging under the weight. At 210 feet (64 m), the frigate USS *Pennsylvania*, built in 1837, was probably the largest ship ever made entirely from wood. The greater efficiency of the later wooden ships, such as the clippers of the nineteenth century, was achieved by improvements in the sails and rigging, but also by increasing the ratio of the length of the vessel to its beam — ships became more streamlined.

The first iron ships
The size limitation was overcome by the introduction of iron, first to provide the frame to which the skin was fixed, but then for the complete construction. Iron ships were starting to appear during the first decades of the last century and, by the middle of the century, steel was taking the place of iron. At the time, the proposal to build iron ships was very controversial. Most people believed that wooden ships floated because wood floats — the idea that they float because they are less dense than the volume of water they displace was not well

understood. It seemed to follow, therefore, that an iron ship would sink because iron sinks. The fallacy of this notion was soon demonstrated, but the traditionalists who favoured wooden ships fought a strong rearguard action and it took some time — and a number of accidents in which iron ships survived better than wooden ships —

before the argument was finally won.

By this time, however, the days of the sailing ship were numbered. Sails had been used by craft plying the Nile, but for a long time the power they supplied was augmented by rowing — they were 'galleys'. Warships, especially, required the additional speed and manoeuvrability provided by oars.

The ancient Greek warships were rowed, but had a supplementary sail as did the Viking longships, the warships that raided north-western Europe in the eighth and ninth centuries. They were powered by oarsmen — up to 10 on each side — and also carried a sail, but the Norsemen also built larger vessels, to carry passengers and

The Portuguese training ship *Sagres* is a fine example of the elegance achieved towards the end of the days of sail.

cargo, which were powered only by sail. Improvements in the design of sails and rigging, which allowed ships to sail faster and at an angle to the wind direction, made oarsmen redundant and although the word 'galleon' is probably derived from 'galley', galleons were not rowed. The increasing complexity of the rigging required much larger crews, but they replaced a still larger number of rowers, and the space needed to accommodate the rowers, with their seats and oars, was freed for other uses — one of which was to provide gun decks.

Steam power

The change came with the development of steam-powered marine engines, and it came quickly. The first steamships, which came into service in the 1820s, were propelled by paddle wheels. This was not a new idea. Anyone familiar with water mills, in which a paddle wheel is turned by water, might have proposed a similar wheel as a means of ship propulsion. Several experimental paddle steamers were constructed during the eighteenth century, as well as paddle-driven ships which relied on manpower. Paddle steamers began to enter regular service in the first decade of the nineteenth century and in 1819 the *Savannah*, a sailing ship fitted with a steam engine, sailed from Savannah, Georgia to Ireland, although it used its engine for only part of the crossing.

Steam power was introduced first into what were essentially sailing ships, but it was not long before the emphasis changed and sailing ships with engines gave way to steamships with sails, and over the years the number of masts and sails declined. Navies were slower to introduce them than merchant fleets, mainly because the large wheel on either side of a paddle steamer was exposed and vulnerable, and it prevented the ship from carrying a full complement of conventional guns. This disadvantage was overcome with the invention of the propeller, whose efficiency was demonstrated most sensationally by the *Great Britain*, designed by Isambard Kingdom Brunel (1806-59) and built at Bristol between 1839 and 1843. It was made from iron, in addition to its steam engine it carried sails on six masts, and it was big — 322 feet (98 m) long. It sank in 1846, off the Falkland Islands, but Brunel had made his point. What remained of the *Great Britain* was salvaged some years ago and, in 1970, returned to Bristol where it is

being restored and is open to the public.

Even so, sailing ships competed successfully with steamships for some time. Steamships had to carry coal, in space that could be devoted to cargo on a sailing ship, and they had to replenish their fuel stocks at coaling stations along their routes. In 1869, the opening of the Suez Canal removed this disadvantage. The route to Asia was made shorter, and so was the distance between coaling stations. Sailing ships, meanwhile, were smaller, slower, and their routes were determined by prevailing winds. Many sailing ships were sunk during the First World War and it was not economical to

replace them. Steel and steam had replaced wood and sail, and the age of the huge, fast, luxurious, ocean liner had dawned.

The *Normandie*, launched in 1932 for the trans-Atlantic service, was 1000 feet (305 m) long and carried more than 2000 passengers at an average speed of more than 30 knots (55 km/h). Following the Second World War, oil replaced coal as a fuel, diesel engines replaced steam engines and, during the 1950s, nuclear reactors were installed — but the technology was abandoned for surface ships because it proved uneconomic. By the 1960s oil had become the principal fuel for transportation, and the combination of plentiful oil supplies, low prices, and the stimulus to the development of air transport provided by the military needs of the Second World War, led to the rapid expansion of air travel. Oil tankers continued to be built to an ever greater size, but passenger-carrying vessels could not compete with the airlines and the ocean liners survived, much reduced in numbers, only by providing luxury cruises.

Submersibles

The two wars also stimulated the development of an entirely different category of craft, the submarine. The idea of a

Today, few ocean liners operate scheduled services, but some manage to survive by offering luxury cruises.

The modern merchant fleet is based on large ships, many of which carry containerized deck cargo in addition to their full holds.

submersible vessel was not new. Robert Fulton, an American engineer, built and tested one, successfully, on the Seine in 1800, and in 1820, an English smuggler offered — at a price — a craft of his design to rescue Napoleon from St Helena. The Emperor died before he had a chance to test the proposal. More submarines were built at intervals throughout the remainder of the century, but, like their predecessors, their inventors had failed to solve some of the formidable problems that faced them. The first submarine to incorporate hydroplanes for stability, to control its depth by regulating its buoyancy, and to be powered below the surface by electric motors was the *Fenian Ram*. It was designed by John Philip Holland (1841-1914), an Irish-born school teacher who migrated to the United States in 1872. The venture was financed by associates in Ireland, who thought the submarine might be used against the Eng-

lish, but Holland soon dissociated himself from his former friends. The first design failed, but he won a contract to design a submarine for the United States Navy and his second attempt, the *Holland*, was a success. Submarines of this design were in the service of many navies by 1900. They used diesel engines to provide power on the surface and recharge the batteries. The snorkel, by which air is obtained from the surface to allow the diesel engines to run below water, was first used by the German navy in 1944.

The dreams of the pioneers have been largely realized. Soviet Alfa-class submarines can descend to 2000 feet (610 m) and travel submerged at 45 knots (83 km/h), and a nuclear-powered submarine can remain submerged for many months at a time. In recent years submersibles have been used increasingly for scientific exploration of the ocean floor.

LIVING AT SEA

The first expedition to explore systematically below the surface of the oceans took place between 1872 and 1875, when a team of scientists sailed aboard HMS *Challenger*, under the leadership of the Canadian oceanographer and biologist John Murray (1841-1914). The team took soundings and used dredges to collect samples of sea-bed sediment in the Atlantic, Pacific, Indian and Antarctic Oceans, and their final report ran to 50 thick volumes. It was the *Challenger* expedition which established the dimensions of the Mid-Atlantic Ridge.

Descending to the sea bed

The *Challenger* explorers did not descend to the sea bed in person. Today, submarines are used for exploration — some carry passengers on sight-seeing excursions — and humans can visit the floors of the deepest oceans. On 23 January 1960, in a 'bathyscaphe' called the *Trieste*, Jacques Piccard, the son of Auguste Piccard, the Swiss inventor of the bathyscaphe, and Lt Don Walsh of the US Navy, dived to 35,800 feet (10,916 m) in the Marianas Trench. In doing so, they established a depth record that cannot be broken, since they visited the bottom of the deepest of all ocean trenches, and they realized one of humanity's oldest dreams. Aristotle mentioned a diving bell, and bells were in use in the seventeenth century, but the

exploration of the ocean floor presented formidable obstacles.

As its name suggests, the diving bell was simply a container, open at the bottom, which was lowered into the water. The human diver entered to breathe the air trapped in it. In the eighteenth century, the English civil engineer, John Smeaton (1724-92), added a pump to change the trapped air, and a modern version of the diving bell is still used. The diving suit, which consists of a modified diving bell — the helmet — attached to a watertight garment, is based on a design patented in 1819 by Augustus Siebe, a German inventor who lived and worked in England. The aqualung, which frees the diver from the restrictions and dangers of an air line linked to a pump on the surface, was invented in the 1870s by Benoît Rouquayrol and Auguste Denayrouze, and called the 'Self-Contained Underwater Breathing Apparatus' — or 'scuba', but it was not until the middle of this century that its technical problems were overcome and the apparatus was perfected.

There is a limit, however, to the depth a diver can reach wearing a diving suit. With every 33 feet (10 m) of depth, the pressure increases by about 14 pounds per square inch (one bar). At about 150 feet (46 m) the pressure is so high that oxygen and

Submarines have been used mainly in war, but they can also provide transport to spectacular underwater scenery. This is HMS *Tiptoe* leaving Portsmouth, England.

(Opposite) One day, industrial raw materials may be obtained from the sea bed or from sea water and refined in factories built on the bed itself.

The ocean floor has many wonders to offer. These bivalve molluscs are living near the Galápagos hydrothermal vent.

nitrogen from the air the diver breathes begin to dissolve into the blood. A rapid ascent causes the nitrogen to form bubbles which can lodge in joints or nervous tissue, causing illness or even death. The traditional remedy is to reduce the pressure very slowly. A diver who spends an hour at a depth of 200 feet (61 m) must undergo decompression lasting three hours. This makes it very expensive to employ divers, although breathing gases that do not include nitrogen (an oxygen and helium mixture is commonly used) can help.

Compression difficulties do not arise if a bathysphere or bathyscaphe is used. These are sealed chambers whose internal pressure is held at its sea-level value. The bathysphere, invented by the American biologist and explorer William Beebe (1877-1962), was first used in 1930. It proved cumbersome, and dangerous because it was suspended by a cable, which might break. The bathyscaphe, which first dived in 1948, is free. Its chamber is attached to the underside of a float containing gasoline, and it has ballast in the form of iron shot held by electromagnets.

The windows of the *Trieste* are of a design that has been copied in most of the submersibles built since. They are thick, shaped like truncated cones, and arranged to provide the crew with the maximum visibility for as far as its searchlights can penetrate the darkness of the ocean depths. One of the most famous submarines to use them, the *Aluminaut*, is designed to reach a depth of 15,000 feet (4575 m). Submersibles are expensive. Some contribute to scientific research, but the main direction of pure research lies in the drilling of cores from the continental shelves and the deep ocean floor. The systematic, international programme to collect cores began with the Joint Oceanographic Institutes for Deep Earth Sampling, and is now the International Programme of Ocean Drilling. Most submersibles are engaged in strictly commercial activities. They examine submarine structures — such as oil platforms and pipelines — and search for minerals. Arms and grabs allow them to collect samples and, because of the darkness in which they work, many samples are needed before a coherent picture of the nature of the sea bed can be compiled.

Submersibles (above) are used increasingly for underwater exploration and could carry tourists. Modern equipment gives divers great freedom of movement. This diver (right) is studying a sea pen (*Sarcophyllum bollons*) 120 feet (37 m) below the surface of Doubtful Sound, New Zealand.

Deep-sea experiments

It is not always necessary to travel long distances or explore large areas. There are circumstances in which it is more useful for divers to spend longer in one place. A submarine is of little use to them. Conven- tional diving can achieve more — or it could were it not for the decompression time. Experiments to increase the time humans could remain on the sea floor began in the 1960s, and were based on providing accommodation in which the divers could eat and sleep and from which they could work, breathing a mixture of oxygen and helium. In 1965, in the 'Pre-continent' experiments led by Jacques-Yves Cousteau, six men lived for three weeks at 330 feet (100 m), and in the United States' 'Sealab' experiments, which followed the 'Man-in-Sea' programme, 10 men spent two weeks at 197 feet (60 m). The Soviet 'Kitzeh' programme also extended the time for which humans can remain at depth. As the experiments progressed, the accommodation that was provided became increasingly comfortable and safe. The ultimate aim is to create conditions in which teams of divers can spend up to a month at a time, working ordinary shifts, at depths of about 1000 feet (300 m) — near the edge of the continental shelf — and need to spend no more than a day or two in decompression when it is time for them to return to the surface.

The development of the offshore oil and gas industries has generated a great deal of experience in working below water. This might allow sea-bed factories to be constructed to extract useful materials from below the bed or from the water itself. The nodules composed of a range of metals and abundant in most seas might be collected, and uranium and deuterium extracted from water.

To the human inhabitants of densely crowded islands the vastness of the ocean must seem to offer limitless space into which they might extend their cities. The idea is much less fantastic than it may sound. In many parts of southern Asia large numbers of people live on boats that are permanently moored to create, in effect, floating cities. This tradition might be adapted to modern needs wherever a suitable expanse of sheltered, fairly shallow water is available.

A large offshore development, with housing, shops, and facilities serving a marina, has already expanded the area of Monaco, and in the Kallang Basin, on the southern side of Singapore City, more than 800 hectares (2000 acres) of land have been reclaimed from the sea for residential and light industrial use. There have been several plans to extend Tokyo into its Bay. One of the most ambitious, by architect Kenzo Tange, consists of a business and commercial centre built on an artificial island and linked by road bridges to large, 50-storey, residential buildings, interspersed with parks and open spaces for recreation. The whole complex would be built over the water.

Japanese designers have also planned to create submarine parks that would be accessible to visitors by means of observation towers. Each tower would stand on the sea bed, with the entrance above the surface. It would contain underwater restaurants and, possibly, observation tunnels, fitted with 'Trieste' windows, extending along the sea bed. Might oil and gas production platforms find new, recreational uses when the fields they exploit are exhausted?

Water and industry

Water is an essential resource, without which we could not live. The difficulties of surviving in a dry desert are well known, after all. We must have water to drink and for washing, and without it our crops will not grow.

In an industrialized society, however, satisfying such domestic and agricultural needs accounts for only a part of the total amount of water we use. In the United States, for example, the domestic supply represents about 10 per cent of all the water used. Agriculture uses 41 per cent, industry 11 per cent, and the production of steam for electricity generation 38 per cent. In Egypt, where agriculture, mining but not the refining of ores, and the financial sector together account for two-thirds of the total value of the gross domestic product, one per cent of water is used domestically, 98 per cent is taken by agriculture, and industry and power generation take the remaining one per cent between them.

The contrast is dramatic but its significance is not quite as it may seem, for water is not 'used' in the conventional sense. Even at home, most of the water we drink or use for washing enters the sewers and thus, treated or not, it is returned to the rivers, the sea, or the air — to the hydrological cycle. If industry requires water, then that water has to be supplied, but it is not lost.

In the United States, water taken into an industrial plant is used, on average, 2.2 times before it is discharged, and a little more than 90 per cent of it is returned to the surface water system. Recycling or regeneration are increasingly common practices. These figures are similar to those found in most industrialized countries. After all, it is difficult to remove water altogether from the hydrological cycle.

(Opposite, top) Large dams are built to generate electrical power, but they sometimes have a serious adverse effect on the environment. (Bottom) Accidents involving oil tankers frequently cause severe pollution of beaches. This tanker has sunk off the Portuguese coast.

Water for steam generation

The large cooling towers that are characteristic of certain industrial landscapes indicate that water is being recycled, usually after it has been regenerated. Water for steam generation is taken from a source, usually a river, although brackish water and sea water can also be used. It is boiled to convert it to steam, and after the steam has been used it must be condensed again, back to the liquid phase. While it is still hot it may be fed back to the boilers to be converted back into steam — this is regeneration. Eventually,

though, the waste heat which is produced but cannot be used, must be released — or the building would become intolerably overheated. There are two methods which achieve this. A 'once-through' system condenses the steam, allows the water to cool inside the plant, and then discharges it directly, replacing it with fresh water. This wastes no water, but a high proportion of the heat that must be dissipated is transferred to the water into which the discharge feeds, and the method is little used in Britain, except for power stations that use

Protecting the environment demands detailed knowledge based on meticulous scientific study, but the presence of abundant wildlife indicates healthy surroundings. This alligator, basking close to a NASA launch pad, is one of 5000 living beside the Kennedy Space Center, Florida, United States.

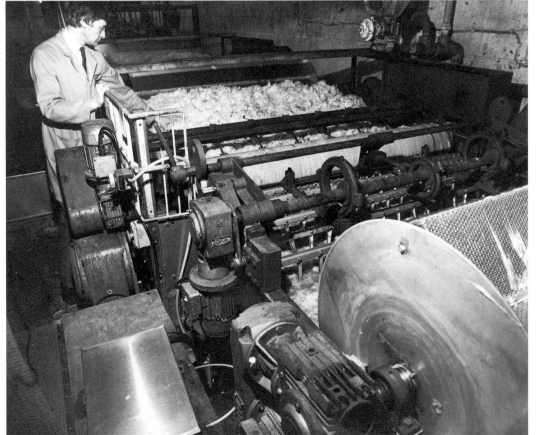

(Above) Large amounts of water are used industrially for cooling. These are the cooling towers of Didcot Power Station, in Oxfordshire, England. (Left) Before it can be spun and woven, wool must be cleaned by washing it in water.

(Opposite, top) Volunteers helping to clear oil from a beach in southern England. (Opposite, bottom) Nowadays, responsible industries take care to protect the environment. This is the Kennedy Space Center, Florida, United States. It is operated by NASA, but much of the total area is managed as a sanctuary for wildlife.

sea water. In a cooling tower, the water is cooled by an upward flow of air, so the waste heat is discharged to the atmosphere, but about 10 per cent of the water is lost by evaporation. Most cooling towers are found beside power stations, but they are also associated with other industries, wherever steam is required — although the cooling towers which are a traditional feature of The Potteries region of Staffordshire, England, are used for air-cooling in connection with ceramics manufacture, which does not employ steam.

Water for cleaning

Washing, as an industrial version of the way clothes are washed at home, is a necessary part of the manufacture of woollen cloth. A fleece contains natural wax and salts from the evaporation of perspiration, as well as dust, earth, burs and other plant material, all of which must be removed before carding and spinning can commence. Traditionally, the larger and more obvious pieces of dirt

are removed by hand and the fleece is then washed in warm, very soft, soapy water — exactly as a woollen garment might be washed. The addition of a little alcohol helps the process by assisting in the emulsification of the grease. Some wool is dry-cleaned, using chemical solvents other than water, but this is expensive and most wool is still washed.

Water is also used industrially to separate different substances from a mixture. Coal, for example, occurs in seams from which it is mined, but the seams are not pure, and when the coal is removed from the mine it is mixed with earth and rock. At one time, the demand was mainly for large lumps of coal and their removal left behind small coal mixed with dirt, much of which was discarded to contribute to the growth of the spoil heaps around the colliery. In those days, coal was mined by hand and miners were paid according to the quantity of marketable coal they obtained, so the larger stones and more obvious dirt were removed

In the froth flotation process, a metal is held by the bubbles, which are skimmed from the surface. Here zinc is being separated at the Nanisivik Zinc Mine, in Baffin Island, Canada.

by the miners themselves. This became impossible as machines took over the mining operation. Today, coal is cleaned before it leaves the colliery site, and the cleaning process uses water to separate materials according to differences in their specific gravities.

The coal is fed into the top of an approximately conical hopper containing a mixture of water and sand. Upward water currents keep the sand suspended in the water. The specific gravity of water is less than that of coal — so coal will sink to the bottom if it is placed in pure water — but the sand increases the specific gravity of the mixture, and the proportion of sand can be adjusted so that the specific gravity of the mixture is slightly higher than that of the desired quality of coal. The coal remains at the top, and impurities which are heavier than the fluid sink to the bottom and are removed.

Mineral extraction

It is a sedimentation process and variations of it — all of them relying on water — are employed widely in mineral extraction. 'Panning' for gold is such a process, in which swirling the mixture to produce a gentle centrifugal effect causes the heavier grains of metallic gold to collect in the centre of the pan — the deepest part — and the lighter particles of impurities to collect at the edges. The production of kaolin (china clay) also exploits this principle, but on a much larger scale. The kaolin is obtained by washing it from the granite in which it occurs, using high-pressure water hoses. The resulting slurry contains kaolin mixed with clay particles and sand grains. The sand, composed of grains that are much larger and heavier than those of the clay and kaolin, is removed by sedimentation. Separating the kaolin from the clay is more difficult. It requires 'froth flotation', a process which is also used to clean very small coal, as well as in the refining of many other mineral products.

The process involves adding to the water a substance, called the 'collector', that will adhere to one component of the mixture but not to others, and that will form bubbles — the froth — when air is pumped through the liquid. The froth rises to the surface and the particles, coated with the collector, adhere to the bubbles, while the uncoated, and therefore wetted, particles tend to sink. The froth is then skimmed from the surface and further washing separates the collector from the material it has collected. Froth flotation is now used in the processing of most metallic ores.

The paper industry

Kaolin was used originally in the manufacture of porcelain. It is still used for that today, but the paper industry provides its biggest market. It is used as a filler, between the fibres of the paper, and as a coating on high quality 'art' papers. Much of the filler kaolin is supplied as a slurry, rather than being dried to a cake or powder, because the paper makers find it more convenient. The manufacture of paper is one of the biggest of all industrial users of water.

A century ago, most paper was made from old rags, which were rotted and then shredded to a pulp. Some paper is still made this way, mainly for producing bank notes and other 'security' papers. Today, however, most paper begins as wood pulp, much of it made from spruce. The bark is removed from the logs, which are then pressed against a rapidly revolving, abrasive drum while water is sprayed on to them. The result is a mixture of wood fibres suspended in water. After screening and cleaning this makes newsprint and other cheap papers. Chemical processing, in which the wood is cut into chips, cooked in steam, and then treated chemically before mixing the fibres with water produces a whiter and more durable paper. In the paper mill, kaolin slurry and bleach are added, and the final mixture is sprayed evenly on to a 'blanket', which absorbs some of the water, to leave a coating of matted, interlocked fibres — wet paper which is gently lifted from the blanket then dried and pressed.

It takes from 100 to 300 tons of water to manufacture one ton of paper. The water is not lost, of course. The finished paper contains very little and after cleaning the used water can be returned to the lake or river from which it was abstracted, but the high demand for water requires that paper mills — like woollen mills — be sited on or close to river banks or lake shores.

It is not always possible to site an industrial operation beside a source of the water it will use. Mineral extraction, for example, must take place where the minerals are found and, although it is technically simple to transport ores for refining elsewhere, it is

(Opposite) The water wheel is still used in many parts of the world. It was the first device to convert the energy of flowing water into power for machinery.

Water vapour occupies a larger volume than the liquid and the expansion, when water boils, is the basis for the steam power that drove the factories and transport of the Industrial Revolution.

expensive because of the usually large amount of waste that must be carried with them — and returned, after refining has separated it, to the place from whence it came. The usual solution to the difficulty is to take the water to the factory, if the factory is unable to locate itself beside the water. Water itself is a commodity that can be transported — as it is transported, through pipes, into and then away from, our homes.

Flowing water

Water can be moved long distances through pipes. Combined with the fact that some industrial raw materials are used in the form of a slurry, consisting mainly of water, this suggests the possibility of using water itself as a transport medium. The technique is used widely to convey materials from one stage in their processing to another. The mixture of water and crushed rock and minerals that are the raw material for cement manufacture are pumped as a slurry from one part of the factory to another, for example, and kaolin travels as a slurry until it is ready to be dried.

Such pipelines can be used over longer distances. In the USSR, a coal-slurry pipeline 161 miles (260 km) long links Belovo and a steel plant at Novosibirsk, and there is a 12-mile (20-km) iron-slurry pipeline in New Zealand.

If you were to stand on a river bank, watching the water flow past carrying leaves and twigs, it might occur to you that the flowing water would exert a force on any stationary object placed in its path. You might then go on to speculate about the possibility of constructing some kind of device that would allow the force of the flowing water to do useful work. No one can know how many inventive people dreamed in this fashion, or for how long, before one of them conceived the first turbine, but water wheels are thought to have been in use up to a century before the birth of Christ.

The principle is simple enough. Essentially, a turbine is nothing more than a wheel with cups or paddles fixed around the rim so that the moving water causes the wheel to turn. Early water wheels were mounted horizontally, with a vertical axis, so they had to be placed at the edge of the water flow. Probably they were used to

pump water for irrigation. Later, more efficient versions were mounted vertically, with a horizontal axis, and used mainly to grind corn, a task they continued to perform until very recently — a few are still working.

Spinning cotton

In 1771, Richard Arkwright (1732-92) opened a mill at Cromford, Derbyshire, for the production of cotton yarn strong enough to be used as warp thread. The spinning was done by a machine of his own design which incorporated a number of earlier ideas — it was not an original invention. It was called a 'water-frame' and was powered by the River Derwent. Arkwright was knighted in 1786, by which time he had become very wealthy, and his many factories employed about 5000 workers. Around 1779, Samuel Crompton (1753-1827) combined the water-frame and the 'spinning jenny', invented in about 1767 by James Hargreaves (1720 or 1721-78) to make the spinning mule, which superseded both its predecessors. All these machines were operated by water power, and their introduction marked the commencement of the Industrial Revolution.

The amount of energy water can deliver depends on the volume of water and its rate of flow — which depends, in turn, on the height through which it falls (known as the 'elevation head'). Sufficient power for industrial use can be harnessed only at a limited number of natural sites, and these are not necessarily located close to sources of raw materials, sea ports, or markets. This does not restrict the use of water power to generate electricity, however, because electrical energy can be carried almost anywhere by cables.

Hydroelectric power

Hydroelectric power — water power — supplies a very significant proportion of the energy needs of many countries. It accounts for 99.5 per cent of all electrical generation in Norway, for example, 94 per cent in Iceland, and almost 71 per cent in Austria. It is the principal source of electricity in many of the less-industrialized countries.

Modern civil engineering techniques have removed the limitation imposed by the natural flow of rivers. Where a river flows through a deep valley it can be dammed to form a lake, and water released near the top of the dam can be channelled past modern, efficient turbines. A 'major' dam is defined as one more than 492 feet (150 m) high, or with a volume greater than 19.6 million cubic yards (15 million cu m), or whose reservoir has a capacity exceeding 12 million acre-feet (14.8 billion cu m). In 1989 there were 59 such dams under construction or recently completed. Many are more than 650 feet (198 m) high, and the Chapeton Dam, on the Paraná River in Argentina, though only 115 feet (35 m) high, will be 139 miles (224 km) long.

Many modern factories have reverted to water power, in the form of hydroelectrically generated electricity, but 150 years ago the shortage of suitable river-bank sites might have halted industrialization, had an alternative not appeared. In 1785, a spinning mill at Papplewick, north of Nottingham, was converted from water to steam power and, by the turn of the century, steam engines were driving factories of many kinds — although as late as 1830 probably half of all textile mills still relied on water power.

People had known for centuries that when water boils confining the expanding vapour causes it to exert strong pressure. The 'aeolipile', described by Hero of Alexandria in about the first century AD, though only a novelty at the time, was a kind of steam engine, but it was not until the seventeenth and eighteenth centuries that designs for practical engines began to appear. Other engineers, the most famous of whom was James Watt (1736-1819), built on these to design the greatly improved engines that were installed in factories, steamships and railway locomotives. The limitation had been removed.

Today, when we travel in cars and aircraft, powered by engines which burn petroleum, when electric and diesel engines power most of our locomotives, and when our means of communication include electronic devices, we may be tempted to dismiss steam and water power as obsolete technologies. This view would be profoundly mistaken. Virtually all of our electrical power is generated by turbines, some turned by the fall of water in a river or from a dam, the remainder by steam, and research continues to be directed towards ways of improving turbine design and efficiency. The water wheel, invented some 2000 years ago, is the direct ancestor of the modern turbine, which continues to make its essential contribution to our way of life.

POLLUTION OF THE ENVIRONMENT

Pollution occurs when a substance, or energy, is introduced into the soil, air, or water in a concentration that is sufficient to harm living organisms. The concentration — the dose — is central to the concept, for there is no substance so poisonous that there is no dose below which it is harmless to all organisms, nor any substance so benign as to be invariably harmless to all organisms at any dose.

Of course, some substances are safer or more dangerous than others. People regard uranium as hazardous because it is both poisonous and radioactive. This is true, but ordinary sea water contains uranium, at a concentration of about three parts per billion, and very small amounts are present in most living tissue. It does no harm because the dose is too low. Sea water also contains common salt (sodium chloride), as does virtually all the food we eat — and we often add pure salt as a condiment. Take enough salt, however, and it may kill you.

Substances that are capable of causing pollution enter the environment from many sources, not all of them linked to human activities. Volcanoes, for example, release very large amounts of ash, which can smother and kill vegetation and obscure the Sun enough to cause a climatic cooling, as well as a range of gases, which can increase the acidity of rainfall or trap radiation and so contribute to climatic warming. Certain species of marine algae emit dimethyl sulphide, which is oxidized to sulphate — a cause of acid rain.

The pollution is temporary because, little by little, the pollutants disperse, diluting their concentration, or they react chemically to form less reactive compounds, and eventually they lose their capacity to pollute. The pollutants we humans release into the environment, by accident or through the deliberate discharge of wastes, experience a similar fate. The pollution continues because the releases are sustained. Were they to cease the pollution levels would fall.

The length of time a molecule or particle remains in the soil, air, or water is its 'residence time' in that medium. By the end of its residence time it has been transformed into a different substance — whose resi-dence time may also be of interest — or has transferred to a different medium. Residence times in the soil tend to be long (years or decades), those in the lower atmosphere short (days or weeks), and sooner or later most substances that survive unaltered to the end of their residence times are likely to reach the ocean.

It may seem improbable that the condition of an ocean can be linked so directly to events which occur deep in the heart of a continent, but consider the fate of a molecule of a gas, say carbon monoxide, emitted in the exhaust of a car. Carbon monoxide has a very short residence time in the air. Within minutes it will have been oxidized to carbon dioxide. As carbon dioxide it may enter a green plant through photosynthesis, but only to be released again when the plant dies and its tissues decompose. Sooner or later it will dissolve in rain water, and become part of a molecule of carbonic acid. The rain will return it directly to the sea, or to the ground and eventually to a river, and so it will find its way to the ocean. Sulphur dioxide, released when fuel containing sulphur is burned, is oxidized to sulphate crystals, on to which water vapour con-denses to form rain drops. Some of the acidity in certain lakes is due to emissions of sulphur dioxide from chimneys hundreds of miles away — and most lakes feed rivers that carry their acidified waters to the sea.

Liquids are likely to be discharged directly into water. Because water was so essential to the development of industry — for power, cooling, or transport — factories congre-gated along river banks where the river provided a convenient conduit for their wastes. By the early years of this century, the concentrations of industrial effluents had risen to levels high enough to kill all organisms in most of the rivers in the more heavily industrialized regions of the world.

Industrial discharges are not the only source of the contaminants which enter the sea. All over the world, communities living near the coast have found the sea the cheapest and most convenient 'sink' into which to pour their sewage, much of it untreated.

Such deliberate release of potentially harmful substances is being brought under

control, albeit slowly. To the extent that the controls are effective, the discharges are reduced or ended — we may hope, permanently. It is much more difficult to prevent accidents from happening because they are not deliberate and, by definition, the best of precautions cannot anticipate eventualities that are unpredictable. In September, 1987, in the Brazilian town of Goiânia, a cancer-therapy machine was stolen from an abandoned clinic and a scrap metal dealer broke open a capsule he found inside it, which contained a pretty blue powder that he distributed among his friends. The powder was caesium-137, and highly radioactive. A large area of the town had to be sealed for decontamination, nearly 250 people were treated for radiation sickness, and four people died.

Accidents at sea

In 1974, a Yugoslav ship, the *Cavtat*, sank in the Adriatic. It was carrying a cargo of tetraethyl lead ($Pb(C_2H_5)_4$), sealed in drums. This is the compound which is added to gasoline to improve its octane rating, and its use is now being phased out because 'leaded' gasoline is the principal source of airborne lead, and it may be harmful to health. As often happens, there were arguments among the owners of the ships, salvage companies, and governments concerning the jurisdiction in which the wreck lay, the allocation of responsibilities, and the financial aspects of recovering the drums. It was April, 1978, before the last of the drums was returned to the surface. By that time some of them had begun to leak, although not sufficiently to cause serious pollution. Tetraethyl lead is insoluble in water. Had there been a major release, probably the compound would have become incorporated in sediments in the immediate vicinity of the wreck and from there, over a number of years, it might have been absorbed by invertebrate animals and so entered the marine food chain.

We may reduce the risk of accidents at sea, but there is no way to prevent them altogether, for the list of possible causes is too long and human fallibility too great. The *Amoco Cadiz*, for example, sank off Portsall, Brittany, on 17 March 1978, because its steering gear failed, but the mechanical failure might not have had serious consequences had the captain, or the captain of the tug which went to assist, called in outside help or warned the authorities of the danger

facing the ship. As it was, the *Amoco Cadiz* drifted helplessly for a day, then ran aground, broke in two, and spilled the whole of its cargo of 1.6 million barrels of oil, mainly light crude, which it had been carrying to Britain from the Persian Gulf. Almost all of the oil drifted on to the Brittany coast.

Such incidents are spectacular, but the harm they do depends only partly on the magnitude of the spillage. Some areas of the world are more susceptible to damage than others. The *Exxon Valdez*, which ran aground on Bligh Reef, in Prince William Sound, Alaska, on 24 March 1989, lost only part of its cargo and spilled only 200,000 barrels of oil, compared with the 1.6 million lost from the *Amoco Cadiz*. The ecological balance of the Alaskan environment is more delicate than that of the Brittany coast, however, and it may be that although the Alaskan spill was much smaller its consequences were more severe.

Oil pollution

Shipping accidents are not distributed evenly throughout the world. They occur only on or close to the main shipping routes — and since the opening of the Suez Canal, many of those routes have led through the Mediterranean. The rapid expansion of the oil industry during this century has increased the Mediterranean traffic as tankers have taken this obvious route between the Gulf, Europe, and the Americas. This has made the Mediterranean especially prone to pollution incidents, and not all of them have been accidental. Unlike conventional merchant ships, oil tankers are specialized. They carry only oil. This means that their journeys to load at the Middle Eastern oil terminals are made in ballast. Before they arrive they must wash out their oil tanks with sea water and, for many years, it was the usual practice to discharge the dirty water, together with residues from the ballast, directly into the sea. This highly polluting operation is now forbidden — there are other ways for tankers to clean their tanks. Lapses still occur, but more rigorous monitoring by aircraft and satellites is making them less common.

Oil is a highly visible contaminant. It floats on the surface of water and when it drifts ashore it coats rocks. Sea birds that dive through it in search of fish also become coated. The oil clogs their feathers, which

(Opposite) Water receives pollutants from many sources, including vehicle exhausts. This is Mexico City which, in Aztec times, relied on an elaborate system of aqueducts to supply it with water, and a unique system of canals surrounding cultivated plots to provide its food.

impairs their insulating qualities, and when the birds try to preen themselves they may swallow lethal amounts of oil. Inshore spills often lead to heavy casualties among sea birds, but their effect on other organisms is not really serious. Because oil lies on the surface, most marine organisms are not exposed to it, and in due course the oil disappears.

Some evaporates. When it emerges at the well head, crude oil is a mixture of hydrocarbons — compounds that consist mainly of hydrogen and carbon — whose volatilities range from that of methane (natural gas), which exists in the gaseous phase at room temperature, to thick bitumen. It is the job of the oil refinery to separate this mixture into its 'fractions', each of which has its particular uses. When oil spills into the sea this separation occurs naturally. Methane is lost, together with ethane, butane and propane, all of which evaporate readily. The gasoline, kerosene and diesel oil also evaporate, and in the end all that remains is the bitumen, as almost solid, brown or black lumps, which are broken up gradually by wave action. Finally they are consumed by bacteria, for which their carbon and other ingredients are a source of nutrients.

This is not to say that oil spills are not

Factory emissions are carried long distances and contribute to marine pollution. These are the chimneys of the Kremlin Power Station, Moscow.

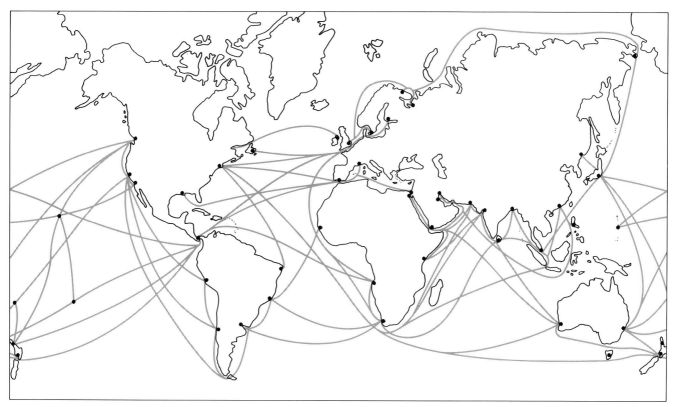

serious, or that we should not do everything within our power to prevent them. Clearly we should, but other sources of water pollution are more damaging and their control is more intractable.

Sea pollution from rivers
Seas are fed by rivers and many of the world's largest rivers flow through densely populated and heavily industrialized regions, and contaminants that leak or are discharged into them may be carried to the sea. The North Sea, for example, receives the waters of the Elbe, Weser, Ems, Rhine, Schelde, Thames, Humber, Tees, Tyne and Forth, which between them drain some of the largest and most important industrial regions in Europe.

The Mediterranean is fed by even more rivers — including the Rhône, Arno and Po. Some of these also drain industrial regions, especially the rivers of Spain, France, Italy and Greece, and they enter the Sea carrying their accumulated loads of detergents, phenols, mineral oil, mercury, lead, chromium, zinc and pesticides.

Agriculture has always been a major source of substances that drain into surface and ground waters, and eventually to the sea. Most of the pesticides in water reach it by this route, although some are washed from the air by rain. Soluble plant nutrients

— principally nitrate and a much smaller amount of phosphate — are carried by water moving through the soil. Modern farming has increased the rate at which nutrients are leached, partly by ploughing up old grasslands to increase the area sown to arable crops and partly by adding fertilizers. The first ploughing of a soil increases its permeability and allows nutrients to be washed from it more readily. Plant nutrients are not pollutants in the conventional sense — they are not poisonous — but in still or slow-moving waters they can stimulate the growth of aquatic plants to such an extent as to choke waterways. When the plants die and decay, their bacterial decomposition may de-oxygenate the water, causing the death by asphyxiation of many aquatic animals. This type of damage is called 'eutrophication' (from the Greek *eu*, 'well' and *trophe*, 'nourishment').

Some of the discharges are of wastes from manufacturing industry, but not all pollution is the result of discharges. Water can be contaminated by substances that are washed from the air, and the mere disturbance of soil and rocks can affect chemical reactions in and around them. Coal seams often occur in surroundings rich in pyrite, or 'fool's gold' (FeS_2) and marcasite, which is chemically identical (but differs mineralogically) as well as other sulphide minerals. Mining lowers

The main shipping routes now criss-cross the world. Although aircraft carry the great majority of long-distance passengers, freight is still carried mainly by sea and international trade depends on merchant ships.

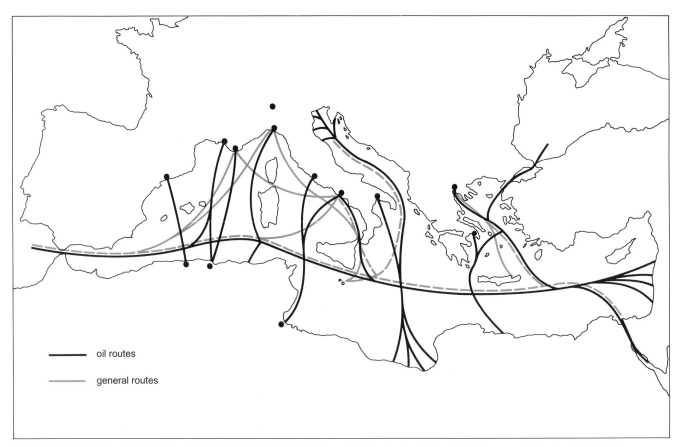

The main shipping routes in the Mediterranean, an almost land-locked sea in which pollutants tend to accumulate. Apart from local trade, large amounts of Middle Eastern oil are carried through the Suez Canal and the Mediterranean to northern Europe and North America. In addition to spillages from ships, four major European rivers, the Rhône, Arno, Po and Ebro, discharge into the sea, carrying sewage and industrial effluent from large industrial cities.

oil routes

general routes

the water table and exposes the minerals to the air. They oxidize to produce ferrous sulphate ($FeSO_4$) and sulphuric acid (H_2SO_4). In the presence of sulphuric acid and air, the ferrous sulphate oxidizes further, to ferric sulphate [$Fe_2(SO_4)_3$], which reacts with the hydroxyl (OH) ions in water to form ferric hydroxide [$Fe(OH)_3$] and more sulphuric acid. The water draining from a coal mine may be rich in iron, very acid and, because of chemical reactions between the acid and substances through which it flows, it is likely to collect other metallic compounds, some of which are toxic. This is not necessarily harmful. A study of a strip-mining region in Kentucky found that the mine water increased the rate of tree growth.

The residue left after the burning of coal is 'fly ash'. It contains heavy metals, especially cadmium, and a proportion of this also enters water.

Salt is spread on roads in winter to remove ice — as the salt dissolves, initially in atmospheric water vapour, it forms a strongly saline solution whose freezing temperature is much lower than that of fresh water. Fairly large amounts are used — about six million tons each winter in the United States, in some places at an intensity

of about 84 tons per square mile (32 tonnes per square kilometre). Most of this salt leaves the roads through the storm drains and finds its way into rivers and lakes. This can lead to significant changes in the chloride content of fresh water, to which many organisms are highly sensitive. Salt is not the only contaminant carried by storm drains. City streets receive soapy water from the washing of cars, water and oil that drip from vehicles, tobacco, and many other substances. Each year, its population of around 500,000 dogs deposits some 20,000 tons of faeces and 840,000 gallons (3.8 million l) of urine on the streets of New York City, to be washed away into the storm drains.

The excretions of dogs are insignificant compared with the very much larger quantity of human sewage that is discharged into coastal waters — much of it raw. Sewage consists mainly of substances marine organisms can utilize as nutrients, so in principle it causes no harm. Once again, it is a matter of the dose, however, and in practice sewage discharges are often harmful because the sewage tends to be highly concentrated in particular areas and can form a sludge that covers the sea bottom and kills most organisms.

Water in motion

Every year or two the newspapers report that, while walking along the sea shore, someone has found a bottle containing a message, with an address hundreds or even thousands of miles away and a surprisingly recent date. At one time such discoveries were considered startling and writers of adventure stories made use of them to rescue their shipwrecked heroes. Sending a message by bottle can hardly be classified as an efficient method of communication, but neither can its arrival on a distant shore be counted as remarkable — and these days the reports tend to be confined to local newspapers.

Apart from upland tarns — shallow lakes which are fed by small streams and lose water only by evaporation — water is constantly moving. We are so familiar with the movement of water that most tarns feature in local legends as magical places and, because no stream carries water from them, bottomless (Dozmary Pool, for example, a tarn on Bodmin Moor in Cornwall, is credited with being the Lake of Arthurian legend). This being so, a floating object cast into the water will travel with the water until it sinks or is removed. Launch a sealed bottle in the Gulf of Mexico and, in a matter of weeks, the Gulf Stream may well carry it all the way to Europe.

We notice sealed bottles because they may contain messages, but anything we discharge into moving water will be carried in exactly the same way. In the past we have made use of this by allowing rivers to remove our wastes. This was not ignorant or careless behaviour for as long as the quantity of wastes did not exceed the cleansing capacity of the receiving water. Organic material, such as human sewage, nourished aquatic organisms and so was recycled. Potentially poisonous substances were diluted, reacted with other substances they met to yield innocuous reaction products, and so were rendered harmless.

Pollution occurred — and it began centuries ago — when, locally, the system became overloaded and the quantity and diversity of aquatic life was markedly reduced. Aquatic organisms are vulnerable to three types of attack. They can be poisoned, asphyxiated, or smothered, and very often the three occur together and compound one another.

When organisms are killed by poison, the bacteria which decompose organic material are usually unaffected. Presented with a vast food supply in the form of the corpses of the poison victims, their populations increase dramatically. Decomposition is largely a process in which carbon is oxidized, and the bacterial activity reduces the amount of oxygen that is dissolved in the water. A pint of even the cleanest, freshest water holds no more than about 0.0007 ounces of oxygen (12 mg/l) and most water holds less, so animals which escaped the poison may nevertheless succumb, some time later, to asphyxiation.

Even an effluent that contains no poison of any kind can deoxygenate water. If the discharge consists of water containing little or no oxygen, as it mixes with the water into which it is introduced it will reduce the overall oxygen content of the water. This most commonly results from the discharge of warm water, because the amount of dissolved oxygen water can hold decreases as the temperature of the water increases.

Sewage discharge

The discharge of sewage, or the leaching of nitrate or phosphate from agricultural land, supplies nutrients to aquatic plants, and when they die their bacterial decomposition reduces the amount of dissolved oxygen. The provision of small amounts of plant nutrients is essential, for plants form the basis of the aquatic food chain, and water that contains no nutrients is lifeless. An

The North Sea also provides important sea routes between Britain and continental Europe and receives discharges from nine major rivers and the Humber estuary (of two combined rivers).

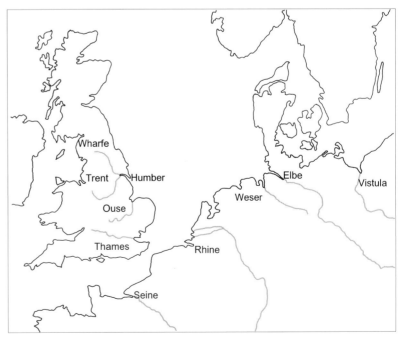

excessive supply, however, may cause oxygen depletion and the asphyxiation of organisms. This is eutrophication and it can occur naturally as part of the ageing process to which all lakes and ponds are prone. They begin as 'oligotrophic' (nutrient-poor) bodies of water, supporting few organisms. Nutrients reach the water, more plants and animals arrive to exploit them, and the water becomes 'mesotrophic' (containing an adequate but not excessive amount of nutrient). As the process continues the water becomes increasingly eutrophic (over-nourished) and the combination of a high rate of transpiration because of the large number of plants, and a high rate of sedi-mentation because of the accumulation of debris as organisms die causes the depth of water to diminish. Eventually the lake or pond becomes dry land. Whether it occurs naturally or as a result of pollution, eutrophication affects only still or very slow-moving water — in small ponds and ditches,

for example. In flowing water, the nutrients are carried downstream before they have time to stimulate excessive plant growth.

Most effluents, including sewage, contain small solid particles that are held in suspension. When the particles settle they may form a dense coating of sludge on plants and on the bed of the waterway. This smothers organisms. The delicate feeding apparatus of invertebrate animals which live on the bed is clogged, and the opaque coating of their leaves inhibits the process of photosynthesis on which plants depend. The sludge contains little or no oxygen and the decomposition of its organic matter, by bacteria that cannot tolerate oxygen, may release gases such as methane and hydrogen sulphide, which are poisonous to many organisms, and which may bubble noisomely to the surface (hydrogen sulphide smells like rotten eggs).

The actual effects of pollution are much more complicated and difficult to predict

These birds live beside the Kennedy Space Center, Florida, United States, where important nature reserves are established on NASA property.

(Opposite) There are still places where industrial effluent is discharged into coastal waters. This outfall is on Humber-side, England.

than this simplified outline suggests. The accidental release of a poison, for example, may have a devastating effect immediately, but provided the water is moving and the incident is not repeated life will soon return. Where the pollution is sustained, aquatic plants and animals vary widely in their susceptibility to poisons and oxygen depletion. Life is not destroyed easily and pollution may not even reduce the total mass of living organisms. What happens is that more sensitive species are lost, their places taken by an increase in numbers among the less sensitive species, and the community as a whole becomes less diverse. A survey of the species present can provide a good indication of the quality of water. The presence of salmon and trout, for example, indicates well-oxygenated water.

Biological oxygen demand
There are many ways of calculating the degree to which water is polluted and the amount of pollution a particular substance may cause. One of the most widely used methods calculates the 'biological oxygen demand', or BOD, in which water is polluted deliberately in the laboratory and the consequences measured. A sample of the effluent is mixed with clean water (the amount of dilution varies according to the nature of the effluent and is determined by experience based on trial and error), and the oxygen content measured in milligrams per litre of liquid. The mixture is then kept in darkness for five days at a constant temperature of 68 °F (20 °C) after which the oxygen content is measured again. The difference between the two measurements represents the amount of oxygen that was utilized by oxidation. A BOD of less than 1 indicates very clean water, at about 5 the water quality is dubious, at 10 it is bad, and at more than 20 the pollution is very severe.

The method has been used for many years, it is accurate and reliable, and in cases of

The nuclear industry complex at Sellafield, in Cumbria, England, adjoins nature reserves owned, managed and protected by the company.

doubt there are other laboratory methods which may be used to check its results. By itself, however, it is incomplete because it does not take account of the volume of water into which an effluent is discharged, or the rate at which the two mix. With rapid and thorough mixing in a large enough volume of clean water any pollutant will be diluted to a harmless concentration. Scientists cannot predict the effects of a discharge until they know where it will occur, and have examined the way the receiving waters move.

The need for such detailed information is obvious in the case of discharges into a river or small lake, but may be less so for discharges into a large lake or the sea. Since a lake the size of, say, Baikal or Superior, or a small sea such as the Baltic contains a volume of water which dwarfs into insignificance the volume of effluent humans are capable of discharging into it, it is tempting to assume that dilution will render pollutants harmless. There are circumstances under which this is so (see page 189) but by no means is it a foregone conclusion. The rate at which two waters mix depends partly on their relative densities. If fresh water is added to denser salt water it will tend to float to the surface with little mixing and then remain there until wave action disperses it. If the discharge is into coastal waters, onshore winds and tides may bring it close to the shore. This is usually what happens in places where beaches are contaminated by sewage that is discharged through an outfall pipe. The pipe releases the sewage offshore and at depth, but it floats to the surface and is returned to the shore before it has had time to disperse.

Movement of the tides

Tidal movements do not affect lakes and barely affect even a sea the size of the Mediterranean, but where they are significant they are much more complicated than they may seem. When you stand on the shore and watch the tide flowing or ebbing, the movement appears to be at right angles to the shoreline. As you face the sea, the tide seems to move directly towards or away from you. It is a natural assumption because, of course, the tide line, which marks the limit reached by the rising water, does run along the shore, parallel to the edge of the sea. In fact, though, this is seldom the way the tide is flowing.

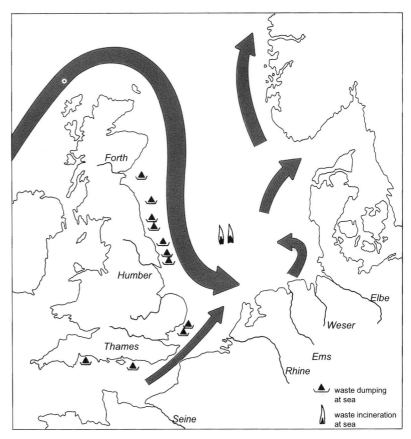

Imagine you have a container, partly filled with water, which you are holding with one hand on either side. If you tilt the container the water level will rise one one side, and on the other side when you tilt it in the opposite direction. The gravitational attraction, mainly of the Moon, which pulls the waters of the oceans to create tidal movements does not tilt the ocean basins, of course, but the effect is much the same. Imagine now that, instead of smooth edges, the sides of your container are as irregular as a coastline, with bays, headlands, and peninsulas. When you tilt the container the water level will rise all along the coastline, but the angle between the direction in which the water flows and the coastline depends on the shape of the coastline itself. It is quite possible — indeed, it is very common — for a stretch of shoreline to lie parallel to the direction of tidal flow, so the tidal movement runs parallel to the shore rather than at right angles to it, although the movement would still appear to be at right angles to a person standing on the shore, because such an observer would see only the rise and fall of the water level. Currents are usually invisible.

Tidal flows around bays and headlands may produce complex patterns of eddies,

The main currents in the North Sea flow in an anticlockwise direction close to the coasts, the largest current flowing southwards down the eastern coast of Britain. Substances discharged into coastal waters are likely to be confined there, carried by the currents. Apart from the major rivers discharging into the North Sea, wastes are dumped inshore of the main current. Incineration of wastes, in the centre of the Sea, probably causes no pollution.

No link with pollution has been positively proved, but when diseased fish are caught in heavily polluted waters reasonable suspicions are aroused. This flounder is from coastal waters of the North Sea.

and the speed of tidal currents is no less variable. Close to shore they commonly reach speeds of about 5 knots (9.3 km/h), but the confinement of the moving water, as in a strait, can produce a 'tidal race' with a speed of up to 10 knots (18.5 km/h). This is why it can be very dangerous to swim off many beaches along coasts where the tidal range is large. It also explains how effluents which are discharged into coastal waters in one place may be returned to the shore somewhere else.

The use of computers in tracing the movement of water

Even where effluents mix well with the water into which they are discharged, the dilution may not be sufficient to render them harmless. They become part of the water that receives them, are carried wherever it may go, and may accumulate somewhere, perhaps a long way from the place where they were discharged, until they reach concentrations that are harmful. In order to discover exactly where water does go, scientists release harmless but brightly coloured dyes, trace their movement and the time that elapses before they become so diluted as to be no longer visible, and use this information to construct detailed maps — usually stored in computers — of water movements in rivers, estuaries, along coastlines and in the open sea. It is a slow,

laborious, and expensive business, but necessary if we are to predict what will happen to substances which are released into water, rather than simply hoping for the best and trying to correct mistakes after they have been made.

Such maps now make it possible, at least for the more heavily industrialized rivers and estuaries and for some sea areas, to locate the best position for an effluent outfall. The computer screen displays a map of the area, the operator keys in such details as the type of discharge and rate at which it will be released, then selects an outfall point on the map. The discharge then appears on the map, and the operator can identify its position after specified time intervals. It may be, for example, that if the discharge is made in certain places the effluent will accumulate because the water simply moves in a circle, and in others that it will flow back across its own outfall, or move towards a point from which clean water is being abstracted. The position of the outfall is altered until the best place for it is found. The system is not infallible — because the data on which it is based may be imperfect or incomplete, and because water movements change over time so the actual conditions must be monitored regularly to ensure that the map uses up-to-date information — but it is a great improvement on guesswork.

Clearly, the location of the discharge is at least as important as the nature of the effluent, and this is as true for the open ocean as it is for a river which flows through a city and on which people rely for drinking water. Washings and ballast from oil tankers, empty containers, and all the other rubbish that is produced on ships and carelessly thrown overboard far out at sea, probably in the tropical North Atlantic, have been accumulating for years in the Sargasso Sea, carried there by the North Atlantic gyre. They probably cause little harm, being unsightly rather than toxic, but, like the sealed bottle containing a message, they provide evidence, if evidence were needed, to support the somewhat commonplace observation that everything we release into the environment must go somewhere.

The movement of water means that the pollution which results from the release of substances into water always occurs locally. This is not to say that moving water does not mingle to some extent with the water adjacent to it, and that pollutants cannot be transferred in this way. They can and are, but only as a kind of leakage from the main concentration, and the leaked pollutant enters a much larger body of water which dilutes it. It is unrealistic to suppose that humans, or their industries, are capable of causing serious contamination of

entire oceans. This is impossible, and the idea may encourage a confusion that could be hazardous, for if it allows us to dismiss as absurd a simple extrapolation from local conditions, which may be bad, to the condition of an entire ocean, most of which is unaffected, we may feel entitled to underestimate the true seriousness of those local conditions.

The North Sea Project

The word 'local' may be applied to an area which is large and which may be of special importance. In recent years there has been much concern over the condition of the North Sea, which we have treated as though it were a bottomless well into which we may safely throw our refuse, regardless of the amount or its composition. The North Sea Project, a detailed study of the Sea, and of the movement and eventual fate of substances entering it, began in 1988 and involved 15 voyages, each lasting 12 days, by the research ship *Challenger*.

Most of the refuse reaches the Sea from the rivers which flow into it, mainly around its southern margins — from England and the countries from France to Denmark and Germany — but also from the air. Each year, for example, about 8000 tons of zinc reach the Sea from the air — over which it is distributed evenly — and a similar

The protection of any sea can be achieved only through the agreement and collaboration of all countries using the sea and bordering it. In the case of the Mediterranean, such agreement was not easily obtained. As the map shows, 19 countries border the Mediterranean proper (including Gibraltar) and, if the Black Sea is included, Bulgaria, Romania and parts of the former USSR must be added. The northern countries are European, the southern Arab, with Israel on the eastern side, some have market economies and others formerly had command economies.

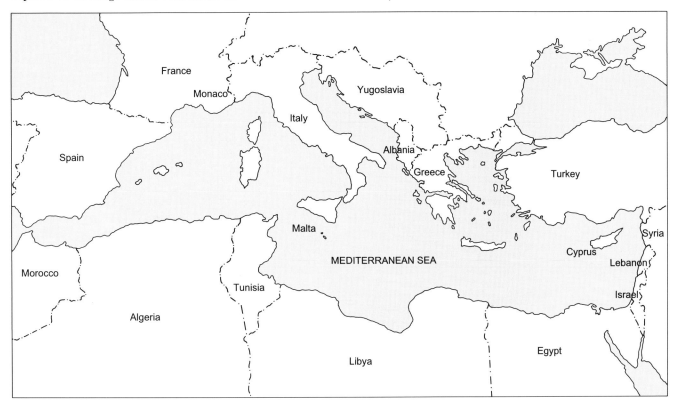

The dumping of raw sewage into the North Sea, seen here, will be banned in 1992 unless it can be shown to cause no harm.

amount from rivers. Other contaminants probably also reach the Sea in equal amounts by air and by river.

The river water is less saline than the sea water and forms a band around North Sea coasts, separated by a distinct boundary from the main body of the Sea, and riverborne pollutants are largely contained within this band. Once in the Sea they are moved mainly by the wind, but wind-driven currents do not flow precisely with the wind. Due to a combination of the Earth's rotation and friction, in the North Sea they move at the surface at about 45 degrees to the right of the wind direction. This angle increases with depth until, at about 330 feet (100 m), the water flows in the opposite direction to the wind. The phenomenon, first reported in 1905, is known as the 'Ekman spiral' after Vagn Walfrid Ekman (1874-1954), the Swedish scientist who discovered it. Overall, the water moves at 90 degrees to the right of the prevailing wind direction. Prevailing winds in the North Sea are from the south-west, so the polluted river water is carried more or less eastwards along the southern margin — driving the pollutants towards the shores of the Netherlands and the Bight, where they accumulate. The main body of the North Sea is little affected, and it is quite true to say that the Sea as a whole is not seriously polluted, but pollution is serious in the coastal waters where it accumulates and

the pollutants reach it mainly from rivers draining the industrial regions of north-west Europe. Fish have been injured by pollutants and polychlorinated biphenyls (PCBs) — compounds used mainly for electrical insulation in large transformers — have been found in the body fats of seals, and some scientists suspect they may have reduced these animals' resistance to infections.

Algal blooms

Over about the last 25 years, large blooms of algae have been observed more frequently in the North Sea. The blooms occur in spring and early summer, possibly stimulated by warm sea temperatures that follow mild winters, and they are fed by nutrients which enter the Sea in pulses from the continental rivers entering between Belgium and Denmark. Most of the algae are 'diatoms' — single-celled plants which protect themselves in a kind of shell made partly from silica, so for them silicon is an essential nutrient. By the middle of summer the stock of nutrients is depleted and the blooms disappear, but while they last they emit enough dimethyl sulphide to contribute about one-quarter of the acidity of rainfall and at their peak, during May and June, they are probably the principal cause of acid rain.

Other algal blooms are a nuisance. *Phaeocystis pouchetii*, which blooms in the waters discharged from the Rhine, lives in vast colonies that form masses of a jelly-like substance which can clog fishing nets. Others, especially *Chrysochromulina polylepsis*, release poisons, and blooms of them are not confined to the North Sea. The Baltic as well as the northern part of the North Sea suffered a large bloom of this species in May and June 1988, and tens of thousands of fish were killed.

Large algal blooms have also been observed during recent years in the central North Atlantic, to the south of Iceland. The cause of these blooms is uncertain, for this is an unpolluted sea area where nutrients should not be especially abundant, but they may be a response to generally higher sea-surface temperatures. The blooms consist mainly of algae belonging to the family coccolithophorids, a group which protect themselves by constructing small plates (coccoliths) from calcium carbonate, so they are removing carbon dioxide from the air. They are among the most prolific producers of dimethyl sulphide. By removing atmospheric carbon dioxide and, through their production of dimethyl sulphide, increasing cloud formation, the coccolithophorid blooms may have a significant climatic effect.

The Mediterranean has suffered for quite different reasons based on its geography. Water enters at the surface through the Strait of Gibraltar and is augmented by rainfall and flows from rivers. Evaporation removes water from the surface at about three times the rate at which rain and rivers deliver it. In late winter, the water in the eastern Mediterranean becomes relatively cool. Its salinity is high — because of the high rate of evaporation of fresh water, salinity increases from west to east — and its increased density causes this water to sink to some 650 to 1970 feet (200 to 600 m) where it forms the current which flows out of the Sea below the surface, mainly into the Atlantic, but also into the Black Sea.

Because water can leave only by evaporation or by a current flowing at a considerable depth, any pollutant which is less dense than water is liable to remain trapped at the surface for a long time. The incoming surface current flows eastwards, slowing as reaches the eastern end of the Sea, and establishes a generally anticlockwise circula-

tion of water. Smaller anticlockwise currents form circular patterns between Spain and Sardinia, in the Tyrrhenian Sea between Sardinia, Italy and Sicily, and in the Ionian Sea between Sicily, Greece and Libya. The currents are not strong, the tidal flow is insignificant, and pollutants that enter from rivers tend to follow the coastlines. Those discharged well out to sea usually mix reasonably well into the upper waters.

Pollution is not a new phenomenon. Historical records of blooms of toxic algae may have been linked with the local enrichment of sea water with nutrients entering as a result of human activity. In modern times, however, the great increase in the populations living around the Mediterranean Basin and in their industrial activities, together with the increase in shipping — especially of oil — that has accompanied industrial expansion, have increased it greatly.

Water extraction

Adverse consequences can also result from the abstraction of too much water from rivers which feed a sea. The Aral Sea, to the east of the Caspian, is fed by two rivers, the Amu Darya and Syr Darya, both of which carry very large loads of sediment. Over the last 30 years water from both rivers has been used for irrigation, reducing the inflow to the Sea, whose level began to fall sharply during the 1960s. Plans for increasing the area of irrigated land, made early in the 1970s, threatened to take all of the water from both rivers, so in time the Sea would disappear. By 1988, the total annual flow entering from both rivers was about 0.5 cubic miles (2 cu km) of water. The complete removal of an entire sea, covering an area of 25,659 square miles (66,456 sq km) should not be contemplated lightly, but the effect was not only aesthetic. Muinak, a town whose people depended on fishing, found itself 50 miles (80 km) inland, and the rivers, which fed the domestic water supply as well as the Sea, was heavily laden with agricultural chemicals and other contaminants which included pathogenic organisms that caused illnesses afflicting some two-thirds of the surrounding population.

The land exposed by the retreating water was covered with a mixture of salt and fine silt which were carried long distances by the wind, damaging the agricultural soils on which they fell. A programme has now been launched to increase the river flow tenfold by the end of the century and to find other sources of water for irrigation.

Dumping

Wastes that are discharged directly into rivers or estuaries, or into the sea from coastal outfalls, may mix slowly with the sea water and are liable to be carried by currents flowing parallel to the shoreline. A similar fate will befall discharges from ships in coastal waters and, since 1 January 1989, international controls issued by the UN International Maritime Organization have stipulated what may and may not be dumped from ships. No wastes of any kind may be thrown overboard within 3 miles (5 km) of land, and plastics and other non-degradable materials may not be dumped anywhere. Depending on their nature and the extent to which they have been treated, other wastes may be dumped provided the ship is more than 12 miles (19 km) or 25 miles (40 km) from land.

These regulations deal with the kind of 'housekeeping' rubbish ships produce. They do not cover the disposal by dumping of industrial wastes or sewage sludge, although it is now forbidden to dump toxic wastes in the North Sea under an agreement by the 25 nations which have signed the Convention on the Prevention of Marine Pollution by Dumping of Wastes and Other Matter (the London Dumping Convention). It seems probable that the dumping and incineration of all wastes at sea will be ended within the next decade.

'Dumping' is an emotive word, suggesting that extremely noxious wastes are simply tipped into the sea. This is more or less what happens to sewage sludge, but it is preferable to discharges into coastal waters and it is less hazardous than it may seem. The dumping takes place well away from land, where wind and wave action accelerate mixing. The organic material disperses and supplies nutrients for marine organisms. Unfortunately, domestic sewage shares a sewerage system that is also used for some industrial discharges which may contaminate it with substances, such as heavy metals, which are toxic and long-lived, so

The *Vulcanus II* is equipped with incinerators for destroying toxic industrial wastes at sea.

there is a possibility that in time these substances could enter a food chain that includes species caught for human consumption. The practice is undesirable for this reason, and also because sewage sludge can be used as a fertilizer or soil conditioner, or as a fuel, so that dumping it is apparently wasteful — although the alternatives may involve heavy capital expenditure or long-distance transport from a city, making such thrift costly.

Industrial wastes are treated differently. They are sealed in secure containers and deposited in deep water, where they sink to the bed. After many years it is possible that the containers may corrode or be broken, leaking their contents. By that time, however, the containers will probably have been buried beneath sediment, so the leakage is not directly into the sea, but into the sedimentary deposits. This will pollute the sediment, but only very locally because chemical compounds do not move very far or very fast under these conditions. Whether or not the resulting pollution causes harm depends on its character, the

depth at which it lies, and on the abundance of life nearby.

The North Sea is shallow, although in the Norway Deep, which extends south as far as the Skagerrak, the depth is up to 2400 feet (732 m). This is well below the thermocline, in the region where water is exchanged with surface water only very slowly, so the chance is extremely remote that any substance escaping at sea-bed level can reach surface waters, and the food chain which might affect humans.

The dumping of more hazardous wastes, including those which are radioactive, has ended. They used to be deposited in much deeper water, beyond the edge of the continental shelf, in the Atlantic. Again, the wastes were sealed in drums. Only low-level radioactive wastes were disposed of at sea. Low-level radioactive wastes consist of such items as clothing, laboratory glassware and empty containers, and come mainly from research laboratories and hospitals. They are only mildly radioactive and their dumping constituted no conceivable risk. Since dumping ceased they are disposed of

The environmental group Greenpeace attempt to prevent waste incineration at sea.

in other ways. British wastes are buried in a landfill site in Cumbria.

The incineration of wastes far out at sea, on vessels equipped with high-temperature incinerators, destroys the more intractable wastes. With proper anti-pollution equipment the practice is harmless, but because it takes place at sea it is difficult to monitor, and onshore facilities are being built to replace the incinerator ships.

Redressing the balance

During the 1960s, public concern over environmental pollution became widespread. Many books were published, on every conceivable aspect of the subject, and there were articles in most newspapers and many magazines, as well as television programmes. The situation was described in the most dramatic, and often lurid, terms and governments were compelled to take notice. The United Nations became involved towards the end of the decade and, in the summer of 1972, it held a Conference on the Human Environment, in Stockholm. The Conference produced a declaration which was presented to, and accepted by, the General Assembly. The Assembly authorized the establishment of a United Nations Environment Programme (UNEP), with its headquarters in Nairobi, as well as 'Earthwatch', a worldwide environmental monitoring system, to be run by UNEP. As part of this, UNEP launched a Global Environment Monitoring System (GEMS). In 1985, UNEP and the Swiss Government jointly founded the Global Resource Information Database (GRID), based in Geneva, which uses computers and software supplied by the US National Aeronautics and Space Administration (NASA) to analyse data.

The United Nations thus established an institutional framework to monitor and coordinate the activities of governments. Monitoring is based partly on surface stations and partly on satellites. The first Earth Resources Technology Satellite (ERTS-1) was launched from the United States in 1972, and in 1975 the programme was expanded in the Landsat programme, using several satellites that transmit photographs of the whole of the Earth's surface with a 98-foot (30-m) resolution. A French satellite, launched in 1986, provides a 33-foot (10-m) resolution for the Système Probatoire d'Observation de la Terre (SPOT).

The larger industrial companies now engage in extensive research to determine the effect their processes and products have on the environment. This ship, taking grab samples for laboratory analysis, belongs to the ICI Group Environmental Laboratory at Brixham, on the south coast of England.

UNEP has no legislative power. When legislation is necessary — to reduce pollution in a river that crosses an international frontier, for example — UNEP can only exhort and try to persuade. Governments, in their turn, can legislate only within the limits of what is technologically feasible and acceptable to their own constituents. Inevitably, progress must seem slow and piecemeal to environmentalist campaigners, yet very real progress has been made and industrialists, in particular, are far less reluctant than they were — and than they are sometimes alleged to be — to reduce the pollution caused by their operations. Many large companies are prepared to make environmental improvements voluntarily, moving beyond their strictly legal obligations, where they perceive a need and opportunity to do so.

Biodegradable detergents
It was the detergent manufacturers who agreed among themselves that all domestic detergents should be fully biodegradable and who, in 1964, all changed simultaneously to a new formulation to achieve this. Until then, most detergents had been based on alkyl benzene sulphonate, a non-degradable compound, and there had been spectacular instances of detergent residues causing foaming in rivers and at sewage treatment plants.

Since 1964, all domestic detergents marketed in Britain, the United States, and most other countries have been fully and rapidly biodegradable. The industry is now seeking an effective alternative to the phosphates, used in most washing powders to soften hard water, which can contribute to the stimulation of undesirable plant growth in some still or slow-moving waters. Also in the 1960s, oil tankers began to use the 'Load On Top' system, in which water used to wash tanks is held in a 'slop tank', mixed with oily ballast water, for at least 72 hours. This allows the oil to separate from it, the recovered oil is added to the next cargo, and the ballast is much cleaner when it is discharged.

The days are long gone when a manufacturer could introduce a product with no regard for the environmental consequences of its manufacture or use. In a developmental process which can take several years, the environmental effects of a new product, together with those of the raw materials from which it is made, the intermediate products formed during its manufacture, and discharges from the manufacturing operation, are tested first in the laboratory and then, under careful control, in the natural environment. This is only partly altruistic, of course, since a product which proved harmful might well be banned, leaving the company out of pocket. ICI, for example, maintains a large and very well-equipped and funded laboratory, at Brixham in Devon, for testing the effects of substances on the freshwater and marine environments. The company will develop a new product only if it is sure to prove environmentally acceptable not only in the country of its manufacture, but in any part of the world where it is likely to be used.

The London Dumping Convention
Individual companies and industries can achieve only so much, however, and it would be a mistake to underestimate the complexity of some of the reforms which are necessary. A series of intergovernmental agreements have been reached that are designed to protect the Baltic and the North Sea. The London Dumping Convention was signed by 25 countries in 1972, and regulates the discharge of substances from ships. The Oslo Convention for the Prevention of Marine Pollution by Dumping from Ships and Aircraft, also agreed in 1972, includes sea-bed operations, and the Helsinki Convention on the Protection of the Marine Environment of the Baltic Sea and the Paris Convention for the Prevention of Marine Pollution from Land-based Sources were both signed in 1974. The Helsinki Convention came into force in 1980 and at its first meeting, the Commission established under its terms determined to halt the discharge into the Sea of polychlorinated biphenyls and, later, mercury. The Soviet Government said that no more untreated sewage would be discharged from Leningrad after 1985, and since 1981, tankers of more than 20,000 tonnes and chemical carriers of more than 1600 tonnes have been required to report their entrance into the Baltic and their subsequent positions.

These agreements established the willingness of coastal states to act in a concerted way to protect their regional marine environments and it encouraged several United Nations agencies to attempt a similar agreement in respect of the Mediterranean.

Work to this end began in 1974 under the auspices of the General Fisheries Council of the Food and Agriculture Organization (FAO). UNEP joined soon afterwards.

The need was great, but so were the difficulties. The Mediterranean receives pollutants from many industries, as well as agricultural chemicals leached from farm land and sewage from coastal communities. Its level of pollution can be reduced only by the collaborative effort of the governments of all the countries bordering the Sea. There are 18 of them: Spain, France, Monaco, Italy, Yugoslavia, Albania, Greece, Turkey, Cyprus, Syria, Lebanon, Israel, Egypt, Libya, Tunisia, Malta, Algeria and Morocco, a mixture of industrialized and less-industrialized, Christian, Islamic and Judaic countries.

Meetings held in Rome, in 1974, led to an intergovernmental meeting which was held in Barcelona early in 1975. The Convention for the Protection of the Mediterranean Sea from Pollution (the Barcelona Convention) was completed and opened for signature on 16 February 1976. It forbade the discharge into the Sea of a wide range of substances, including organosilicon compounds, all petroleum hydrocarbons, all radioactive wastes, and acids and alkalis, but it did not specify their source. A meeting was held in Athens, in 1977, to discuss pollution from land-based sources and a third protocol to the Convention, covering agricultural chemicals, sewage, and factory wastes, and

banning the discharge of lubricating oils, plastics, radioactive substances, arsenic, cadmium and carcinogenic compounds, was signed in 1980 by all the Mediterranean states except for Albania.

An international agreement achieves nothing unless it leads to action and the Barcelona Convention called for an 'Action Plan', to be drawn up and implemented by the signatories, initially in the form of a nine-year monitoring programme. In July, 1980, for the first time for several years, all Mediterranean beaches were reported to be safe for bathing.

The success of the Barcelona Convention and its predecessors encouraged UNEP to develop a Regional Seas Programme to protect other seas — known as 'regional seas' — that are almost land-locked or whose waters mix only slowly with those of the oceans. In each case, conferences are held to bring together representatives from all the coastal states. When the governments reach agreement a convention is signed, and then its implementation is up to the signatory governments — which by then have recognized the need to act. The North and Baltic Seas have their own conventions and, in addition to the Mediterranean, the Regional Seas Programme now covers the Caribbean Sea, Red Sea, Gulf of Aden, Persian Gulf, the south-west and south-east Pacific, and the coastal waters of West, Central, and East Africa and East Asia.

The UNEP Regional Seas Programme aims to reduce the pollution of almost landlocked seas and then to protect them by international agreement. UNEP has identified nine seas, or parts of seas, it considers to be in need of such protection.

1 Mediterranean
2 Kuwait
3 Caribbean
4 West and Central Africa
5 East Africa
6 East Asia
7 Red Sea and Gulf of Aden
8 South-west Pacific
9 South-east Pacific

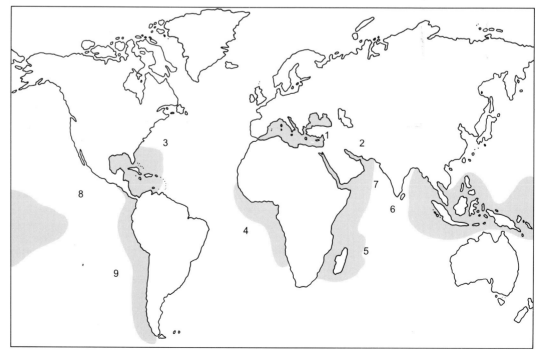

INDEX

Acknowledgements

The publishers wish to thank the following for supplying photographs for this book:

Page 2 Planet Earth; 3 RIDA/David Bayliss; 6 Mary Evans Picture Library; 8 Mary Evans Picture Library; 9 Mary Evans Picture Library; 10 Hutchison Library; 11 NASA; 15 Robert Harding Picture Library/G and P Corrigan; 19 U Ackermann (top); 19 Hutchison Library/M Macintyre (bottom); 20 Oxford Scientific Films (OSF)/Andrew Plumpire; 22 Hutchison Library; 24 RIDA/David Bayliss; 25 Richard Garratt Design; 29 Hutchison Library/Chris Johnson; 32 M Allaby; 33 Unichrome; 34 OSF/Martin Chillmaid; 37 Shell; 39 NASA/Science Photo Library; 40 NASA/Science Photo Library; 42 Hutchison Library/Pierrette Collomb; 43 RIDA/David Bayliss; 44 Hutchison Library/J L Peyrohavre; 48 OSF/Jack Dermid; 53 NASA GSFC/Science Photo Library/Dr. Gene Feldman (top); 53 Premaphotos Wildlife/R.A. Preston-Mafham (bottom); 54 Seaphot/Planet Earth Pictures/Alex Williams (top); 54 Richard Garratt (bottom); 56 Hutchison Library/Julia Davey; 57 OSF/eter Parks; 59 OSF/Peter Parks; 65 South West Water/Brian Lessware; 66 Anthony Burton; 67 Fortean Picture Library/Paul Broadhurst; 68 Planet Earth Pictures/Duncan Murrell; 70 OSF/Steve Littlewood; 71 Premaphotos Wildlife/K. G. Preston-Mafham; 72 Hutchison Library; 75 Hutchison Library; 83 OSF/Rodger Jackman; 84 Planet Earth Pictures/Gilbert van Ryckevorsel; 90 Hutchison Library/John Wright; 92 Planet Earth Pictures/Robert Hessler; 96 Hutchison Library/Michael Macintyre; 97 Hutchison Library; 98 OSF/Peter Parks; 101 Hutchison Library/Brian Moser; 105 NASA; 106 National Film Board of Canada (top); 106 Frank Gibson (bottom); 110 Hutchison Library/P Goycolea; 114 NASA; 123 Bord Failte/Irish Tourist Board (top); 123 National Film Board of Canada (bottom); 124 RIDA/David Rolls (top); 124 Hutchison Library/Simon McBride (bottom); 126 Miss S M Postle; 130 Hutchison Library/Bernard Regent; 131 Hutchison Library; 136 Hutchison Library; 137 Hutchison Library; 138 RIDA/R Moody; 141 Highlands and Islands Development Board; 142 Hutchison Library; 144 OSF/Dr Raymond Parks; 150 Hutchison Library/Bernard Regent; 151 Hutchison Library/Michael Macintyre; 152 Bord Failte/Irish Tourist Board; 153 British Waterways Board Photo Library; 157 Hutchison Library/Melanie Friend (top); 157 Hutchison Library/Bernard Regent (bottom); 158 Hutchison Library/T E Clark (top); 158 Hutchison Library/RG Williamson (bottom); 160 Times Newspapers Limited; 164 Ajax News and Feature Service/Jonathan Eastland; 166 Ajax News and Feature Service; 168 Ajax News and Feature Service/Jonathan Eastland; 169 Ajax News and Feature Service/Jonathan Eastland; 170 Seaphot/Planet Earth Pictures/Robert Hessler; 172 National Film Board of Canada (top); 172 OSF/Kim Westerskov (bottom); 174 NASA; 175 Hutchison Library/Carlos Frelre (top); 175 Greenpeace/Bijlsma (bottom); 176 The Environmental Picture Library/P Glendell (top); 176 NASA (bottom); 177 Hutchison Library/Mick Rock (top); 177 International Wool Secretariat (bottom); 178 Shell; 180 Richard Garratt Design; 181 Hutchison Library/V Southwell; 184 Hutchison Library/Liba Taylor; 186 Hutchison Library/Liba Taylor; 190 The Environmental Picture Library/A Greig; 191 Hutchison Library/John Downman; 192 Hutchison Library; 194 Greenpeace/Richard; 196 The Environmental Picture Library/P Fryer; 198 Greenpeace/Van der Veer; 199 Greenpeace/Vennemann; 200 ICI plc.